ETHICS IN THE FASHION INDUSTRY

ETHICS IN THE FASHION INDUSTRY

V. Ann Paulins

OHIO UNIVERSITY

Julie L. Hillery

NORTHERN ILLINOIS UNIVERSITY

FAIRCHILD BOOKS

AN IMPRINT OF BLOOMSBURY PUBLISHING INC

BLOOMSBURY

NEW YORK · LONDON · NEW DELHI · SYDNEY

Fairchild Books

An imprint of Bloomsbury Publishing Inc

1385 Broadway   50 Bedford Square
New York   London
NY 10018   WC1B 3DP
USA   UK

www.bloomsbury.com

FAIRCHILD BOOKS, BLOOMSBURY and the Diana logo are trademarks of Bloomsbury Publishing Plc

First published 2009
Reprinted 2014

© Bloomsbury Publishing Inc, 2009

Library of Congress Cataloging-in Publication Data
Library of Congress Catalog Number:
2008924282

ISBN: PB: 978-1-5636-7533-1
      ePDF: 978-1-6289-2775-7

GST R 133004424

Cover Design: Bruce Cayard
Compositor: Precision Graphics
Illustrations: Bruce Cayard
CD-ROM Development: high medium graphic design

Printed and bound in the United States of America

Dedication

This book is dedicated to my son, Matt, and other future decision makers who have the ability to improve our world through ethical leadership.
—VAMP

This book is dedicated to my mom, Linda, who through her actions has always taught me to think of how others are affected by my actions. Thanks, Mom.
—JLJH

February 14, 2008. We will never forget. Forward, together, forward.
—VAMP AND JLJH

Contents

Extended Contents

CHAPTER SIX

RESPONSIBILITIES AND LIABILITIES IN A COMPLEX INDUSTRY 135

Preface

As we began writing this book, the headlines in a recent newspaper included "teacher fired for having sex with student," "coach arrested for drunk driving," and "twelve-year-old boy killed by gunshot." The first two of these headlines are related to unfulfilled expectations connected to employment. All of the situations are related to judgment in the decision-making process. Unfortunately, these random headlines are fairly typical of the daily news. Furthermore, these situations have far-reaching implications for the future interpersonal relationships of those involved. People are evaluated on their credibility, integrity, and ability to make decisions based on their past behaviors. Making good decisions versus poor decisions is the root of ethics.

Clearly, evidence emerges each day that substantiates the need for awareness of ethical issues. We believe that it is important to keep in mind that ethics would be irrelevant without the human element. When people become involved in interactions with one another, they must make decisions about honesty and how they treat others. Within a professional setting such as a business or in an educational institution people make decisions about what level of attention and care they give to the tasks at hand, what they produce and how they produce it (whether it is a wool coat or a research paper), and how they present their work to others. If we never had to deal with people, we would not have any reason to worry about ethics.

This is a book about the relationships between functions in the textiles, apparel, and retailing complex and the people who make those functions happen. The human element is explored in terms of decisions-making processes leading to outcomes that have ethical implications. Our goal, as a result of this book, is to empower students who will soon become professionals in this industry to make good decisions. In addition, the accompanying CD-ROM features a thorough overview of the text, including activities, quizzes, case studies, and resources for each chapter. (The following icon appears in the margin next to each CD-ROM reference ⊚.)

We hope this book and CD-ROM help them become informed about the industry, aware of controversial issues within the industry, in touch with their own ethical constructs and personal comfort levels with activities in the industry and within their work environments, and aware of potential consequences or benefits of their actions as they work through the decision-making process.

In the words of Upton Sinclair, "it is difficult to get a man to understand something when his salary depends on his not understanding it."[1] We believe this sentiment applies to many ethical decisions that are made in the workplace, with the appropriate course being to seek understanding and ultimately improve the environments in which we work and live.

ENDNOTE

1. Sinclair, U. (1934). I, *Candidate for Governor and How I Got Licked.* Published by the Author, Station A, Pasadena, CA.

Acknowledgments

Much appreciation to the Fairchild team whose direction and vision made this textbook possible. We owe particular recognition to Senior Development Editor Jennifer Crane, Senior Production Editor Liz Marotta, and Executive Editor Olga Kontzias. Your guidance and support throughout this process has been truly invaluable. We also appreciate the work and valuable suggestions from the reviewers for our book, who made this a better product; the careful copyediting by Nancy Reinhardt; and the assistance offered by Rachel Recker and Megan (Thiele) Demianiuk in preparing this book.

Special thanks to all of the companies who contributed materials for our book . . . especially those who set themselves apart by modeling the highest standards for ethical practices.

We also thank Robert Hillery of High Medium Communication Design for transforming our ideas into the CD-ROM that accompanies this book.

ETHICS IN THE FASHION INDUSTRY

Chapter 1

Ethics in Everyday Life

THE OBJECTIVES OF THIS CHAPTER ARE TO:

- Introduce the concept of ethics

- Gain familiarity with the history of ethics and major philosophers who have contributed to ethical theory

- Explore various approaches that can be used to address ethical dilemmas

- Connect ethical applications for decision making in the fashion industry

ethics (eth´iks) *n.* **1** the study of standards of conduct and moral judgment; moral philosophy **2** a treatise on this study **3** [*with sing. or pl. v.*] the system or code of morals of a particular person, religion, group, profession, etc.[1]

The human ability to make choices based on values separates people from animals, which act on instinct alone. You have the ability to form your own judgment, based on your knowledge and perspective, and then to make decisions and carry out behaviors. Ethics are about making decisions that are right versus wrong. Ethics exist because we have choices. Ironically, our choices are complicated because what we *want* to do may not be what we *ought* to do. The easiest course of action is often not the most ethical. We tend to act in favor of our own best interests, sometimes at the expense of a better organizational, group, or societal outcome. Furthermore, people's beliefs and values about what is right and what is appropriate often differ. Therefore, you and your friends, family, or co-workers may not always agree on the right, or the best, choice. Nevertheless, because we are able to make choices, we are also saddled with the responsibility of being accountable for our actions.

FIGURE I.I

Ethics involve doing the "right" thing. How we determine what is right versus what is wrong depends on our culture, our morals, and our values. Culture includes elements of our environment such as family, religion, ethnicity, geographic origin, and the times in which we live. Our morals develop as we learn certain beliefs. As we place various levels of importance on our beliefs and on virtues we deem important, our values are formed.

People's choices regarding their behaviors may have ethical roots. The contexts in which choices are made determine whether ethics are involved. For example, the decision to use a pencil instead of a pen to write a note has no ethical consequence. Clothing, food, and entertainment choices are not usually rooted in ethical thought and corresponding decisions. Sometimes though, even seemingly benign actions may have ethical benefits or consequences. Consider that you might choose a modest versus body-hugging suit for work, eat a vegetarian sandwich, and decide to watch a *Sex in the City* rerun. It is likely that you have selected your attire for its appropriateness as a reflection of your company when you meet with clients. You might have strong feelings about harming animals, or you might prefer the taste or the nutritional content of the vegetarian sandwich. Your entertainment selection might reflect your indifference to watching promiscuous sexual behavior on TV or you might have been outvoted by others with whom you share a television. These examples demonstrate how the context of situations can affect the way ethics are applied to decisions.

Decisions that you make throughout your life have increasing social or personal consequence as you begin to act on behalf of organizations and employers. You may place a greater level of importance on some areas of decision making than others based on your opportunities, experiences, and point of reference. The choices to date co-workers, claim travel expenses that are allowable but not used, return a shirt you have already worn, turn in a term paper written by someone else, or secure a manufacturing contract for your employer with an overseas company that hires children as laborers all have varying degrees of social and personal consequences. Your career satisfaction will be influenced by the fit between your values and those of your corporate work environment. Furthermore, the beliefs and values that shape your decisions, in both your personal life and in the workplace, should mesh or else you will experience a great deal of conflict between the two. Your personal ethics affect your feelings toward situations at work and the specific decisions you ultimately make. An awareness of the potential ethical application of decisions you make will enhance your ability to make choices that appropriately reflect your own values and those of your employers.

Knowing that responsibility accompanies decisions is sometimes enough motivation to do the right thing. Though we might choose to do the right thing for its virtuous outcome alone, it is important to realize that making appropriate (or inappropriate) choices also shapes both our personal and professional reputations. As a student, you are beginning to move from making decisions that are mostly personal to taking on responsibilities for decisions that are or will be made on behalf of organizations or in a workplace. As you accept leadership positions—whether as president of a student organization or as the manager of a retail store—your personal values will serve as your point of reference for decisions and behaviors that you exercise in a professional capacity. Your decisions in the workplace must reflect the values of your employer if you expect to advance in your career.

Ethical decision making can be practiced and improved. You are encouraged, as you read this book, to reflect often on your own ethical base, and to think about how you will approach opportunities to make ethical decisions in the future. In the same manner that you work to enhance other skills, the ability to recognize ethical dilemmas, anticipate others' reactions to your decisions, and identify appropriate criteria on which to base your decisions can be improved with attention and experience. The time to begin developing this skill is now, rather than after you have entered the professional arena, where you will be expected to make appropriate and complicated decisions on behalf of your employer.

DO ETHICS CHANGE OVER TIME?

According to some observers, we do not exercise ethical living today in the way others have in the past. Moral education is not a foundation of our academic curriculum as it historically had been (and many of us have heard how, for hundreds of years, trustworthy and binding business deals were done with simple handshakes and verbal agreements). On the other hand, many practices that were commonly accepted in our ancestors' culture, such as racial and gender segregation, slavery, public hangings, and corporal punishment are considered unethical behaviors in today's society. Worldwide, cultural values and ethical perspectives vary widely. We cannot assume that our own ethical constructs are the same as those of other cultures. Our perspectives on ethics are influenced by current and local culture—which are shaped by the way we view relationships and process information. Ethics itself is not a unique concept to our modern world, but the way we understand ethical applications is influenced by the world around us. Our current technological tools, such as television and computers connected to the World Wide Web, enable us to be aware of cultural conflicts as they unfold. Unprecedented news coverage is offered to political movements that have generated modern perspectives and approaches toward racial, gender, and sexual orientation equities. These issues are further brought to light through popular media, including primetime television and popular magazines. It is likely that sheer awareness of human rights and dignity issues has advanced our ethical views as a society. Over time, human rights issues have been championed in the United States and throughout the world. As different areas and aspects of politics and business develop, views toward what is and is not ethical behavior in those realms are formed. For example, in the United States, constitutional rights are continually being reinterpreted to reflect the values, ethics, and laws of the current citizenry. Consider the laws and the standing of women and people of color before the law, for example, in 1776 when Thomas Jefferson wrote, "All men are created equal," compared to our laws now.

VALUES, EMOTIONS, AND ETHICS

The human ability to feel emotions such as compassion, shame, humiliation, sympathy, affection, jealousy, and anger complicates our decision-making process with respect to ethics. Decisions are often rationalized because of our feelings about situations. Obviously, our ability to reason can be strongly influenced by our emotions. Decisions made by impassioned people are often shortsighted or later regretted. Awareness of ethics, through identification of a set of basic, universally accepted values, can counter the tendency to act purely in response to emotions. It is commonly agreed, even across cultures, ethnicities, age groups, and religions, that there are some actions that are ethical and others that are unethical. These are known as moral absolutes. For instance, it is good (ethical) to be honest, fair, trustworthy, sympathetic, kind, respectful, dependable, broad-minded, and generous.

Conversely, it is universally accepted that it is wrong, or unethical, to kill, lie, steal, cheat, be unfaithful, harm others, and be cruel. This categorization of "right" and "wrong" behaviors is relatively straightforward, but specific situations often develop within complicated contexts and we can become tempted to modify our interpretations of these universal values. Complicated situations are exacerbated by emotions in a variety of ways. We may decide that it is acceptable, or even preferable, to tell a lie in an effort to spare another's feelings. We may rationalize that it is okay for a mother to steal in order to feed her children. We may even decide it is acceptable to humiliate someone we believe is deserving of such cruelty as a "payback" for his or her behavior toward us or someone else. When we begin to modify the basic foundation of our core values and beliefs or when our values do not match those of others in our environment, ethical dilemmas emerge. Ethics are complicated because humans are complex beings who feel emotion, bring multiple perspectives to situations, are influenced by others, often disagree with one another about the proper course of action, and tend to rationalize inappropriate behavior.

Several factors are particularly likely to complicate ethical decision making. One of these is money. People tend to be motivated by the prospect of making money. Greed is a reality in both personal and corporate situations. Ethical decisions are particularly difficult when the unethical choice has direct monetary benefits. The second common complicating factor is power. People tend to be influenced by those who are more powerful than themselves. Furthermore, people tend to seek ways to be powerful and power is often abused. When someone in power has expectations for outcomes that might more easily be achieved through unethical behaviors (such as increasing sales yet decreasing payroll), making the right decision becomes more difficult. For example, when a boss instructs a subordinate to achieve a certain sales goal and exerts power in the relationship by saying that failure is not an option, the known consequence (termination or demotion) for not meeting the goal may prompt the employee to compromise ethics because the more ethical decision (and corresponding action) does not achieve the goal. Third, people have tendencies to crave recognition and value success. Ego often gets in the way of ethics. Short-term achievements that bring recognition and accolades support egos, but may be gained through unethical behaviors.

Society does not readily reward ethical behavior. In fact, ethical behavior is routinely punished, particularly in the short term, in corporate environments. Kathryn Ruemmler, a former accountant at Enron, the Houston-based energy company that imploded in 2001 after corporate malfeasance, testified in March 2006 that she felt discriminated against because of her ethics during her employment prior to the company's collapse. Three well-known whistle-blowers—Sherron

Watkins of Enron, Coleen Rowley of the FBI, and Cynthia Cooper of WorldCom— were recognized by *Time* magazine as its 2002 Persons of the Year for their ethical behavior. Prior to their public recognition, each woman risked her job security and privacy by making unethical workplace behavior known to her CEO, Director,

---

BOX 1.1

HEADLINES AND NEWS STORIES WITH ETHICS CONTENT

- Hundreds of customers line up at Anya Hindmarch's New York and Los Angeles stores to buy the "I'm not a plastic bag" white canvas shopping tote (*Women's Wear Daily*, June 21, 2007, p. 8).
- A Pennsylvania state court judge approved a class-action lawsuit against Wal-Mart Stores, Inc. by Pennsylvania employees who claim the company pressured them to work off the clock (*Wall Street Journal Online*, January 12, 2006).
- Ethical fashion is broadening its scope as major European retailers respond to heightened consumer concerns about apparel manufacturing that damages the environment or violates human rights (*Women's Wear Daily*, May 3, 2006, p. 6).
- A jury found Martha Stewart guilty on all four counts of obstructing justice and lying to investigators about well-timed stock sales, and the former stockbroker turned style-setter could face years in jail (*CNNMoney.com*, March 5, 2004).
- Diesel U.S.A. won a permanent injunction and final judgment on consent against Chic Lady Ltd. and its owner for copyright infringement (*Women's Wear Daily*, January 11, 2007, p. 11).
- The House passed a minimum wage increase that many retailers maintain would adversely impact specialty stores and small chains and diminish opportunities for low-skilled workers (*Women's Wear Daily*, January 11, 2007, pp. 1, 3).
- With the IRS putting the kibosh on tax-free awards show swag, celebrities can no longer get their nails painted, hair styled, faces preened, and backs massaged without forking over hard-earned cash to Uncle Sam (*Women's Wear Daily*, August 25, 2006, p. 6).
- As shoplifters use high-tech scams, retail losses rise (*Wall Street Journal*, October 25, 2006, pp. A1, A12).
- Shoppers have something new to worry about this holiday season: A scam targeting gift-card buyers that could leave you without any gifts (*The Columbus Dispatch*, pp. A1, A4).

and board, respectively. Richard Lacayo and Amanda Ripley reported in *Time* that "whistle-blowers don't have an easy time. Almost all say they would not do it again. If they aren't fired, they're cornered: isolated and made irrelevant" (p. 33).

ETHICAL DILEMMAS AND APPROACHES TO ETHICS

An ethical dilemma occurs when the "right" choice is not the easiest, the least expensive, the one agreed upon by a group of decision makers, the course specified to you by others in power, or the decision you are inclined to make. Ethical theorists have identified useful approaches to ethical dilemmas (although these approaches can appear contradictory at times) as those dilemmas are explored in an effort to reach decisions. When you find yourself wrestling with a decision and know that given choices will have unique and potentially consequential outcomes, you are involved in a decision-making dilemma. A variety of cases are presented in the CD-ROM that accompanies this book. The cases provide opportunities for you to analyze decisions and the decision-making processes that have been made by others who have faced ethical dilemmas in the fashion industry. In addition, by familiarizing yourself with the situations in the cases, you will engage in the process of ethical decision making.

Various approaches have been developed as guidelines to determine the right (or ethical) decision for these types of situations. These approaches can be contradictory because the underlying principle or value identified in a given approach may be on the action itself or on the outcome of the decision, which can be associated with multiple behaviors. A variety of approaches and their origins are described in this section. What is good or right depends largely on what the decision maker considers important, or values most. Having an awareness of numerous ethical approaches will empower you to more thoughtfully explore your values and gain a greater understanding of the complexity of ethical decision making.

Virtue Approach

Plato and his student Aristotle, both fourth-century BC Greek philosophers, approached the concept of ethics with the perspective that life is based on a series of actions, and we should strive to be good, or virtuous, in our actions. Plato encouraged prudence, courage, temperance, and justice as a means toward happiness, which he considered the ultimate achievement in life. Aristotle further developed that line of thinking, theorizing that all decisions are made with the goal of happiness in mind. The Virtue Approach provides a context for behaviors in which people should make decisions that will enable achievement of happiness and well-being of themselves and others. Therefore, the Virtue Approach to ethics incorporates the values of honesty, trustworthiness, fairness, courage, faithfulness, and loyalty. The Virtue Approach simply expects that we do the right thing for the sake of well-being and to ultimately achieve happiness.

John C. Maxwell, in his book *Ethics 101*, suggests that we exercise ethics by choosing to practice the Golden Rule—treat others as we wish to be treated. The Golden Rule offers an "ethic of reciprocity" approach whose origins are traced to the gospels of the New Testament in the Christian Bible; this ethic is also associated with most religious faiths, including Buddhism, Islam, Judaism, Hinduism, and Native American spirituality. The Golden Rule, or the ethic of reciprocity, requires that we value and respect others to the degree we value and respect ourselves, and when this occurs, our decisions and actions will necessarily be ethical. This is an example of the Virtue Approach to ethics.

An ethical code that primarily values the good treatment of people is care-based, reflecting an underlying concern for others that shapes decision making. Good ethics can be good business too. For example, Howard Schultz, chairman and CEO of Starbucks, effectively argues in his book, *Pour Your Heart Into It*, that providing health-care benefits to all employees is not only a good thing to do for the employees, but it also has the corporate benefit of reducing turnover—which therefore reduces recruiting and training expenses. Schultz leads Starbucks by making decisions that reflect the company's core values, which include respect and human dignity. Starbucks' care-based method of applying ethics uses the Virtue Approach.

Common Good Approach

The works of Plato and Aristotle laid the foundation for the Common Good Approach, which is really a derivative of the Virtue Approach. This approach prescribes the course of action that most benefits society rather than an individual person. Using this approach, the right decision is the one that advances the well-being of the most people possible, hence the common good.

Starbucks provides health benefits to both part-time and full-time employees. This keeps some employees from becoming dependent on state and federal programs for health care. The company believes this decision is in its best interest in the long run; it therefore is a solid business decision even though it results in greater expenses for benefits than are borne by competitors. This decision reflects a concern for the common good of society by providing a greater number of people with health care than would otherwise be covered. Therefore, it was ethical for the company's Board of Directors to endorse the policy. The Common Good Approach is a care-based philosophy that uses an ends-based approach. That is, the outcome of the decision to provide health benefits is the criterion that provides the most good for the most people.

Utilitarian Approach

An approach to ethical decision making that focuses on whether the outcome of a decision will be good in terms of creating well-being versus harm for others is known as the Utilitarian Approach. Like the Common Good Approach, this is also an ends-based approach because the focus of the decision is the desired outcome. The utility of a decision is weighed in terms of benefits over consequences, and the impact of the action should be applied to all people affected by the decision, whether the outcome is direct or indirect.

Although the roots of Utilitarianism can be traced to the ancient Greeks, modern philosophers Jeremy Bentham and John Stuart Mill developed the theory in the nineteenth century. The gist of Utilitarianism is that the greatest amount of good is achieved for as many people as possible. The end result of the action rather than the action itself is used to determine whether the goal has been achieved. The decision is weighed in relation to the value of the end result of the action.

The Utilitarian Approach is reflected the decision-making structure used by Levi Strauss & Co. between 1997 and 2002, when it systematically closed its U.S. manufacturing facilities and moved production overseas. The company desired to sell merchandise at reasonably low prices—a goal that matches most consumers' desire for low prices. In fact, many consumers can afford only moderately priced jeans. Levi's blue jeans personify the concept of democratized fashion, so it is important to the company that its products remain affordable to mainstream America. Its ability to offer moderately priced denim and other casual wear to American consumers produces an outcome that is considered beneficial to many customers. Therefore, the decision to use foreign labor and close manufacturing plants in the United States to reduce the cost of merchandise was rational and appropriate if the value of affordable garments outweighs the value of employment for three to five thousand workers. If you agree that the benefit for millions of consumers to have access to low prices by keeping the company financially healthy and able to offer moderately priced merchandise outweighed the benefit of saving thousands of jobs (likely only in the short term), then the company's decision was rational when the Utilitarian Approach is applied.

The decision to fund voluntary social compliance audits at apparel factories can be seen as another example of the application of ethics using the Utilitarian Approach. While it is costly for companies such as Levi Strauss & Co., The Gap, and Nike to hire social compliance auditors who monitor labor practices in the factories producing their goods, this activity also creates numerous benefits. The resulting value and cost of ensuring (or at least making a good faith effort) that laborers are working in an environment where local laws and global standards are enforced are benefits measured not only by the well-being of employees but also by the reputation and financial performance of the companies. Failure to monitor compliance could result in consequences that far outweigh the cost of social compliance audits in terms of the bad publicity that would accompany disclosure that unhealthy and inappropriate labor conditions are associated with the manufacture of the companies' products.

Principled Approach

Immanuel Kant, an eighteenth-century ethicist, presented an approach to ethics based on the belief that a person's intentions or motives are primary in determining the right action. The Principled Approach is based on the concept of deontological (religious) ethics; this perspective reasons that people have a duty to perform according to commonly agreed-upon, rational, structured guidelines. This is a rules-based approach. According to this theory, our culture and experiences within our environment frame a context in which we develop expectations of others. Such expectations are so embedded in our makeup that we do not need to be told what the right course of action is. Kant advocated that praise be offered to people who exhibit goodwill in their decisions (even when the eventual outcome was negative or bad) and blame to those whose motives are not well intended. This approach developed into the Principled Approach, where decisions are based on what one *ought* to do, founded in responsibility toward duty and intended goodwill. Using this approach, people make decisions based on the best use of information that is available at the time.

Wal-Mart's decision to sell only edited songs by musicians such as Eminem, Kid Rock, Nellie, and others is based on the Principled Approach. Wal-Mart sees itself as a company that has a responsibility to offer wholesome products that are not offensive to the general consumer market. It is exhibiting goodwill toward its customer base by stocking shelves with merchandise that will not offend shoppers, according to the company's guidelines of what is considered offensive. This decision allows Wal-Mart to exercise ethics that reflect the company mission to be a family-friendly retailer—a duty to their customers that has been established as a cornerstone of the company. As Don Soderquist explained in his book *The Wal-Mart Way*:

> As a family store, we made merchandising decisions that cost us sales because they were in conflict with our values and our heritage. We chose not to carry certain magazines that we did not find appropriate for family. We decided that we should not stock CDs that had suggestive pictures on the cover or vulgar words in the lyrics; the same rule applied for games and videos (page 87).

In the 1970s, textile manufacturers began using TRIS, a chemical that enabled children's sleepwear to conform to the U.S. federal safety standard by making those garments flame retardant. The decision to use TRIS could be considered an ethical decision at the time it was initiated. Manufacturers of children's sleepwear desired to offer apparel that met minimum safety standards for flame-retardant fabrics, an end that clearly benefited consumers. Later, TRIS was found to be a carcinogen. After this information became available, the ethical decision to withdraw the chemical from the market was made. The initial decision to use the chemical, however, was a correct ethical decision within the Principled Approach, where manufacturers of children's sleepwear had a duty to implement a safety feature in their products. Kant's philosophical perspective would negate blaming manufacturers for using TRIS because the decision to do so was well intentioned and based on the information that was available at the time.

The concept of a duty to report unethical behavior is also an example of applying the Principled Approach. Have you ever wondered what your obligation is when you observe unethical behavior such as shoplifting or the misuse of a timesheet? Using the Principled Approach you would surely conclude that it is understood by you and others that you have a duty to report the behavior. Your reporting of the behavior will contribute to society's well-being in the long run by reducing shrink for the retailer and making a contribution toward lower prices for customers. After all, if you were the store owner, you would want others to tell you about a dishonest employee. As a consumer, you will benefit through lower prices when shoplifting is minimized.

Rights Approach

John Locke, a seventeenth-century philosopher, believed that people are born free and with certain natural rights. Furthermore, Locke believed that no one has the right to deprive another person of his or her rights. His work provided the foundation for the Rights Approach, which is based on the value that lives are important enough to warrant protection of basic rights. During the Age of Enlightenment (*Siècle des Lumières*) in the eighteenth century, philosopher Jean Jacques Rousseau introduced the concept that a social contract, guided by cultural norms, obligates people to respect the rights of others. The right to information, privacy, consent, freedom, liberty, and property are some examples of the basic rights that should be protected. This is another example of a rules-based approach; it also contains elements of a care-based philosophy.

President John F. Kennedy introduced four fundamental consumer rights to Americans through the implementation of a Congressional consumer protection program in the early 1960s. These rights were the right to safety, the right to be informed, the right to choose, and the right to be heard. Subsequent presidents have added the right to a clean environment, the right to consumer education, and the right to redress, or to seek reparation for injury. An awareness of these consumer rights is important as decisions that influence commerce are considered.

When companies promise not to sell customer lists—to respect the right for privacy from other unsolicited marketers—those companies are implementing an ethical decision based on a Rights Approach. The McDonald's Corporation came under fire in 2001 when it was publicized and confirmed that beef extract was used in the oil the company used in the production of its French fries, a presumably vegetarian menu item, even though in 1990 the company had said it used pure vegetable oil. The right of consumers to know full information about their consumption choices was violated, leading many people to conclude that McDonald's had executed an unethical decision.

In the United States, the concept of individual rights and freedom is widely understood and accepted. When apparel retailer Abercrombie & Fitch introduced T-shirts with slogans such as "Two Wongs will make it white" and "It's all relative in West Virginia," citizens protested. A highly publicized plea came from West Virginia Governor Bob Wise, who felt that the rights of all people to be treated with respect and dignity had been violated. Similarly, when a tavern owner in Mason, Ohio, placed a sign in his front window that said, "For service, speak English," the Ohio Civil Rights Commission cited discrimination, a violation of consumer rights.

Protesting these businesses' actions reflected ethical decision making based on the Rights Approach. Responses to these complaints reflect the organizations' values of the Rights Approach.

Fairness (Justice) Approach

John Rawls, an American philosopher, authored *A Theory of Justice* in 1971. He argued that justice is fairness. The Fairness Approach to ethics is based on how fairly or unfairly actions benefit or burden others. Using this approach, decisions should be based on people being treated fairly so that justice prevails. To be ethical, situations must be balanced for all participants. This means that there should not be an imbalance in power or information for one person or organization that would unfairly disadvantage others. "Fair" does not necessarily mean "the same," but there should be symmetrical balance for all parties involved. In other words, a double standard is inconsistent with an ethical choice. If one party has more information or has a different set of guidelines than another, good ethics cannot be achieved.

Martha Stewart's legal troubles in 2004 resulted from a situation where fairness was an issue. She and her former stockbroker Peter Bacanovic were convicted of obstructing justice and lying to investigators after a sale of stock (ImClone) happened in response to inside (unfair) knowledge about the precarious future of the stock's value. Ironically, Stewart's avoidance of an estimated loss of approximately $50,000 pales in comparison to the financial setbacks resulting from the impact that legal trouble on her company, her future business endeavors, and her professional reputation. Similarly, former Ohio State University marketing professor and consumer behavior expert Roger Blackwell's professional reputation and career were affected when he was convicted of illegal activities related to stock trading in 2005. Through his position on the board of Worthington Foods, Blackwell learned of an impending buyout by the Kellogg Company. He then shared the information with friends and family members who, with that unfair advantage due to the inside knowledge of company activities, profited through the purchase of Worthington Foods stock, whose value rose dramatically after the buyout. When the playing field is uneven, certain people and companies will benefit at the expense of others who do not have the benefit of inside knowledge. Because a fair market system is valued in the United States, behavior exploiting an unfair advantage is considered not only unethical, but also illegal. The U.S. Securities and Exchange Commission's insider trading laws are based on the Fairness Approach to ethics.

BOX 1.2

"WAL-MART GROUP, UNIONS TAP ACTIVISTS TO PROMOTE CAUSES"

Two back-to-back hires of activists—one made by a union coalition and the other by a group funded by Wal-Mart—show how management and labor are using PR campaigns and the aura of the civil rights movement to seek public support for their positions.

On February 25, [2006], Working Families for Wal-Mart announced that it had hired veteran activist Andrew Young to serve as chairman of the group's steering committee. Working Families for Wal-Mart, which is funded by Wal-Mart, is paying Young through a contract with his consulting company, Goodworks International. Seven days later, the Change to Win Coalition, a group of seven unions that spun off from the AFL-CIO last year, said it had hired Frank Clemente, former director of Public Citizen's Congress Watch in Washington, D.C., as its issues campaign director.

Each of these hires is an attempt to raise public awareness of their causes, observers say. Twenty years ago, employers and unions focused more on getting employees of specific companies to hear their pleas, but in today's political climate, public opinion is much more important, says Lowell Peterson, an attorney at New York-based Meyer, Suozzi, English, & Klein, which represents unions.

But whether these two men are just figureheads or will actually accomplish something remains to be seen, says Ken Goldstein, an economist at the Conference Board. "I'm skeptical that they can get beyond all of the inertia right now," he says.

SOURCE: Jessica Marquez, *Workforce Management*, April 10, 2006, Volume 85, Issue #7, page 10.

Our capitalist economy is based on the right of consumers to freely choose what they purchase and from whom. Ethics questions arise when large companies dominate the market because they develop an unfair advantage over their competitors. The result of this situation can be an inability for new merchants to enter the market, resulting in a loss of choice to consumers, and a potentially inflated cost of goods in the market. Antitrust legislation requires that companies not monopolize competition (a violation of consumers' right to choose in a free enterprise market). Antitrust legislation was first introduced in the United States during the presidency of Benjamin Harrison with the Sherman Antitrust Act in 1890, named for Senator John Sherman. At that time, there was growing public concern about giant corporations, particularly oil and tobacco companies. The Sherman Antitrust Act provided a definition of unfair business practices and established an investigative body to observe and monitor corporate activity. In 1914, under the leadership of President Woodrow Wilson, the Clayton Antitrust Act clarified the existing antitrust laws and specifically prohibited predatory price cutting, price fixing, ownership of stock in competing companies, and individuals from serving as directors of competing companies. Furthermore, the Clayton Antitrust Act supported workers and labor organizations and specifically stipulated that boycotts, strikes, and picketing activities were legal. The Federal Trade Commission (FTC) was established in 1914 as the regulatory agency empowered to investigate corporate practices.

More recently, Microsoft Corporation was embroiled in antitrust lawsuits because it holds an enormous, and some people would argue unfair, share of the computer software market in the United States. In 2005, Microsoft settled an antitrust suit brought by the U.S. Department of Justice by paying $775 million to rival IBM, and extended an additional $75 million in credit toward deployment of Microsoft software at IBM in an effort to enhance a competitive marketplace. Antitrust legislation, based on the Fairness Approach to ethics, exists in an effort to ensure a competitive environment that is fair for companies to enter into and that provides justice for consumers.

The ongoing relationships between business leaders and laborers continue to create tension in the marketplace and work environments. Unions, also known as bargaining units, have been established in many industries to create and regulate fair labor practices. Although unions are well entrenched in the U.S. manufacturing sector, there have been relatively few successful unionizations of retail employees. The debate continues regarding the need for unionization and with respect to the value of the outcomes that bargaining units contribute to retailers and other companies. In general, corporations clearly resist employee movements to unionize, yet many employees view unions as vehicles to receive increased fair employment and benefits. The ethics of union and anti-union activities are connected to perspectives and interpretations of fairness and justice.

ETHICS IN APPAREL PRODUCT DEVELOPMENT AND RETAILING

The fashion industry produces and markets a huge range of merchandise that accommodates a variety of consumer preferences, many of which have ethical foundations. For example, an organic grocery store has emerged that pleases those consumers who prefer to make pesticide-free and other environmentally friendly shopping choices. Inexpensive apparel is available at many stores partly because many consumers do not choose to make production issues (such as low wages and sweatshop conditions) a priority in their shopping behaviors. Other retailers, many of which are college and university spirit shops influenced by their consumers, provide only merchandise that is certified as not having been produced in sweat-shops. Essentially, every marketplace and its merchandise are in some way the result of an ethical consideration or decision.

Companies in the fashion industry are constantly wrestling with various ethical issues. There seems to be no limit on the emerging situations that present ethical dilemmas in this industry. Examples of both good and poor ethical decisions abound. It is important to note that the examples in this book sometimes present companies in positive (ethical) perspectives; other examples describe unethical situations or actions. The intent is to illustrate how complex ethics are, even for high-profile companies, and to demonstrate that a person or a company is not necessarily all ethical or all unethical.

As ethics issues are presented throughout this book, you are encouraged to consider the variety of approaches to ethics that are part of the decision-making processes. You will have the opportunity to explore situations where ethical dilemmas have been handled well, others where considerations of ethics were not fully developed, and some that have had disastrous outcomes. The accompanying CD offers a series of cases that present situations with ethical dilemmas. These cases offer you the opportunity to consider a particular situation, analyze the actions that have been taken in response to that situation, and offer alternative solutions that might improve the outcome in terms of an ethical application.

You are responsible for your decisions and for your own personal behaviors. And, ultimately, you will be making decisions in the fashion industry, many of which will have ethical implications. The decisions you make are up to you, but it is important that you use care and deliberation as you form them. After all, you alone are responsible for your actions; however, you are not the only one who will live with the outcomes. Your professional reputation will be built on the decisions you make. We encourage you to keep the variety of ethical applications in mind. Remember too that circumstances can change as new information emerges, new technologies develop, or personal opinions change. As a professional in the fashion business, you should consider ethical dilemmas from a variety of perspectives. What if you are the business owner? What if you are a manufacturer—or a buyer? What if you are the customer? Would your ethical conclusions be different? Why or why not? Fred Rogers, of *Mr. Rogers' Neighborhood*, wrote in *The World According to Mr. Rogers: Important Things to Remember* (2002), "You rarely have time for everything you want

BOX 1.3

"8 COLLEGES SIGN ON TO ANTI-SWEATSHOP PLAN BUT WORRY OVER ANTITRUST ISSUES"

At least eight institutions have publicly endorsed the principles behind a proposal that calls for colleges to require that apparel bearing their logos be made only at factories that pay employees a living wage and have legitimate unions. But those colleges have stopped short of backing the proposal to the letter.

At issue is whether doing business with certain factories, while freezing out others that do not comply with the new rules, violates antitrust laws. United Students Against Sweatshops, a national network of student labor activists that introduced the proposal [in fall 2005], is lobbying college administrators to back what is called the "designated-supplier program."

All eight institutions that have signed on—Duke, Georgetown, Indiana, and Santa Clara Universities, Smith College, and the Universities of Connecticut, of Maine at Farmington, and of Wisconsin at Madison—are members of the World Rights Consortium, an independent monitoring organization that would oversee the program.

"We believe strongly that this is a program with significant merit that reaches our overall goal to eliminate sweatshop labor," said Julie Bell-Elkins, associate dean of students at the University of Connecticut and leader of its anti-sweatshop efforts. "But if we're going to proceed . . . we want to make sure that it's just and it's legal."

Under the designated-supplier program, companies licensed to produce college apparel must use factories where workers are treated fairly. The companies would pay more than the industry norm for the goods they buy from those factories, so that the factories could then pay workers a living wage.

Students say sweatshop conditions would begin to disappear if, in return for respecting workers' rights, a designated group of factories received a steady stream of college-apparel business and fair prices for their work.

The Worker Rights Consortium, which comprises 152 member institutions and works closely with such activist groups as United Students Against Sweatshops, would determine which factories the licensees could use. The companies would have to get at least 25 percent of their goods from those factories the first year the program became official. That proportion would go up to 50 percent the next year, and to 75 percent the third year.

SOURCE: Audrey Williams June, *The Chronicle of Higher Education*, March 17, 2006; page A38. © *Chronicle of Higher Education*, printed with permission.

Box 1.4
ETHICS IN THE WORKPLACE

Interviews with almost 2,000 employees at U.S. public and private companies of all sizes for the Ethics Resource Center's (ERC) 2007 National Business Ethics Survey® show disturbing shares of workers witnessing ethical misconduct at work—and tending not to report what they see. Conflicts of interest, abusive behavior, and lying pose the most severe ethics risks to companies today. Over the past year, more than half (56 percent) of employees surveyed had personally observed violations of company ethics standards, policy, or the law. Many saw multiple violations. Forty-two percent of employees who witnessed misconduct did not report it through any company channels. ERC President Patricia Harned indicated that, "There is a strong sense of futility and fear among employees when it comes to reporting ethical misconduct, and that increases the danger to business. More than half of employees who witnessed but did not report misconduct believed that reporting would not lead to corrective action. More than a third of non-reporters feared retaliation from at least one source, but [ERC] research shows that having a strong ethical culture virtually eliminates retaliation."

"Employees at all levels have not increased their 'ethical courage' in recent years," Harned said. "The rate of observed misconduct has crept back above where it was in 2000. And employees' willingness to report misconduct has not improved, either. The good news is that the rate of misconduct is cut by three-fourths at companies with strong ethical cultures, and reporting is doubled at companies with comprehensive ethics programs."

The types of misconduct most frequently observed by employees were:

Lying to employees, customers, vendors, or public; observed by 25 percent
Putting own interests ahead of the organization; observed by 22 percent
Abusive or intimidating behavior toward employees; observed by 21 percent
Internet abuse; observed by 16 percent
Discrimination; observed by 14 percent
Stealing; observed by 11 percent
Sexual harassment; observed by 10 percent
Improper hiring practices; observed by 10 percent

SOURCE: The Ethics Resource Center, report released November 28, 2007. Available: http://www.ethics.org. Reprinted with permission of the Ethics Resource Center.

in life, so you need to make choices. And hopefully your choices can come from a deep sense of who you are" (p. 32). Our hope is that the process of working through this book will prepare you to face ethical dilemmas, particularly those in the workplace, with confidence and appropriate consideration.

QUESTIONS FOR DISCUSSION

1. How often do you experience ethical dilemmas in your decision making? What types of ethical dilemmas (both personal and professional) have you faced?

2. Discuss and describe some key ethical issues that have been presented in (a) recent news coverage, (b) popular television shows, and (c) movies. How do societal views of these ethical situations develop in response to media coverage?

3. How do you interpret the statement, "All men are created equal"? Explain your response and apply an appropriate ethical approach to your response.

4. In your opinion, what are the most unethical practices that you are aware of in the fashion industry?

5. In your opinion, what are the most ethical practices that you are aware of in the fashion industry (or in other businesses)?

6. Do unions have a value to add to the manufacturing industry? What about the retailing industry? Explain your response.

7. What is your comfort level in making decisions that have ethical implications? Provide your level on a scale of 1–10, and explain your position.

8. Offer examples of decisions you have made using the various approaches to ethics (Virtue, Utilitarianism, etc.)

9. Find a current news article describing an ethical dilemma in the fashion industry. Identify and discuss the decision maker's approach to addressing the situation. What specifically about this situation created the ethical dilemma?

REFERENCES AND SUGGESTED READING

Agins, T. (April 9, 2002). Levi Strauss will slash 20% of workers, shut six plants. *Wall Street Journal*. Retrieved on March 15, 2006 from http://online.wsj.com

Call that a joke? A state gets shirty about a t-shirt. (April 3, 2004). *Economist*, 371(8369), 33–34.

Cohen, R. (2003). *The good, the bad and the difference: How to tell right from wrong in everyday situations*. New York: Broadway Books.

Dao, J. (March 23, 2004). T-shirt slight has West Virginia in arms. *New York Times*, 153(52797), p. A16.

Dobrin, A. (2002). *Ethics for everyone: How to increase your moral intelligence*. New York: John Wiley & Sons, Inc.

Huntsman, J. M. and Cavuto, N. (2005). *Winners never cheat: Everyday values we learned as children (but may have forgotten)*. Upper Saddle River, NJ: Wharton School Publishing.

Kaufman, L. (April 9, 2002). Levi Strauss to close 6 U.S. plants and lay off 3,300. *New York Times*, 151(52073), p. C2.

Kidder, R. M. (2003). *How good people make tough choices: Resolving the dilemmas of ethical living*. New York: HarperCollins Publishers.

Lacayo, R. and Ripley, A. (December 30, 2002/January 6, 2003). Persons of the year. *Time*, 30–33.

Maxwell, J. C. (2005). *Ethics 101: What every leader needs to know*. New York: Center Street.

Mellert, R. B. (1995). *Seven ethical theories*. Dubuque, IA: Kendall/Hunt Publishing Company.

Missner, M. (2004). *On ethics*. Belmont, CA: Wadsworth-Thomson Learning.

Mutschler, A. S. (July 4, 2005). IBM, Microsoft resolve antitrust issues. *Electronic News (North America)*, 51(27).

Rogers, F. (2003). *The world according to Mr. Rogers: Important things to remember*. New York: Hyperion.

Sanders, E. (May 4, 2001). McDonald's confirms its French fries are made with beef extract. *Boston Globe*. Retrieved on March 12, 2008 from http://www.commondreams.org/cgi-bin/print.cgi?file=/headlines01/0504-02.htm

Schultz, H. and Yang, D. J. (1997). *Pour your heart into it: How Starbucks built a company one cup at a time*. New York: Hyperion.

Soderquist, D. (2005). *The Wal-Mart way*. Nashville, TN: Nelson Business.

Tortora, P. G. and Collier, B. J. (1997). *Understanding textiles* (5th Ed.). Upper Saddle River, NJ: Prentice Hall.

Turner, G. and Mitchell, M. (September 2005). Where are you from?: Does it influence your ethical outlook? *Retail Education Today*, 26(1), 8–13.

Witness felt discrimination at Enron for questioning financial reporting. (March 1, 2006). *Wall Street Journal*. Retrieved on March 15, 2006 from http://online.wsj.com

ENDNOTES

1. *Webster's New World College Dictionary*, Fourth Edition, p. 488.

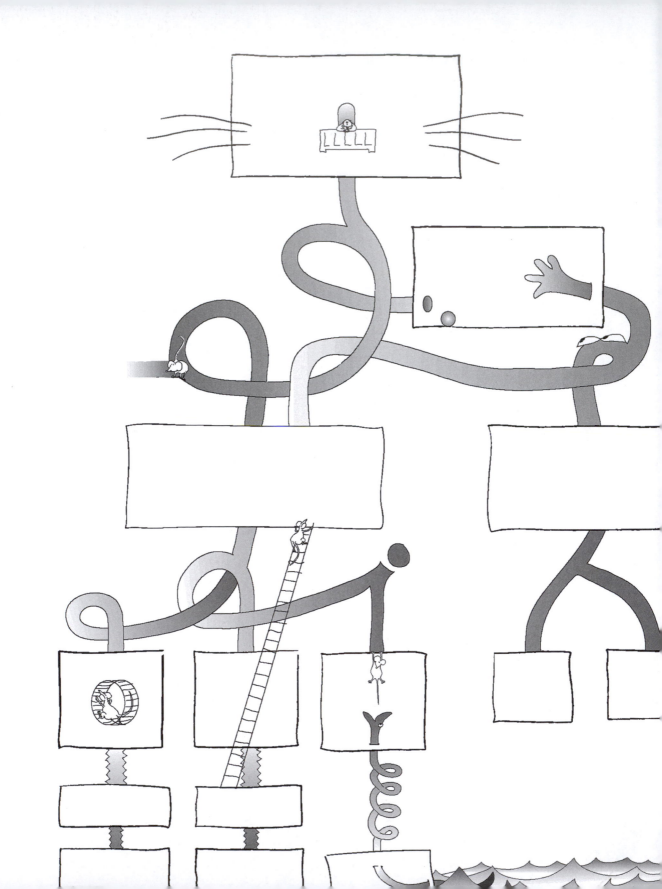

Chapter 2

Corporate Culture

THE OBJECTIVES OF THIS CHAPTER ARE TO:

- Define what is meant by "corporate culture"
- Explore the relationship between corporate culture and decisions made within the business
- Identify how corporate culture influences employee satisfaction and productivity
- Recognize the influence of corporate culture on customers' perceived image of companies

Corporate culture can be defined as the environment found at a company, or more simply, as the company's "personality." Another widely accepted definition for corporate culture is the way things get done around here (Deal and Kennedy, 1982). Corporate culture, which sets the standards for the company, includes factors such as morals, values and beliefs, ethics, and expected behavior.

Consumers today demand not only quality products from fashion retailers; they also demand that companies remain socially responsible to their employees and to the communities where they operate. In response, companies are increasing efforts to promote and ensure a positive corporate culture. Several studies (Fiertag, 1999; Hall, 1999; Kersten, 2006; Verschoor, 2005) have addressed the impact that a strong ethical corporate culture has on consumers' behavior. For example, two-thirds of people consider a company's ethical stance when purchasing products; 71 percent said that if a company was investing in non-ethical areas, it would negatively affect their decision to buy shares of that company's stock; and 58 percent of consumers reported that they would boycott a brand if that company used child labor to make its product (Hall, 1999).

"Ok honesty is the best policy.
Let's call that option A."

FIGURE 2.1

Just as corporate culture is shown to affect consumers, it is perhaps even more important to the company's employees and prospective employees because workplace atmosphere and expectations are related to job satisfaction. Fiertag (1999) found that people will do more and be more motivated if they like their employer, are shown respect, have two-way communication with management, and are involved with decisions. All of these factors give employees a sense of empowerment, which also contributes to job satisfaction. This is important because, as reported in a 2006 issue of *Harvard Business Review*, only 50 percent of U.S. workers are satisfied with their jobs. In fact, job satisfaction has been steadily dropping for the past 15 years. Workers continually report a lack of personal fulfillment with their job, a lack of acknowledgement for their efforts, work/life imbalance, and a lack of influence with their supervisors. The conclusion is that the general dissatisfaction is due to poor leadership (management) and a bad work environment (Kersten, 2006). The values that shape corporate culture contribute to the work atmosphere.

In another study addressing the relationship between managers and job satisfaction, Lee and Gao (2005) examined organizational commitment among retail employees. They tested a model on the relationships among two facets of commitment (affective and continuance), two areas of work outcome (effort put into work and the propensity to leave), and three facets of job satisfaction (pay, co-workers, and supervisors). The researchers found that satisfaction with pay and supervisors significantly increase both forms of commitment and significantly decreased employees' propensity to leave the company.

Other examples of how the corporate culture affects employees include the company dress code, the number of hours and the schedule that employees are expected to work, the amount and type or interaction with management and other employees, and the training and development employees are offered. In a recent study (*New Trends*, 2004), new college graduates reported seeking employers with ethics, and the rash of recent corporate scandals (e.g., Enron, WorldCom, Saks) has led graduates to rate integrity as a top criterion for choosing an employer. In the same study, having ethical business practices was rated in the top five. Obviously, both of these elements have an important role in shaping corporate culture.

Yet another reason that corporate culture is important is because of the impact it will have on employee expectations and behavior. In 2005, the Ethics Resource Center (ERC), released results of its National Business Ethics Survey (NBES). More than 3,000 American workers participated in the study; the findings suggesting that less wrongdoing and more reporting of misconduct are associated with a superior ethical culture. In fact, even in the presence of a formal ethics and compliance training program, which 69 percent of the employees reported having, the strength of the ethical culture was a more important factor in employee behavior. Employees in companies with weak ethical cultures reported a much higher level of observed unethical behaviors as compared to those with a strong ethical culture: 70 percent versus 34 percent! (Verschoor, 2005). After the ERC conducted its 2007 Survey, the center announced that workplace ethical misconduct had deteriorated to pre-Enron levels despite attempts to encourage more ethical behavior. However, organizations with strong, positive programs that help create a "corporate culture of ethical action and policies" reduced the risk of unethical employee behavior (Gebler, 2006).

COMPANY MISSION AND VISION STATEMENTS

Consider the following advertisement for a sales position:

> Seeking experienced salesperson who enjoys working in a cut-throat environment where no training is offered, has no desire to advance, enjoys being bullied by supervisor, will not expect any praise for a job well done, and will be reprimanded frequently for performing above expectations.

Chances are that if you saw this advertisement you would not be interested in working for this company, and obviously, no company would place such an ad if it was serious about finding motivated salespeople. However, we have all heard stories about people working in positions such as this, or we may have even been unfortunate enough to find ourselves in this type of environment!

It is difficult to determine the corporate culture of a particular company without actually working for that organization. However, a company's mission statement, values statement, or vision statement often provides important clues as to the company's culture and ethical stance. Such statements, and discussions concerning the company's core values and expectations, are often included in the annual report and are also posted on the company's Web site. A mission statement describes the purpose of the company, the vision statement articulates what the company expects to do (or be) in the future, and the values statement indicates what criteria (such as diversity, honesty, respect, etc.) are important to the company. Given the increasing emphasis on corporate ethics, many companies today have developed additional ethical statements that specifically address ethical expectations and standards. Box 2.1 includes two such examples of mission/vision statements.

Target Corporation, which is continually mentioned as one of the top socially conscious companies in America, places such an emphasis on promoting a positive corporate culture that it produces a yearly Corporate Responsibility Report. This document addresses issues such as the company's stand on environmental issues, employee diversity, social responsibility, volunteerism, product offerings, and business conduct. Target's philosophy began almost 100 years ago when company founder George Dayton established a corporate foundation to give back to the community. In 1946, Target strengthened its commitment to this cause when the company's management formalized the policy to contribute 5 percent of its income to the communities in which the company does business. Target's Corporate Responsibility Report can be found at www.target.com.

MAKING DECISIONS THAT INVOLVE WORKPLACE ENVIRONMENT

Let's now take a closer look at what specific factors companies consider in setting policies, which ultimately define their corporate culture. For our purposes we have chosen to discuss these under three broad topics: treatment of employees, ethical responsibilities to others, and vendor relationships. As you read these discussions, try to identify some of the underlying ethical issues for each topic.

TREATMENT OF EMPLOYEES

Many issues that involve employees and help to shape the corporate culture are also ones that can be viewed from an ethical standpoint. Two examples are: Are employers ethically obligated to provide health-care benefits? and What is a fair wage?

BOX 2.1

MISSION, VISION, AND ETHICAL STATEMENTS FROM STARBUCKS AND PATAGONIA

Starbucks's Mission Statement:

Establish Starbucks as the premier purveyor of the finest coffee in the world while maintaining our uncompromising principles while we grow.

The following six guiding principles will help us measure the appropriateness of our decisions:

1. Provide a great work environment and treat each other with respect and dignity.

2. Embrace diversity as an essential component in the way we do business.

3. Apply the highest standards of excellence to the purchasing, roasting and fresh delivery of our coffee.

4. Develop enthusiastically satisfied customers all of the time.

5. Contribute positively to our communities and our environment.

6. Recognize that profitability is essential to our future success.

SOURCE: http://www.starbucks.com

Patagonia's Mission Statement:

Build the best product, do no unnecessary harm, use business to inspire and implement solutions to the environmental crisis.

SOURCE: http://www.patagonia.com

Patagonia's Environmental Activism Statement:

Our definition of quality includes a mandate for building products and working with processes that cause the least harm to the environment. We evaluate raw materials, invest in innovative technologies, rigorously police our waste and use a portion of our sales to support groups working to make a real difference. We acknowledge that the wild world we love best is disappearing. That is why those of us who work here share a strong commitment to protecting undomesticated lands and waters. We believe in using business to inspire solutions to the environmental crisis.

SOURCE: http://www.patagonia.com. Reprinted with permission.

Benefits and Wages

Prominent in the news today is the availability of health care for individuals and families in the United States. Therefore, it is no surprise that this is an issue facing all companies large or small, including fashion and retail businesses. In general, companies must decide whether they will offer health-care benefits (e.g., medical, dental, vision, etc.) to their employees, and if so, to whom (full-time versus part-time) and at what cost to the business (company pays 100 percent versus partial contribution). Starbucks is one company that is known for offering health-care benefits to all employees who work 20 or more hours a week. When asked about this policy during an interview on CNBC's *American Made* TV series, company CEO Howard Schultz said, "It's the right thing to do." He explained that when he was growing up, his family lost everything because his hardworking father was hurt on the job and had no benefits. Based on that experience, he vowed that none of his employees would ever suffer those same circumstances. (See Box 2.1 for Starbucks' mission statement; notice that the first guiding principle mentions the treatment of employees).

Wal-Mart, on the other hand, has continually come under scrutiny for numerous employee policies, including the lack of "fair" employee benefits. In fact, the state of Maryland proposed a law in 2006 that would have required companies with more than 10,000 employees to spend at least 8 percent of their payroll on health benefits. Although the lawmakers claimed that they did not intend to single out Wal-Mart when they proposed the law, the retail giant was actually the only company in the state that the law would have affected (Wagner and Barbaro, 2005). The proposed law subsequently failed to pass, but as a result of the controversy, Wal-Mart now allows part-time workers to enroll their children in a low-cost health-care plan. This policy applies to more than half of the company's employees (Ellis, 2006).

Employee wages are another issue prevalent in the workplace today that affects the corporate culture. Two particular issues are "equal pay for equal work," and the idea of a "fair" or "living" wage. Recently, the Supreme Court set a 180-day deadline (from the date of the unlawful employment practice) for employees to claim under Title VII of the Civil Rights Act that they are being paid less because of their race, sex, religion, or national origin (Associated Press, 2007). Opponents of the ruling argued that this time restriction is too stringent because many people may not realize that discrimination has occurred until after 180 days. Additionally, new employees may be reluctant to speak up right away (within the timeline set) even if they are aware of a discrepancy.

In another discrimination suit, a jury awarded $2 million to a former Wal-Mart pharmacist after finding that the retailer had underpaid her, and then fired her based on her gender. The employee alleged that she was fired in reaction to her demand that the company pay her the differential in wage and bonuses compared to her male counterparts. She also claimed that the company had reprimanded her for reporting missing drugs to the U.S. Drug Enforcement Administration (Reuters, 2007).

The second issue concerning wages has to do with what constitutes a "fair" wage. Legislation signed by President George W. Bush in May 2007 increased the federal minimum wage by 70 cents each summer until 2009, when all minimum-wage jobs will pay no less than $7.25 an hour (Holland, 2007). Many individuals and organizations in the United States had lobbied for this change because the previous wage of $5.15 was not enough to keep those workers earning that amount from living below the poverty level. The fashion industry has been notoriously criticized for low wages and poor working conditions, especially in the manufacturing sector. American Apparel, a California T-shirt manufacturer and retailer, bases pay on employee performance in an attempt to maintain a positive corporate culture and to keep employees happy. Pay amounts, on average, are around $12 an hour, which is far above California's 2007 minimum wage of $6.75. Anti-sweatshop activists praise the company's CEO, Dov Charney, as a pioneer in the treatment of garment workers. In addition to the increased pay scale, employees can buy subsidized health insurance for $8 a week, are entitled to English lessons, and receive subsidized meals and free parking. Charney believes that keeping his employees happy has, in turn, led to the incredible success of his company. But Charney is not without critics, and is actually facing several sex discrimination lawsuits ("Face Value: Dov Charney, the hustler," 2007), discussed in greater detail in Chapter 3.

Diversity in the Workplace

Diversity is also an important topic for many corporations today. Although laws are in place concerning discrimination and equal opportunity in the workplace, many companies also promote themselves as being welcoming of all, regardless of race, age, sexual orientation, gender, or religious affiliation. One company that is cited numerous times in the media for its diverse workforce is PepsiCo, Inc., which owns Frito Lay. PepsiCo recognized the increasing ethnic diversity in the American marketplace and realized that the company needed a way to better understand those markets. Steven Reinemund, chairman and CEO of PepsiCo, explained to an audience at the Stanford Graduate School of Business how hiring diverse employees and creating separate advisory boards for Hispanic, African-American, and Asian market segments enabled the company to create a competitive advantage in the marketplace (Chang, 2004). Specifically, PepsiCo was able to gain a large portion of market share with minority-targeted products such as Lay's guacamole chips aimed at Hispanics; a wasabi-flavored snack aimed at Asians; and Code Red, a cherry Mountain Dew aimed at African Americans (Hymowitz, 2005; Chang, 2004; Schneider and ElBogh-dady, 2003). Although PepsiCo is not a fashion-related business, the company's example is one that should be recognized by all types of organizations. Nordstrom, the Seattle-based upscale department store chain, was named in 2007 to *Fortune* magazine's list of the most admired companies due in part to the company's effort to make employee diversity a key priority. In 1988, people of color made up 24 percent of its staff; in 2007 this had increased to 41 percent. In Nordstrom's managerial ranks, 31 percent are currently people of color and 72 percent are women.

On the other hand, another popular apparel retailer, Abercrombie & Fitch, settled in 2004 a lawsuit brought by the U.S. Equal Employment Opportunity Commission (EEOC) for nearly $50 million alleging that the company's hiring practices discriminated against women and minorities. In A&F's attempt to promote its "all-American" image, the company was accused of hiring and favoring employees who had the "Abercrombie Look," which is typified by blond-haired, blue-eyed males who are skinny and tall. As part of the settlement, Aber-crombie was ordered to institute policies promoting diversity in its workforce and its marketing campaign, appoint a Vice President of Diversity, hire 25 recruiters to seek minority employees, and cease the practice of primarily recruiting at all-white fraternities and sororities. Additionally, all managers are now trained in discrimi-nation prevention ("Landmark Abercrombie," 2005; Osterman, 2005; Safer, 2004). The A&F Web site now includes a *Diversity and Inclusion* section with the following introductory statement from Mike Jefferies, the company's chairman and CEO:

> Diversity and inclusion are key to our organization's success. We are deter-mined to have a diverse culture, throughout our organization, that benefits from the perspectives of each individual.

In another more recent discrimination suit, Nike, Inc. agreed to pay $7.6 million to settle a race discrimination lawsuit filed by current and former African-American employees of its Niketown store on Michigan Avenue in Chicago. The employees alleged that African Americans, including members of the Chicago Bulls basket-ball team, were subjected to greater monitoring and scrutiny in the Chicago store. Nike settled the case out of court denying any wrongdoing. However, critics believe that the company settled out of court to avoid potentially damaging media. Nike has a huge following among African-American youth, and the company also uses high-profile African-American spokespersons such as Michael Jordan and Kobe Bryant (Sachdev, 2007).

Companies address diversity not only in terms of their employees but also in their choice of a target market and their customer-focused marketing materials. Wal-Mart came under fire in 2006 from such conservative groups as the America Family Association because the corporation had joined the National Gay and Lesbian Chamber of Commerce and had also donated to the organization Out and Equal, which promotes gay rights in the workplace. These actions were viewed by conservatives as counter to Wal-Mart's principles, which have been understood to be implicitly Christian and previously included bans on music CDs with explicit lyrics and magazines featuring indecent pictures on their covers. This was actually quite an interesting protest because it was the first time that consumers on the more conservative side of the spectrum (the "right") were the ones criticizing Wal-Mart. The company announced plans in June 2007 to curb its support of gay, lesbian, bisexual, and transgender (GLBT) groups because of the protests (Gunther, 2007). This decision will no doubt provide more fuel for liberal consumers (such as those who run the WakeupWalMart.com Web site), some of who have been continually critical of the company for its low wages, lack of equitable employee benefits, and manufacturing/outsourcing practices. Based on these, and numerous other critics, Wal-Mart has added low-cost health care for employees, increased diversity among its employees, and embarked on environmental programs (Crary, 2006).

Companies also address diversity through their marketing and advertising materials. The ethnicity of the models used in advertisements is often scrutinized by consumers. Controversies in the past have centered on Abercrombie and Fitch's exclusive use of blond, blue-eyed, white models; in the 1980s Benetton was criticized for ads portraying relationships between blacks and whites. In October 2007, a panel discussion titled "Out of Fashion: The Absence of Color" was held at the New York Public Library. Identified barriers to diversity on fashion runways and in fashion publications ranged from designers wanting models to appear anonymous to better highlight the clothing to the topic of racism. David Ralph, a model agent and member of the panel, reported that the October 2007 issue of the magazine *Marie Claire* used one black model in a six-page spread, *W* magazine showed one black model in a 20-page spread, and no black models were included in the fashion spreads of that month's issues of *Vogue, Harper's Bazaar, Glamour, Cosmopolitan, Allure, Lucky,* and *Elle* (Feitelberg, 2007). Today many retailers, apparel designers, and fashion publications select models who are ethnically diverse to reflect our culture and the consumer markets, but more conscientious inclusion is needed to accurately reflect the consumer marketplace.

Dress Code

Requirements concerning employee dress directly affect company culture and employee morale. Some companies have strict dress codes; others are more lax in this area. Casual Friday, a day when a company allows its employees to "dress down," became popular in the 1990s, and continues at many American businesses. Some corporations have adopted this type of comfortable dress as acceptable for every day, while others have decided against this policy all together because of problems with employees dressing inappropriately (e.g., flip-flops, halter tops, jeans, etc.) and because of negative customer and client perceptions associated with a casual or unkempt appearance. As previously indicated, some companies have very specific expectations (and standards) for what employees should wear to work. In a variety of work settings, consistency in employee dress (uniforms, for instance) can provide convenience through quick visual identification (for example, most consumers recognize Target employees because of their uniform of khakis and red polo shirts).

Wal-Mart recently announced it would replace employees' familiar "How may I help you?" blue vests with blue polo shirts and khaki pants. After test-marketing the new polo shirts, the company reported that its employees like the new shirts because they projected a more professional image and made the employees feel more like a team. With this change, Wal-Mart provides each employee with two shirts and reimbursement for one pair of pants or a skirt. The company also set up an employee Web site where additional items can be purchased at discounted prices (Dow Jones Newswire, 2006). Most fashion retailers expect employees to wear current clothing as publicity for their store merchandise and to reflect its image. This requirement can create an economic hardship for employees, but many people consider the employee discount to be a perk of the job.

Of course a dress code can also involve specifics about general appearance, not strictly clothing. For example, are male employees allowed to have facial hair? What is the company policy concerning the display of tattoos? Are women required to wear cosmetics? In 2000, a lawsuit tested company policies requiring women to wear makeup to work. When a 20-year employee of Harrah's Casino in Reno, Nevada, was fired for refusing to follow the company's "Personal Best" policy that specified women must wear lip color, face powder, blush, and mascara, she filed a discrimination lawsuit. She alleged that the policy was demeaning and discriminatory in that men were not required nor allowed to wear makeup. However, much to the chagrin of many women's rights activists, the court upheld Harrah's requirement for females to wear makeup, holding that the company's policy did not impose an undue burden on female employees. Therefore the court also ruled that Harrah's was justified in its firing of the employee for refusing to follow the company policy. Members of the hotel industry association in California hailed the ruling because it gave an employer the right to establish grooming standards, which they feel are important in service industries (Colb, 2001; Osterman, 2005).

Environment of the Workplace

The environment at any workplace is affected mainly by the interaction among the employees. For example, how do peers and management interact? Is there a specific chain of command that employees must follow, or does the management team maintain an open-door policy with subordinates? Is the management team supportive, or do they communicate with employees largely through criticism or reprimand? Are new ideas welcome, or are they viewed as threatening? Is the environment fun for employees, or is it highly competitive? Does management take credit for others' work? Does management genuinely celebrate staff members' individual or collective accomplishments, or does achievement result in jealous or snide comments? The situations reflected by these types of questions contribute to either positive or negative cultures.

According to a recent study, more than 90 percent of adults experience some type of workplace abuse during their careers and the larger the company, the more likely verbal abuse is to occur. Verbal abuse, which is intended to harm the target (e.g., employee), includes profanity and hostile remarks concerning competence, gossip, and rumors. Such a corporate culture is obviously undesirable and companies need to be especially aware of this because this atmosphere will hinder employee performance, decrease morale, and consequently cause high turnover of staff members.

The work environment can also be reflected in the way employees treat customers. Considering that 80 percent of customers who stop doing business with companies is the result of poor attitudes from employees, it is imperative that retailers and merchandisers do everything possible to create a positive and nurturing work environment. Corporations should promote positive attitudes among their managers; research suggests that employees' behaviors will reflect those modeled by their manager (Christopher, 2007; Johnson and Indvik, 2006).

Yet another issue that will affect employee morale, and consequently the corporate culture, is the physical workspace. For employees in a corporate setting, does their workspace include an office with a door and a window, or do all employees work in cubicles? How are these assignments made? Many times these decisions are made based on rank and promotion. Obviously, the physical working environment can influence job satisfaction and productivity, and therefore ultimately the company's bottom line. Employees who have a sense of equity in regard to their workspace assignment are more likely to see that aspect of their jobs in a positive light.

Another consideration is décor in the personal workspace. If the employee has a desk, or a personal workspace, is he or she allowed to display personal items such as family pictures? Some companies do not allow such displays because they feel it does not reflect professionalism. Others encourage employees to make a personal statement with their desks and workspace areas; the thinking is that it makes the employees more comfortable and hopefully more productive. Policies regarding personal workspaces reflect company culture, and should be noted and considered when determining a potential fit as an employee.

Perks

In order to attract employees during the past few years, many companies have begun offering special services such as on-site gyms or memberships to health clubs, child care, flexible working hours, on-site massage therapists, the option of working from home, and gourmet cafeterias. Many also sponsor after-hours get-togethers and lavish parties. Such perks generally have a positive effect on morale, reflecting a corporate culture that values employee well-being and making a statement for the company and its mission. For example, in 2001, Abercrombie & Fitch opened a new $130 million, 300-acre "campus" outside Columbus, Ohio. The campus features a gym, ATM, drop box for photo development, a bonfire pit, and a chalkboard in the cafeteria that lists employees' birthdays. All of these features not only emphasize teamwork but are also designed to make young employees feel at home. At the grand opening celebration (hosted by CEO Mike Jeffries, who wore flip-flops and cutoffs), guests enjoyed a frat-house party atmosphere complete with kegs of beer and a live band playing near the bonfire. Jeffries pointed out to journalists in attendance that the campus was designed to reflect both the A&F target customer, who is a college student, and also the ideals of its young employees, many of whom are fresh out of college (Torkells, 2001).

ETHICAL RESPONSIBILITIES TO OTHERS

Although the previously mentioned issues specifically involve employees, most companies also have policies in place regarding their ethical responsibility to others, or policies that promote the "good" of the community. Three areas, "Being Green," the "Treatment of Animals," and "Charitable Contributions and Causes" (e.g., cause-related marketing), are moving to the forefront in today's business world.

Being Green

As we are writing this book, one of the hottest topics of interest is the environment. This is partly due to the documentary *An Inconvenient Truth*, which millions of people around the world have seen. Consumers are increasingly interested in supporting retailers and manufacturers having practices that are environmentally friendly, or *green*. This has become so important that Hall (1999) reports that companies with *green* corporate practices see dividends paid to the stockholders increase an average of 5 percent.

J. C. Penney Company, Inc., as part of its "Matters of Principle" policies, includes a section on environmental responsibility. Some recent programs that have been implemented to reflect these standards include the elimination of unnecessary packaging materials, the use of recycled materials for gift boxes and catalog shipping cartons, reduction in paper usage, waste management, and energy conversation. Due to its energy management and reductions in greenhouse gases, the U.S. Environmental Protection Agency named J. C. Penney Company, Inc. as the "2007 ENERGY STAR® Retail Partner of the Year" (see http://www.jcpenney.net/company/awards/energystar.pdf).

Another way that retailers are addressing environmental issues is in the design of their stores. For example, in March 2007 Wal-Mart opened a second high-efficiency supercenter in Rockton, Illinois. The store, which is expected to use 20 percent less energy than a typical supercenter, features integrated heating, cooling, and refrigeration systems, along with lighting innovations. The new prototype is modeled after two experimental stores in Texas and Colorado. Some of the special features include water-source heating, cooling, and refrigerated system; energy-saving motion-activated lights in refrigerator and freezer cases; sensor-activated, low-flow faucets in restrooms; colored concrete floors that reduce the need for harsh cleaning agents used for carpets; and baseboards and chair rails that are made from recycled plastic. Wal-Mart executives believe it is good business to protect the environment while also lowering energy costs—a savings that can be passed along to customers ("Wal-Mart opens," 2007).

Another example of green store design is the Green Exchange (see www. green-exchange.com), an eco-friendly shopping center set to open in 2008 on Chicago's

North Side. The center is in a renovated lamp factory and will feature stores carrying sustainable clothing, organic cotton, building supplies, and various other *green* retailers. It is the first business development in the United States of its kind and features priority parking for hybrid cars; bike racks; a green roof; and high-efficiency windows, doors, and HVAC system ("Shop and Save," 2007).

Patagonia, an outdoor clothing manufacturer and retailer, has built its company around sound environmental policies, which are clearly reflected in its mission statement (refer to Box 2.1). All of the sports the company promotes are what Patagonia terms "motorless sports" such as hiking, surfing, snowboarding, and skiing. Additionally, its 1 *percent For The Planet* program provides the motivation for any business—large or small—to donate at least 1 percent of annual net revenues to environmental organizations worldwide. To date, participants in the program include restaurants, musicians, wineries, and graphic design and advertising firms.

Treatment of Animals

A continuing debate for the fashion industry is the ethical treatment of animals as related to its product offerings and designs. Activist groups, such as PETA (People for the Ethical Treatment of Animals), believe that animals have rights and should not be abused for the sake of fashion. Consequently, these groups continually pressure companies to promote causes reflecting concern for animal welfare. Historically, PETA focused on banning fur in fashion, but recent campaigns include those against the use of leather, animal testing, and some farming methods involved in the production of textiles and fibers.

In addition to these campaigns, PETA also promotes designers who follow their philosophy concerning the ethical treatment of animals. For example, the PETA.org Web site reports that "many top designers, including Tommy Hilfiger, Ralph Lauren, Calvin Klein, Stella McCartney, Betsey Johnson, Marc Bouwer, Rebecca Taylor, Kenneth Cole, and others, have chosen to take a compassionate stand and rid their lines of fur—or have never used fur at all." Due in part to PETA's tactics, both fur and leather manufacturers have formed their own associations to educate consumers about their products and to help counteract the bad publicity. In addition, many cosmetic companies promote the fact that they do not test their products on animals.

In one of PETA's most recent campaigns, the Australian farming practice known as "mulesing" has come under attack for its unethical treatment of sheep. PETA describes mulesing as a method that involves carving huge strips of flesh off the backs of anaesthetized lambs' legs. However, in a recent full-page ad in *Women's Wear Daily*, the Australian Wool Industry (AWI) defended this practice stating that mulesing prevents the lambs from suffering flystrike, a deadly disease that, without mulesing, would claim an estimated three million sheep a year. Additionally, the public service ad stated that the Australian Veterinary Association (AVA) accepts the practice because it promotes the health and well-being of the sheep. After four days of mediation, the AWI recently agreed to drop its two-year-old lawsuit against PETA, while PETA agreed to temporarily suspend its worldwide activities against the AWI. Actions of PETA against the AWI included calls for boycotts of any retailer selling products made of mulesed wool. The retailers targeted included Abercrombie & Fitch, J.Crew, and Benetton. Additionally, PETA recruited celebrities such as singer Pink and Australian actress Toni Colette to promote that cause. With the settlement, both sides claimed victory (Huntington, 2007). Regardless, in any situation involving animal rights, companies must decide their ethical position, and consumers must decide whether it matters enough to keep them from purchasing a company's products.

Charitable Contributions and Causes

Many companies have long recognized the positive relationship between participation in charitable causes and good business. Events and initiatives rooted in community development build respect among employees, community members and leaders, and consumers of company-produced products and services (Paulins and Hillery, 2005). Consequently, almost all large retailers today support charitable causes and sponsor programs aimed at improving the lives of others. Known also as *cause-related marketing*, these programs often receive free publicity and can therefore make significant strides in promoting goodwill for the retailer. Such programs of goodwill are often promoted to prospective employees as a way to present the company culture in a positive light. Box 2.2 outlines some specific examples of charitable causes and programs either supported or created by retailers and apparel merchandisers.

Hall (1999), however, offers a warning with regard to cause-related marketing: it must be viewed as sincere and aligned with the company's core ideology, as well as the cause it supports, he asserts. Otherwise, consumers may have a negative response because they believe the company is involved with the charity to create a positive customer response rather than actually believing in the cause itself.

CHARITABLE CAUSES AND PROGRAMS OF SELECTED RETAILERS AND APPAREL COMPANIES

Macy's Inc.

Macy's is the sponsor of many charitable events, including "Passport," which raises money for HIV/AIDS, "For the Love of Her Life," which funds research for breast cancer, and "The American Heart Association's Go Red for Women Program," which raises women's awareness of heart disease.

SOURCE: http://www.macys.com/store/about/community

American Eagle

American Eagle works with The Student Conservation Association (SCA) to encourage high school and college students to volunteer their time to help protect parks and restore the environment. American Eagle sponsors events put on by the SCA and also provides volunteers with official SCA clothing. American Eagle also works in collaboration with Big Brothers Big Sisters, which provides mentors for children. American Eagle launched the fundraising event "Bowl for Kids Sake" in 2006, which has already raised thousands of dollars to keep the Big Brothers Big Sisters program alive.

SOURCE: http://www.aebetterworld.com

H&M

H&M and UNICEF signed a 3-year co-operation deal in 2004 that includes an education project for girls in developing countries and a project to prevent the spread of HIV among young people in Cambodia.

SOURCE: http://www.hm.com/us/corporateresponsibility/wesupport

Kohls

Kohl's Cares for Kids is a program that aims to help children stay healthy by means of injury prevention and immunization programs. The Kohl's Cares for Kids program also offers a scholarship program for young volunteers and sells special merchandise, whose profits have raised more than $85 million since 2000 for the Kohl's Cares for Kids programs.

SOURCE: http://www.kohlscorporation.com/CommunityRelations/Community

BOX 2.2 continued from page 40

CHARITABLE CAUSES AND PROGRAMS OF SELECTED RETAILERS AND APPAREL COMPANIES

Patagonia

Patagonia cofounded The Conservation Alliance in 1989, with the goal of encouraging companies in the outdoor industry to support environmental organizations in their efforts to protect threatened wild lands. To date the groups funded have saved over 34 million acres of wild lands and 14 dams have been either prevented or removed—all through grassroots community efforts.

SOURCE: http://www.patagonia.com/web/us/contribution

Sears

Heroes at Home is a program Sears Holdings has created in partnership with Rebuilding Together in response to an urgent need to assist military families facing hardship. Rebuilding Together, the nation's largest all-volunteer home rehabilitation organization, is committed to bringing warmth, safety, and accessibility to homeowners who do not have the financial or physical resources to complete home repairs and other necessary improvements.

SOURCE: http://www.searsholdings.com/communityrelations/hero

JCPenney

JCPenney has created the JCPenney Afterschool Fund, which provides children in need with after-school programs to foster their academic, physical, and social development. This program raises awareness of the need for after-school programs; JCPenney sells promotional items (such as the High School Musical 2 soundtrack) in its stores to raise money for the program.

SOURCE: http://www.jcpenneyafterschool.org

GAP

GAP has partnered with The Global Fund to create a new brand, Product(Red). Half of the profits from Product(Red) merchandise is given to the Global Fund, which helps women and children affected by AIDS in Africa.

SOURCE: http://www.gap.com

Box 2.2 continued from page 41

CHARITABLE CAUSES AND PROGRAMS OF SELECTED RETAILERS AND APPAREL COMPANIES

TJMaxx

For over 20 years, TJMaxx has been in partnership with the Save the Children program. This program advocates for the health of children and focuses on early childhood development, literacy, and physical activity and nutrition programs. For $1, TJMaxx customers can donate to help this cause.

SOURCE: http://www.tjmaxx.com/oneforchange_charity.asp

Eddie Bauer

Eddie Bauer has established the "Add a Dollar, Plant a Tree" program, which has raised over $5 million by asking customers to give one dollar in addition to their purchase, which is used to plant trees in urban areas or areas that have been affected by natural disasters.

SOURCE: http://investors.eddiebauer.com/responsibility/forests.cfm

Maurice's

Since 2005, Maurice's has donated over $600,000 to the American Cancer Society through in-store promotions and Relay for Life teams. Maurice's sells bracelets and plush dogs with 100 percent of the profits going toward the American Cancer Society.

SOURCE: http://www.maurices.com

Younkers

Each spring and fall, Younkers hold a "Goodwill Sale" in which customers receive coupons to use at Younkers if they bring in used clothes to be donated to Goodwill. Goodwill offers training and job placement for people who are experiencing barriers to employment. Younkers also makes charitable donations to causes such as The United Way and the Holden Comprehensive Cancer Center at The University of Iowa.

SOURCE: http://www.younkers.com/category/our+community/goodwill+sale.do

Box 2.2 continued from page 42
CHARITABLE CAUSES AND PROGRAMS OF SELECTED RETAILERS AND APPAREL COMPANIES

Target

Target participates in many charitable activities, many within the areas of education, arts, and keeping families safe. One example of this involvement is the company's partnership with The Salvation Army, in which Target provides grants and volunteers to local chapters in order to help with issues such as disaster relief.

SOURCE: http://sites.target.com/site/en/corporate/page

Bloomingdale's

Bloomingdale's has adopted "The Little Pink Campaign to Fight Breast Cancer," which is a program that has raised $180 million since it was established in 1993 by Evelyn Lauder. During the month of October, national breast cancer awareness month, Bloomingdale's sells special "Pink" merchandise. For every dollar of Pink merchandise sold, a minimum of 85 cents goes to breast cancer research and programs.

SOURCE: http://www.bloomingdales.com

POLICIES GOVERNING VENDOR BEHAVIOR AND RELATIONSHIPS

In 1995, following government investigations into sweatshop conditions and incidents of child labor by some manufacturers of products for the American marketplace, Federated (now Macy's, Inc.) adopted a stringent Vendor/Supplier Code of Conduct that articulates specific standards and requirements for any vendor doing business with Macy's, Inc. Box 2.3 contains the preface page for the Macy's, Inc. Vendor & Supplier Code of Conduct, which provides an overview of the company's policies. Today, most large companies have similar policies regarding the behavior of their vendors in the manufacturing of the company's products. Most of the statements address issues concerning compliance with labor laws, environmental issues, factory conditions, and product labeling. For example, J.C. Penney Company, Inc. addresses vendor selection and compliance (in part) in the following:

> In selecting suppliers, JCPenney tries to identify reputable companies that are willing and able to conduct their business in conformity with all applicable legal requirements and the high ethical standards espoused by JCPenney (www.jcpenney.com).

Box 2.3

PREFACE FOR MACY'S, INC. VENDOR AND SUPPLIER CODE OF CONDUCT

This Vendor/Supplier Code of Conduct sets forth the commitment of Macy's to do business only with those manufacturers and suppliers that share its commitment to fair and safe labor practices. It applies to all suppliers and/or contractors providing merchandise to Macy's Merchandising Group or any of Macy's department [or specialty] store subsidiaries.

This Code of Conduct is divided into three parts. Part I sets forth the general principles upon which the Vendor/Supplier Code of Conduct is based. Part II sets forth the standards that will be used in evaluating compliance and Part III presents methods for the evaluation of vendor/supplier compliance with the Code of Conduct.

The Vendor/Supplier Code of Conduct defines our minimum expectations. Since no Code can be all-inclusive, we expect our vendors and suppliers to ensure that no abusive or exploitative conditions and practices or unsafe working conditions exist at the facilities where our merchandise is manufactured. As set forth in Macy's Statement of Corporate Policy, which has been distributed to all Macy's vendors, the company will not tolerate any vendor or supplier that directly or indirectly, through its subcontractors, violates the laws of the country where the merchandise is manufactured or knowingly violates the standards established by Macy's. Macy's will take appropriate action in accordance with its policy upon notification of such violation.

A copy of this Vendor/Supplier Code of Conduct, translated into the native languages of the workforce, should be prominently displayed within each facility where Macy's merchandise is being manufactured.

SOURCE: The Macy's, Inc. Code of Conduct is available in its entirety at http://www.macysinc.com/company/minc_code_of_conduct.pdf. Reprinted with permission.

Retailers also have policies that govern vendor relationships in terms of selling their products to the company. And many companies, such as T.J.Maxx and Von Maur, prohibit their employees from accepting gifts from vendors because employees could then feel a sense of obligation or pressure to buy products from those vendors. A statement published in *Daily News Record* (November 7, 2005) explained the policy concerning gifts at The TJX companies. The full-page statement, which was addressed to manufacturers and suppliers, explained that associates were prohibited from accepting any types of "gifts, gratuities, payments, or favors of any kind" because, in TJX's view, such gifts "tend to shake the moral structure of the firmest business foundations." Other companies have a similar "zero-gifts" policy such as Wal-Mart, which will not even allow its employees to pick up "freebies" at trade shows (Hisey, 2002). Other companies let their own employees accept gifts—as long as the value of the gifts is less than a certain monetary amount (e.g., less than $100). Regardless of the company policy (and although the consumers may never consider this), it does affect employees' interaction with vendors, and in turn, sets the tone for another aspect of corporate culture.

Manufacturers may also establish codes of behavior in order to clarify their relationships with retailers. In fact, manufacturers formed the Vendor Coalition for Equitable Retailer Practices. According to Donald Kreindler, an attorney at the law firm at which the group had its first meeting in June 2005, the goal of this organization is to "create a better partnership with the retail community so both retailers and their vendors can make a fair profit." This coalition was formed primarily in response to a scandal at Saks in 2005. In this case, vendors were charged millions in fraudulent "markdown money"—the funds that department stores deduct from vendors' payments when goods don't sell briskly enough. (This case is discussed further in Chapter 3 to illustrate unethical behavior on the part of employees.) With the formation of this coalition, and in order to prevent further instances of such behavior by retailers, vendors stated that they simply wanted to view retailers as partners and not adversaries (Young, 2005).

In conclusion, virtually all operations and interactions within a company affect its corporate culture. The atmosphere resulting from the corporate culture affects how employees feel about the company, which subsequently affects how they behave in matters relating to productivity and ethical decisions and behaviors. In general, the best companies to work for continually focus on keeping their employees happy, are employee-centered, and have lower turnover. People-centered companies are also more profitable than those that focus solely on profit (Hall, 1999). On the other hand, when companies face scandals involving the unethical behaviors of employees, consumers often react negatively to the news. For example, Saks' profits dropped 20 percent after its scandal involving markdown money (Kratz, 2005), which is discussed in more detail in Chapter 3.

Of course, as with any ethical question, the "right" or "best" action is often not clear-cut. For example, consider the case of mulesing. Is the procedure worth the protection that the wool industry claims it offers to the animals? Another case in point: Are the excellent wages paid at American Apparel enough to counterbalance the work atmosphere that has led to sexual discrimination lawsuits pending against the company? (See Chapter 3 for further discussion.) The opening bash at

BOX 2.4

WHAT DO COLLEGE STUDENTS AND NEW GRADS LOOK FOR IN AN EMPLOYER?

Students responding to NACE's 2006 Graduating Student & Alumni Survey listed their criteria for choosing an employer as follows:

1. Enjoying what I do

2. Integrity of organization in its dealings with its employees (treats them with honesty and fairness)

3. Ethical business practices (doesn't cut corners or break any laws)

4. Good benefits package

5. Stability (provides secure future)

SOURCE: Reprinted from 2007 Job Outlook, with permission of the National Association of Colleges and Employers (NACE), copyright holder.

the A&F corporate headquarters may sound like a great time but what about the discrimination suit it agreed to settle? Wal-Mart offers great prices but at what expense to its employees? There are no easy answers. Consumers can speak loudly with the dollars they spend (or do not spend) at a particular company. Prospective employees should consider at least some of the factors that contribute to the corporate culture of a particular business when weighing career opportunities. It all depends on what is most important to the individual and how well companies match up with those priorities. Box 2.4 provides an overview of the factors college students look for when considering a possible employer.

QUESTIONS FOR DISCUSSION

1. Can you think of other factors that contribute to corporate culture that are not mentioned in the chapter? Explain how they may pose ethical issues for companies.

2. Considering the discussion of corporate culture, what are your three most important issues when seeking an employer? Explain your answer.

3. What unethical behavior have you witnessed at school or at a job? Why do you think people engage in such behavior?

4. List three reasons why you think it is important to report unethical behavior at work.

5. Why do you think that so much observed unethical behavior goes unreported?

6. Do you think Wal-Mart and other large companies should be obligated to pay a portion of employees' health care? Why or why not?

7. What are your thoughts concerning Casual Friday? Do you think it hurts the image that people have of a company?

8. Do you agree or disagree with the ruling in favor of Harrah's, which requires women to wear makeup to work? Explain your answer.

9. Besides the examples given in the book concerning corporate social responsibility, what are some others you are aware of?

10. Identify at least five charitable causes supported by retailers other than the ones discussed in this chapter.

11. Why do you think companies need to have a vendor code of conduct?

12. Now that you know about the settlement of the discrimination lawsuit against Abercrombie & Fitch, does it change the way you view that company's "diversity and inclusion" statements and practices listed on its Web site? Do you believe A&F is sincere in its efforts—or did the company do this solely because it was ordered to?

REFERENCES AND SUGGESTED READING

Asacker, T. (2004). Ethics in the workplace: Start with honesty. T + D, 58(8), 42–44.

Carli, D., Frink, D., Jones, D., Kachura, P., Rusoo, R., Sanger, et al. (2007). *Best practices: It's good to be green (Part 6 of the SmartReply Benchmarking Series)*. Retrieved on March 12, 2008 from http://www.smartreply.com

Chang, H. (May 2004). A more diverse workforce is good for business at PepsiCo. Retrieved on March 12, 2008 from http://www.gsb.stanford.edu/news/headlines/vftt_reinemund.shtml

Christopher, B. (February 2007). Are we having fun yet? Attitude and peak performance in the workplace. *Business Credit*, 109(2), 63–64.

Colb, S. (January 11, 2005). Makeup requirements for female employees violate anti-discrimination law: Why a federal appeals court erred in ruling to the contrary. Retrieved on March 12, 2008 from http://www.findlaw.com/colb/20050111.html

Crary, D. (November 21, 2006). Conservatives plan to protest Wal-Mart's outreach to gays. *Associated Press*.

Deal, T. & Kennedy, A. (1982). *Corporate cultures: The rites and rituals of corporate life*. Reading, MA: Addison-Wesley Publishing Co.

Dow Jones Newswire (October 20, 2006). Wal-Mart dress code replaces blue vest with polo shirt. Retrieved on March 12, 2008 from http://www.wakeupwalmart .com/news/20061020-djn.html

Ellis, K. (July 20, 2006). Health law aimed at Wal-Mart overturned. *Women's Wear Daily*, 3.

EPA names JCPenney 2007 ENERGY STAR® Retail Partner of the Year. Retrieved on March 12, 2008 from http://www.jcpenney.net/company/awards/energystar.pdf

Face value: Dov Charney, the hustler (January 6, 2007). *The Economist*, 382(8510), 55–56.

Feitelberg, R. (October 17, 2007). Panel urges runway, fashion ad diversity. *Women's Wear Daily*, p. 4.

Fiertag, H. (December 13, 1999). Environment: the foundation of motivation. *Hotel & Motel Management*, 214(21), 48.

Gebler, D. (May 2006). Creating an ethical culture: Values-based ethics programs can help employees judge right from wrong. *Strategic Finance*, 29–34.

Gunther, M. (June 22, 2007). Plugged-in: Wal-Mart shuns gay groups. Retrieved on March 12, 2008 from http://money.cnn.com/2007/06/22/magazines/fortune/ pluggedin_gunther_walmart.fortune/index.htm

Hall, J. (1999). Corporate ethics and the new commercial paradigm. *The Journal of Brand Management*, 7(1), 38–47.

Hansen, R. (2007). Uncovering a company's corporate culture is a critical task for job-seekers. Retrieved on March 12, 2008 from http://www.careerdoctor.org/ Randall_Hansen_career_articles.html

High court limits pay-discrimination claims: Ruling favors employers in disputes with workers. *Associated Press*, May 29, 2007. Retrieved on March 12, 2008 from http://www.msnbc.msn.com/id/18920357/

Hisey, P. (May 2002). Retail: The state of ethics. *Retail Merchandiser*, 42(5), 17–18.

Holland, J. (July 24, 2007). Minimum wage will rise today. *Washington Post*, p. D03.

Huntington, P. (July 5, 2007). Australian wool industry, PETA come to terms. *Women's Wear Daily*, 16.

Hymowitz, C. (November 14, 2005). The new diversity. *Wall Street Journal*, p. R1.

Johnson, P. and Indvik, J. (2006). Sticks and stones: Verbal abuse in the workplace. *Journal of Organizational Culture, Communication & Conflict*, 10(1), 121–126.

Kersten, E. (February 2006). Why they call it work. *Harvard Business Review*, 66–67.

Kratz, E. (August 22, 2005). Marked down: How fashionable Saks Fifth Avenue swapped style for scandal—and turned itself into a bargain-priced takeover target. *Fortune*, 103–108.

Landmark Abercrombie & Fitch discrimination settlement (April 2005). Retrieved on March 12, 2008 from http://www.calchamber.com/hrc.html

Lee, K. and Gao, T. (2005). Studying organizational commitment with the OCQ in the Korean retail context: Its dimensionality and relationships with satisfaction and work outcomes. *International Review of Retail, Distribution & Consumer Research*, 15(4), 375–399.

Osterman, R. (August 22, 2005). Should women be required to wear makeup on job? *The Athens [Ohio] Messenger*, p. 5.

New trends (September 2004). T + D, 58(9), 13.

Paulins, A. and Hillery, J. (2005). CAREERS! *Professional development for retailing and apparel merchandising*. New York: Fairchild Publications.

Reuters (June 21, 2007). Jury awards $2M to ex-Wal-Mart worker. Retrieved on March 12, 2008 from http://money.cnn.com/2007/06/21/news/companies/walmart_suit .reut/?postversion=2007062110

Sachdev, A. (July 31, 2007). Nike to pay 400 Chicago employees $7.6 million to settle discrimination suit. *Chicago Tribune* (Business Section), 3.

Safer, M. (Producer). (November 24, 2004). *60 Minutes*: The look of Abercrombie [television broadcast]. New York: CBS News.

Schneider, G. and ElBoghdady, D. (July 27, 2003). In a global market, it takes all kinds: More companies are finding employee diversity is good for business. *Washington Post*, p. K02.

Shop and Save (July/August 2007). *Sierra*, 92(4), 26.

TJX (November 7, 2005). To our manufacturers and suppliers: Statement of policy concerning gifts. DNR, 13.

Torkells, E. (June 25, 2001). Abercrombie & Fitch. *Fortune*, 143(14), 198.

Valas, E. (April 2007). The best companies focus on employees. *Dealerscope*, 49(4), 28.

Vandervelt, I. (Executive Producer). (April 17, 2006). *American made* [television broadcast]. New York: CNBC.

Verschoor, C. C. (2005). Ethical culture: Most important barrier to ethical misconduct. *Strategic Finance*, 87(6), 19–20.

Wagner, J. and Barbaro, M. (April 6, 2005). Maryland passes rules on Wal-Mart: Insurance bill obligates firms on health spending. *Washington Post*, p. A01.

Wal-Mart opens second "high-efficiency" unit store in Northern Illinois (March 15, 2007). *Progressive Grocer*. Retrieved on March 15, 2007 from http://www.allbusiness. com/ retail-trade/food-stores/4263691-1.html

Young, V. (June 27, 2006). Angry vendors form coalition. *Daily News Record*, p. 4.

Chapter 3

Management, Supervision, and Workplace Issues

THE OBJECTIVES OF THIS CHAPTER ARE TO:

- Identify a variety of ethical workplace issues relevant to the fashion and retailing industries

- Understand the realm of ethical decisions that affect workplace satisfaction and work productivity

- Explore ways to approach workplace ethical dilemmas to achieve appropriate and optimal outcomes

---

One of the greatest challenges for businesses is to recognize that employees may bring personal values into workplaces that do not align with those of the organization. Further complicating the matter is the human ability to rationalize practically anything. Research has shown that individuals tend to view others based on their *behaviors*, whereas they view themselves based on their *intentions* (James, 2002). Therefore, companies interested in maintaining a high ethical standard throughout their operations, including the work environment, need to provide structured workplace opportunities to reconcile individuals' preexisting values with the values implicit in a formula for workplace success. In other words, companies need to equip employees to apply the organization's values (not theirs) when making business decisions (Lagan, 2006). A recent example of this involved Walgreens, in which four of its pharmacists in the St. Louis area were disciplined for not filling prescriptions for an emergency contraceptive pill (i.e., the "morning after" pill). The pharmacists, who were placed on unpaid leave, cited religious and moral objections to filling the prescriptions, but Walgreens claimed that the four

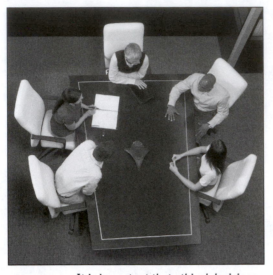

FIGURE 3.1   It is important that ethical decisions are made in the workplace.

were in violation of a state law. In states where there is no law prohibiting the actions taken by the pharmacists, Walgreens' policy says that pharmacists can refuse to fill prescriptions to which they are morally opposed. However, they must also take steps to have the prescription filled by another pharmacist or store ("Pharmacists disciplined," 2005). Situations such as this, where service providers act independently of store or company policy, introduce serious challenges for retailers. Consider the sales associate who does not want to sell fur coats or the brand representative who is opposed to promoting diamonds mined in South Africa. The individual ethical decisions of employees can have significant impacts on the well-being of retailers' bottom lines and reputations.

INTRODUCTION TO ETHICAL BEHAVIOR AT WORK

A big challenge facing young professionals as they transition into their careers is how to best handle the many ethical issues the corporate world will introduce. According to an article in *Retail Merchandiser*, ethical issues for retailers are expected to increase in the years ahead (Hisey, 2002), making preparation for such challenges essential. Just like any other business venture, the increase in ethical dilemmas is partly driven by the tremendous pressure on retailers to perform and to meet sales projections.

Although the retail industry has been considered a relatively "clean" sector, it has certainly not been without its own ethical scandals. Several examples of unethical behavior include the collapses of Phar-Mor and Crazy Eddie's in the 1990s due to stock fraud; Wal-Mart being publicly scandalized for the sale of foreign-made products billed as "Made in the USA," and more recently, for unfair employee wages and benefits; Sears' use of high-pressure sales tactics with automotive consumers to sell more expensive brakes and batteries rather than lower-priced products that were better suited for their particular vehicles; Saks, Inc.'s involvement in fraud-ulent chargebacks with many of the company's key vendors; and Abercrombie & Fitch for illegal hiring practices (selecting employees based on their appearance).

As previously mentioned, a key reason for misbehavior in the retailing arena is the incredible pressure companies are under to perform at profitable levels. These pressures, and sometimes unrealistic goals, often give employees strong tempta-tions to cheat and lead them to ethical lapses. Ken Clark (2006), in a cover story for *Chain Store Age*, reported that experts believe bad behavior manifests as mistreat-ment of employees by management, mistreatment of customers by employees, and employees behaving badly toward the company. For example, in order to meet sales projections, managers will sometimes put undue pressure on salespeople resulting in questionable sales techniques being used with customers (see Chapter 8 for further discussion on this topic). Such pressures can result in unhappy employees, which may lead them to commit petty theft, timecard fraud, substance or alcohol abuse at work, and perform careless recordkeeping (Clark, 2006). This situation should be taken very seriously by retailers because, according to a report released by the National Retail Federation (NRF) and the University of Florida (Giovis, 2007), retailers in the United States lost a record $41.6 billion in 2006 to employee theft, fraud, shoplifting, and internal accounting errors! This figure represents an 11.2 percent increase over 2005, with the losses remaining at about 1.6 percent of total annual retail sales.

Wal-Mart recently reported experiencing an increase in shrinkage and suggested that employee theft, paperwork errors, supplier fraud, and shoplifting could be increasing. It was estimated that Wal-Mart would lose $3 billion in 2007 to such behavior. Analysts tie the increase to three factors: first, in 2006 Wal-Mart decided to no longer prosecute minor (less than $25) shoplifting cases in order to concentrate on organized shoplifting rings. The second factor is the reduction in loss-prevention staff and the redesign of their jobs, making them more admin-istrative and less active. Third, is the perception and/or proof of mistreatment of employees—for example, poor pay/benefits and gender discrimination—as the reason for shrinkage (see also the discussion of this in Chapter 2). One former employee of the company stated that, although she was not the type to steal, she was so unhappy with the mistreatment of co-workers that when she saw others walking out of the store with bags of unpaid merchandise, she simply turned her head rather than reporting it (D'Innocenzio and Kabel, 2007).

From a human-interest perspective, it is intriguing that in many cases of uneth-ical behavior, a variety of players at several different levels can agree to go along with bad behavior. A number of studies suggest that such observations are not surprising (Gurchiek, 2006; Millage, 2005; "Whistleblowing," 2006). For example, a survey conducted in 2005 by the Ethics Resource Center (ERC) found that over half of the 3,000 U.S. workers polled had observed at least one type of ethical misconduct in the past year, but only 47 percent of them had reported it. Abusive or intimidating behavior toward employees (21 percent) and lying to employees, customers, vendors, or the public (19 percent) were the two most common types of misconduct observed by the respondents. The top three reasons given by Gurchiek and Millage for not reporting the bad behavior were:

1. Belief that the organization wouldn't take appropriate action to correct the misconduct

2. Fear that one's supervisor or management would retaliate

3. Distrust that whistle-blowing efforts would be treated confidentially

Although it may be surprising that unethical behavior goes unreported, this is most likely due to the fact that "whistle-blowing" can be very risky. In fact, studies have shown that up to 95 percent of whistle-blowers lose their jobs when they report a problem! If retained, they are often made to feel so uncomfortable that they leave their jobs on their own. This creates a type of "catch-22" for employees because if they read and sign a code of ethics, usually they are obligated to report violations; however, reporting the problem can have serious consequences for the whistle-blower rather than for the person committing the ethical violation. In a recent survey by LRN, an ethics research and consulting firm, about one-third of the workers who took part said they didn't report an unethical incident they had witnessed, and of those, 14 percent said they were not confident about how it would be handled if they had reported the incident (Gogoi, 2007).

Although most students have work experiences in environments that practice and encourage good ethical behavior (Paulins, 2001), future retail managers and apparel product development supervisors are, unfortunately, introduced to myriad workplace dilemmas early in their careers. In a survey of merchandising interns (Paulins and Lombardy, 2005), students reported ethical dilemmas in the areas of management, selling, employee relationships, professionalism, policy implementation, stealing, and honesty. The "top five" universally recognized ethical dilemmas reported, in terms of their ratings of severity by another group of internship students, were employees stealing money, employees stealing merchandise, racism, pornography in the workplace, and suspicion of theft that goes unreported. These activities are clearly inappropriate in the workplace; however, the behaviors that were rated less ethically problematic are also worthy of exploration and discussion because they present greater controversy and conflict for the employees involved. Identified among the least problematic ethical dilemmas were employees using merchandise holds against company policy; lying to customers about how clothing and accessories look on them in order to make sales; employees taking items such as paper, pens, envelopes, and postage for personal use; managers adopting "favorite" employees who are assigned more desirable tasks; and supervisors engaging in romantic relationships with subordinates. The fact that these behaviors ranked among those that are unethical indicates the presence of principles in future fashion industry leaders, but the fact that these issues were rated as minor could be problematic if a person actually finds him- or herself embroiled in such a controversy.

Ethics orientation and training was found to be a component of students' retail merchandising internships for 43 percent of students in a study conducted several years ago (Paulins, 2001). Ethics training activities included reviewing codes of conduct, attending seminars, watching relevant videos, and signing policy adherence forms. Although this study found that in general students and supervisors reported good ethics being practiced in the field, interestingly, supervisors had a significantly more positive view of the ethical environments in which they work than their interns. This difference contrasts somewhat with a longitudinal study (Glenn and Van Loo, 1993) that found, when comparing students and practitioners, the former consistently make less ethical choices than the latter. These findings present an opportunity to explore whether students' initial interpretations of ethical environments change over time as they become "acclimatized" to the workplace, and whether managers rationalize behaviors in different ways than their interns. Whether behaviors accurately reflect attitudes is another important area of inquiry. This also raises the question of whether students go into workplaces with sufficient information to make appropriate ethical choices. You, the reader, are encouraged to think about the ethical environments of your workplace and to evaluate the way your approach to ethics may or may not change. This can be particularly difficult for interns and employees new to their positions, so it is important to consider possible problems in anticipation of ethical dilemmas.

> **Box 3.1**
>
> **CORPORATE POLICIES/POSITION: BUSINESS ETHICS—MACY'S, INC.**
>
> - Each Federated associate and any member of an associate's immediate family will avoid any situation that creates, potentially creates or gives the appearance of creating a conflict between the associate's personal interests and the interests of the Company. Further, no Federated associate or any member of an associate's immediate family will request or accept—or direct others to request or accept—gifts, gift certificates, discounts, gratuities, or any other item of significant value (including services of any nature) from any vendor, supplier or resource with whom Federated or any of its divisions has an existing or potential business relationship.
> - No Federated associate or member of his or her immediate family is permitted to have any financial or other interest direct or indirect in any of the Company's suppliers or other companies with whom Federated has business dealings. This requirement applies regardless of whether the associate has any direct Company-related business dealing with the supplier or vendor. If an associate becomes involved in such business dealings with a company in which the associate or a member of his/her immediate family holds a financial or other interest, the associate is required to disclose to the Company any such holdings. Disclosures of potential conflicts of interest are to be made to the Office of Compliance immediately upon their origination, as well as annually on the Business Ethics Statement. Ownership of a small minority interest in a publicly owned company whose shares are traded through normal markets will not ordinarily give rise to a conflict.
> - Within reasonable bounds, Federated associates are not permitted to requisition Company property, funds or personnel—or use Company time, facilities or equipment for personal use—without proper authorization and reimbursement.
> - No Federated associate shall disclose to anyone outside of the Company, or use in other than the Company's business, any confidential information relating

CORPORATE CODES OF ETHICS

In order to provide guidelines for employees concerning their expected behavior, most major retailers have developed a code of ethics. These written statements usually provide employees with general guidelines for making decisions; some also define forbidden behaviors. Macy's, Inc. specifically spells out its corporate policies of expected behaviors for each associate in terms of discrimination, conflicts of

Box 3.1 continued from page 56
CORPORATE POLICIES/POSITION: BUSINESS ETHICS—MACY'S, INC.

to the Company's business or future business plans unless such disclosure is specifically authorized in advance by the Company.

- A Federated associate may not use for personal advantage or enable others to use material, non-public information about Federated or any company with whom Federated or its divisions have a business relationship.
- Federated and its divisions will take appropriate steps to avoid and correct, or to monitor and control, hazardous workplace conditions when they exist.
- It is against Company policy for any associate, male or female, to unlawfully harass another associate.
- The Company prohibits the use or possession of illegal drugs or alcohol by an associate in the workplace, including working under the influence of such substances.
- Unlawful discrimination in any form will not be tolerated within the Company. The Company will be proactive in keeping the workplace free of such discrimination.
- The Company encourages associates to participate in constructive charitable causes and with established community organizations whose missions are to better the quality of life for persons in the communities in which our associates live and work.
- Federated and its divisions will annually target a percentage of their pre-tax earnings for such charitable contributions, believing that it is fundamentally good business to support the communities that support us.
- Federated and its divisions will strictly adhere to all federal, state and local laws governing campaigns and elections. No corporate funds will be used for political contributions in support of any party or candidate in any federal, state or local election.

SOURCE: http://www.federated-fds.com/company/ethics.asp. Reprinted with permission

interests, use of drugs and alcohol, personal use of equipment during work hours, and the disclosure of confidential company information (see Box 3.1 for Macy's, Inc. Corporate Policies/Positions concerned with individual associate behavior).

JCPenney also outlines its expectations for employee behavior; this includes three key principles that address compliance under the law, conflicts of interest, and preservation of company assets. All managers and associates are required to

BOX 3.2
THE JCPENNEY IDEA

1. To serve the public, as nearly as we can, to its complete satisfaction.

2. To expect for the service we render a fair remuneration and not all the profit the traffic will bear.

3. To do all in our power to pack the customer's dollar full of value, quality, and satisfaction.

4. To continue to train ourselves and our associates so that the service we give will be more and more intelligently performed.

5. To improve constantly the human factor in our business.

6. To reward men and women in our organization through participation in what the business produces.

7. To test our every method, and act in this way: "Does it square with what is right and just?"

SOURCE: Davis, G. L. (2004). Business ethics: It's all inside JC Penney grounded in golden rules of business conduct. *American Journal of Business, 19,* 7–10. Reprinted with permission.

read and electronically sign a certificate of compliance (Davis, 2004). Furthermore, the company outlines "The JCPenney Idea," presented in Box 3.2.

Experts agree that creating strong ethical environments should be the top priority of all companies, even those without formal ethics programs (Vershoor, 2005). Schwartz (2004) reports that the mere existence of an ethical code alone will not positively affect employee behavior; for that type of company, possessing such a code may expose it to criticisms of mere "window dressing" if the company does not actually promote the ethical culture outlined. In fact, Valenti (2002) states that ethics' codes are sometimes more of an insurance policy for companies rather than a true commitment to their employees. A company can greatly reduce the amount of fines it might have to pay for employees who break the law by having a code of ethics in place.

The results of the 2005 National Business Ethics Survey (NBES) showed that less wrongdoing and more reporting of misconduct is associated with a superior ethical culture. In fact, the presence of a formal ethics and compliance program has less impact than an ethical culture, although the 2007 NBES found that companies with ethics programs in place had fewer employee problems in terms of unethical behaviors and decision making. An ethical company culture also helps prevent many causes of unethical behavior, including stress, perceived powerlessness, organizational culture, injustices, and labor-management issues (Kidwell and Koshcnowski, 2005).

The previous discussion highlights the importance of making sure you are in the right work environment so that you are less likely to witness behavior that makes you uncomfortable. As Daniel and Brandon (2006) state, you should never underestimate the importance of a good job fit, and moreover, one of the major contributing factors to a bad job fit is holding opposing views on etiquette or ethics. (Chapter 10 discusses this in greater detail.)

Although many people do not feel comfortable reporting unethical behavior, Ryan (2006) provides some suggestions about what employees can do when they encounter tough situations at work. She suggests that people listen to themselves and heed "gut" feelings. Second, she advises that if something does not feel right, it is probably a good idea to simply say, "I feel uncomfortable with this [decision/action]." Stating this will be more difficult for some people than others, but for the person who does speak up, it may be easier to live with that decision. The cost of not saying anything includes living with the regret of not doing what the person believed to be the right thing. In situations where unethical behaviors are scrutinized, people who were aware but silent can be held responsible by their companies for harboring important information and may face negative career repercussions. Of course, only the employee can know about his or her particular situation and what consequences speaking up may likely bring. If that person is in a positive environment, while the speaking up may make others uncomfortable or frustrated, the person is likely to be rewarded in the long run for following the company ethical code. Gary Davis former vice president for Human Resources at JCPenney, believes that each individual in a company, and particularly those in leadership roles, is responsible for building integrity and should do so in a positive way on a daily basis through every interaction with customers, co-workers, and superiors (2004). If the "emperor has no clothes,"[1] it's probably best to say so even though it will require a lot of courage. The goal is for a person to be able to look back on his or her professional life and feel good about his or her decisions and their positive effect on others. Remember too that building a reputation of integrity is a lifelong process—and one bad decision can wipe out years of work! To begin developing

BOX 3.3

WORKPLACE VALUES FOR STUDENTS TO PRACTICE DAILY

1. Honesty: Everyday you should tell the truth, even if doing so may shed negative light on you or your behaviors.

2. Quality: Do the best job you can in everything you do. Go above and beyond!

3. Reliability and Dependability: Show up when you say you will and be prepared to contribute to your class or group meeting. Show people that they can count on you!

4. Respect: If you want it, you have to give it and earn it!

5. Mutual Support: Take care of your teammates and classmates from an emotional standpoint. Be there when they need you.

6. Sense of Urgency: Get the job done in a timely manner but do it right and take your time as necessary.

7. Fairness: Everyone wants to be treated fairly but everyone defines it differently. What is your definition? Remember, life isn't always fair but at work you will need to decide what "fairness" is and distribute it as evenly as possible.

SOURCE: Davis, G. L. (2004). Business ethics: It's all inside JCPenney grounded in golden rules of business conduct. *American Journal of Business, 19,* 7–10. Reprinted with permission.

good workplace habits, Box 3.3 provides suggestions to help you start practicing positive workplace values.

On a related note, most people do not feel comfortable saying no to a boss who asks them to do something questionable (Valenti, 2002). Workers today do not want to make waves at work for fear that they will be alienated from their co-workers or even fired. Perhaps one of the best recent examples of this situation in the apparel retailing industry is the case of Saks Fifth Avenue. In 2005, Saks Fifth Avenue, Inc. was embroiled in a major scandal involving unethical behavior on the part of the company's senior executives, management, and members of the buying staff. In other words, people at all levels were allowed to act unethically without anyone speaking up. On a basic level, the scandal involved the improper collections of markdown money in the estimated amounts of $8.2 million from 1996 to 1998 and $26 million from 1999 to 2003 (Young, 2007). Markdown money is a common practice in the retailing industry today and is basically money given back to the retailers (buyers) by a vendor in situations where the vendor's merchandise had to be marked down in order to sell. Because markdowns lower the profit margin for the retailer, the buyer will try to negotiate a new lower price with the vendor on the marked-down merchandise to meet their projected level of profit. The difference in the negotiated new price and the old price (i.e., the markdown money) is deducted from the next season's order. This can place tremendous pressure on the vendor because failure to comply can result in the store placing no further orders. An even bigger problem in the case of Saks is that it collected markdown money for merchandise that was either not marked down at all, or was marked down to a lesser degree than what it claimed. The increased revenue it collected from vendors was reflected positively in Saks profit reports until information about this situation was revealed (Hogsett, 2005; Kratz, 2005 and 2006). Once the scandal surfaced, eight bridge department buyers were confronted and escorted out of the Saks store offices. Additionally, the company's Chief Administrative Officer, a Senior Vice President, and the Chief Accounting Officer were fired. Other firings and resignations also occurred in the months following (Moin and Young, 2005). After the scandal, Saks profits fell by more than 20 percent while competitors in the luxury market saw strong gains (Hogsett, 2005; Kratz, 2005 and 2006). By the time Saks had settled charges in the case with the Securities and Exchange Commission (SEC) in 2007, it had repaid vendors $48.2 million for reimbursement of markdown allowances and interest and had publicly faced a charge of violating the Securities and Exchange Act of 1934. Young (2007) reported that, according to the SEC complaint, "improper accounting by Saks resulted in aggressive financial targets the company set for its SFA division, and some SFA buyers believed they were expected to achieve their targets by deceptive means, if necessary." Saks continues to suffer from the negative impact of its actions. The interesting fact remains that nobody working at Saks formally spoke up while the unethical behavior was occurring!

Another high-profile retailer, Home Depot, discovered that four of its flooring buyers and merchandise managers received approximately $1 million in kickbacks from vendors for displaying their flooring products prominently in Home Depot stores. In addition to firing these employees, Home Depot instituted a zero-tolerance gift and entertainment policy for vendor-merchant relationships (Schultz, 2007).

Current Issues in Workplace Ethics

Just as the Saks scandal dominated the fashion industry news in 2005 and 2006, several other issues, including workplace bullying, sexual harassment, and appearance, are in the forefront today.

WORKPLACE BULLYING.   Although most of us may think of bullying as something that was left on the school playground, it is actually quite common in today's workplace. According to the Workplace Bullying Institute (WBI) (http://Bullying Institute.org), "workplace bullying: (a) is driven by perpetrators' need to control the targeted individual(s), (b) is initiated by bullies who choose target, timing, place, and method, (c) escalates to involve others who side with the bully, either voluntarily or through coercion, and it (d) undermines legitimate business interests when bullies' personal agendas take precedence over work itself." Bullies in the workplace display intimidation tactics such as screaming, yelling, and threatening others with termination or retaliation. They are also likely to make unreasonable job demands, constantly criticize performance, purposely exclude certain employees from meetings or necessary information, and block promotions. Just over 80 percent of bullies are those in a supervisory role, and 84 percent of targets by bullies are women. Although women and men are equally likely to be bullies, female bullies are more likely to target other women rather than men (Brunner and Costello, 2003). This suggests that females working under a female supervisor, a common situation in the fashion industry and the retailing field, are more likely to encounter bullies at work. However, Elias (2004) reports that more than 90 percent of all adults are likely to experience workplace abuse over the span of their careers.

In recent studies specifically examining bullying behavior, 80 percent of 800 respondents reported being bullied at work ("How to: beat the bullies," 2007) and nearly 45 percent of respondents reported having an abusive boss (Leonard, 2007). Although the causes for bullying vary, bullies are usually people with low self-esteem and when women in power bully other women, it has been suggested that they do so in order to protect the power base that they have already achieved. Bullies often will target those they feel most threatened by or inferior to. It is therefore not uncommon for overachievers to be targeted by bullies. Sadly, this often keeps other competent women from advancing. Furthermore, the female bully also serves as a poor role model for working women (Brunner and Costello, 2003).

Amble (2007) reports that one of the factors contributing to workplace bullying is that companies stress market processes, individualism, and the importance of managers over workers. However, many bullies do so simply because "they can." At the time of this writing, there is no U.S. law that specifically prohibits bullying (Canada, however, has recently passed an anti-bullying law in Quebec). As the issue becomes more prevalent and receives more national attention, workplace bullying will most likely be addressed in the courts. Nearly 65 percent of American workers surveyed believe that employees in the United States should have some legal recourse (Leonard, 2007). Several states have currently introduced anti-bullying legislation, an effort that is being driven by the Workplace Bullying Institute.

Despite the absence of law to protect against bullying, the wise employer will actively prevent it. Bullying, when allowed to continue, results in turnover, low morale, absenteeism, reduced credibility, and loss of reputation. The cost of replacing an employee who leaves because of bullying can be as high as 150 percent of the former worker's salary when taking into account the recruiting, training, and lost productivity costs (Amble, 2007). Furthermore, those being bullied can experience depression, insomnia, alcohol and drug abuse, decreased productivity, elevated stress levels, and diminished job satisfaction (Elias, 2004). Bullied employees will also often refocus their energies from workplace productivity to self-protection and decide to "punish" their employer by not coming to work, lowering the quality of work, or quitting (Johnson and Indvik, 2006). For suggestions on how to deal with bullying, see Box 3.4.

SEXUAL HARASSMENT.   Another issue closely aligned with workplace bullying, and which often includes bullying tactics, is sexual harassment. Sexual harassment is broadly defined as any unwanted sexual attention. According to Frank Till, the five categories of sexual harassment include:

1. Generalized sexist remarks or behavior.

2. Inappropriate and offensive, but essentially sanction-free, sexual advancements.

3. Solicitation of sexual activity or other sex-linked behavior by promise of rewards.

4. Coercion of sexual activity by threat of punishments.

5. Sexual assaults.

Box 3.4

WHAT CAN YOU DO IF YOU ARE BEING BULLIED AT WORK?

1. *Talk to someone you can trust.* Bullies often operate with the confidence that people will not speak up because of the fear of retaliation. Therefore it is important to speak up. If you do not feel comfortable speaking directly to the bully, find someone in authority who you trust to help you and who can investigate your situation. Most importantly, you cannot allow the bully to intimidate you because this will allow the bullying to continue.

2. *Document, in detail, all occurrences of bullying.* Some bullies are foolish enough to e-mail threats, or demonstrate their bullying through written communication; all of which you should print, put in a folder, and take home for safekeeping. For incidences where you do not have written or documented evidence, you should keep a detailed log of specifically what happened and how it made you feel. You should also note any workdays you missed, or illness(es) you believe you suffered because of the stress and pressure caused by the bully. It is very important to document everything in case you need to defend yourself against being fired, or if you file a grievance or lawsuit. Sometimes just letting others know you have "evidence" will deter future bullying and may even prompt management to address the problem before any formal action is taken.

3. *Do not blame yourself.* Bullying is an expression of a person's need for control and generally has nothing to do with the actions of the person being bullied. That

Younger, unmarried, females are more likely to experience sexual harassment than their older, married counterparts (Norton, 2002). Because two-thirds of retail sales personnel employed in the clothing, accessories, and general merchandise sectors are females under the age of 24, the risk of sexual harassment is greater than in other industries (U.S. Department of Labor, 2006). Workman (1993) found that 73.5 percent of female undergraduate students with fashion retail experience had experienced some type of sexually harassing behavior. Ten years later, the study was replicated (Leslie and Hauck, 2003) and concluded that sexual harassment continues to be a critical issue in the industry. The researchers also noted that, based on the current findings, it is possible that *three-fourths* of the graduates of retail and apparel merchandising programs will experience sexual harassment in the workplace! Because the

Box 3.4 continued from page 64
WHAT CAN YOU DO IF YOU ARE BEING BULLIED AT WORK?

is why most verbal abuse will take place in a one-on-one meeting where there are no other witnesses. In fact, many co-workers may actually blame the person being bullied because the "nice" person in power is not bullying them nor have they ever seen that person bullying anyone. Consequently the employee being bullied will not receive any validation of what is happening to him or her, which may result in self-blaming.

4. *Attend training classes.* If the bullying continues, you may want to sign up for assertiveness training classes and attend stress management classes. Learning how to better cope with the situation, while boosting your self-esteem, will help you identify strategies for addressing the bully and will also give you confidence to ward off any future workplace bully.

5. *Change jobs.* If the situation becomes intolerable and starts affecting you mentally or physically (usually it is both!), consider finding another position. Even though the situation is not your fault, you should not stay in a position that is having a negative affect on you. Companies are always looking for good employees, so there is no reason to stay at a company that allows bullying and verbal abuse to continue. Sometimes it is better to cut your losses and move on rather than to risk retaliation and further bullying. Only you can decide what is best for you!

majority of the cases reported tended to be the least severe types of sexual harassment, the authors of the study suggest that companies—at minimum—provide assertiveness training in how to deal with sexual harassment in an "informal" way. The informal methods for dealing with the unwanted sexual attention include avoiding the harasser, ignoring the behavior, and making a joke of the behavior. When victims were asked why they did not report the incidences or take more formal action, they responded that they thought it would make their workplace environment more unpleasant or that nothing would be done about it. Findings from the same study (Leslie and Hauck, 2003) also indicate that people who do not face sexual harassment report a more positive work environment than do victims, and that the former group also feel more positive than victims about their department's effort to stop sexual harassment.

A recent and noteworthy example of sexual harassment and sexual issues in the workplace can be illustrated by the case of Dov Charney, the CEO and founder of American Apparel Company. Specializing in casual clothes for men, women, and children, American Apparel opened its first store in 2003. The company's growth has been impressive since then; in 2007 the company had 143 stores in 11 countries with estimated sales at $300 million. American Apparel is known for its moderately priced (about $12), brightly colored T-shirts, as well as sweatshirts, underwear, and jeans. As discussed in Chapter 2, Charney has been praised for his anti-sweatshop manufacturing policies and for paying his employees significantly more than the minimum wage. He also provides employees with health insurance, shares of stock, English lessons, and subsidized meals ("Face value: Dov Charney, the hustler," 2007). However, in spite of all the good press surrounding Charney, his company may be best known for the sexually explicit image it has acquired through its advertising campaigns and through Charney's personal conduct. Box 3.5 provides a brief list of some actions and strategies that critics of American Apparel find offensive. Due to the atmosphere at American Apparel, four former employees have filed sexual harassment lawsuits against Charney claiming that he disgusted them with dirty talk and gestures, sexualized the workplace, made their life miserable, and fired them when they complained. To date, three of the cases have been settled and one is still pending ("Face value: Dov Charney, the hustler," 2007; Dean, 2006; Wolf, 2006). As a result of the lawsuit, and to prevent further sexual harassment cases, all employees of American Apparel are now required to sign an agreement stating that they realize that part of their job involves sexual language and visuals (Wolf, 2006). Dozens of young people contact American Apparel every week wanting to be part of the company's ads and thousands continue to pursue careers with the company at the retail level.

Codes and Regulations for Appearance

One of the more controversial ethical issues in the fashion industry today continues to be the impact it has on promoting eating disorders and an unhealthy lifestyle (see Chapter 7 for a discussion of issues related to advertising images). Although the fashion industry has been criticized for years for its promotion of an unachievable beauty ideal, in 2006 the death of Brazilian model Ana Carolina Reston at 23 from anorexia served to amplify the debate over the use of ultra-thin models. At the time of her death Reston weighed 88 pounds. Critics allege that clothing designers' use of underweight runway and print models encourages eating disorders such as

WHY ARE THE CRITICS MAD AT DOV CHARNEY AND AMERICAN APPAREL?

- Dov Charney, CEO and founder of American Apparel, decorates his office with vintage *Playboy* magazines, and pages ripped from a "Girls of Polynesia" calendar, which is also the merchandising theme in American Apparel's retail stores which feature covers from erotic magazines such as *Oui* and *Penthouse*. Among the stores offerings, besides T-shirts and underwear, are paperback books containing collections of erotic Japanese photos.
- Mr. Charney has been known to have his store managers call together store employees and tell them that they no longer work at American Apparel because their appearance does not fit the image of the store.
- Sexuality is at the core of American Apparel's ad campaign. The majority of the images found in the company's ads are taken by Mr. Charney and feature friends, employees, and people off the street. Most are in sexually explicit poses; some of which are in the shower or in bed; lounging on a sofa with legs spread, and are frequently wearing only one item of clothing. On occasion the models featured are Mr. Charney's girlfriends, whose pictures are taken on his bed suggesting that they were taken during a sexual encounter.
- American Apparel's Web site was cited by Adult Video News, a trade publication aimed at the porn industry, as one of the best soft-core Web sites. The Web site features sexually implicit pictures of American Apparel models, and at one point also featured a video of Mr. Charney walking around his office and workplace in nothing but his underwear.
- During an interview with a *Jane* magazine reporter, when the conversation turned to sexuality and masturbation, he decided to provide the reporter with a demonstration as the interview continued.
- Dov Charney does not believe in marriage, monogamy, nor is he ashamed to acknowledge consensual sexual relations with his employees. He also encourages employees to have sex with each other because he believes it enhances the creativity within his company.

SOURCES: Dean, J. (September 2005). Dov Charney, like it or not. *INC* magazine, 124–131; Face value: Dov Charney, the hustler (January 6, 2007). *Economist, 382*(8510), 55; Wolf, J. (April 23, 2006). And you thought Abercrombie and Fitch was pushing it? *The New York Times Magazine*, Section 6, 58.

Box 3.6

CFDA GUIDELINES FOR HEALTHY MODELS

- No models will be under 16 years of age
- Education in the industry concerning the warning signs of eating disorders
- Models with eating disorders should be given professional help and not allowed to work again until given a doctor's permission
- Develop workshops on the causes of eating disorders and raise awareness of the effects of smoking and tobacco-related disease
- During fashion shows, healthy food and snacks should be provided along with banning alcohol and smoking

SOURCE: Guidelines reprinted with permission of Steven Kolb, Executive Director, Council of Fashion Designers of America (CFDA).

anorexia and bulimia. However, many fashion designers feel that they are being unfairly targeted and that they are not solely responsible for the growing number of young women suffering from such disorders.

Regardless of who is responsible, the controversy has resulted in changes for the industry. The first city to place restrictions on model size was Madrid, Spain; in 2006 the city instituted a minimum Body Mass Index[2] of 18 for all models. And beginning in 2007, all models participating in Milan fashion shows were required to obtain a license before they could do shows or shoots. The license, which guarantees the health of the model, is issued by the Chamber of Fashion, the Association of Fashion Service, Milan city officials, the Associazione ServiziModa (Assem—the Association of Modeling Agencies in Milan), and a group of doctors, nutritionists, psychologists, and other experts. The guidelines for obtaining the license state that the models cannot be under the age of 16 and must have a Body Mass Index (BMI) of at least 18.5. The license has been called an "ethical code of self-regulation" (Zargani, 2006) because it reflects concern for the health of the models and also for the well-being of the young people who see them as role models for beauty. Additionally, plans are underway to include nutrition and physical activity courses in Italian modeling schools (Zargani, 2006).

In the United States, the Council of Fashion Designers of America (CFDA) issued voluntary guidelines for fashion models in anticipation of NYC Fashion week in February 2007. These guidelines, which are suggestions and not binding, are outlined in Box 3.6. Although many concerned industry observers believe the guidelines are a step in the right direction, critics believe that they do not go far enough because they are only "suggestions" with no method for enforcement, and they do not set a BMI as was done in Madrid and Milan (Critchell, 2007a, 2007b; Johnson, 2007).

After the CFDA released its guidelines, some fashion designers (such as Karl Lagerfeld) stated that they would not be dictated to by different fashion organizations and that they were not planning to make major changes in their hiring practices for upcoming shows. And many designers believe that the responsibility for screening models falls primarily on the modeling agencies (Staff, 2007). However, Lynn Grefe, chief executive of the National Eating Disorders Association (NEDA), responded to the issuance of the guidelines by saying, "This is long overdue. I consider this a workplace issue. You have this industry that has really not been looking out for the health and welfare of those who are in it" (Johnson, 2007).

THE ROLE OF THE MANAGER IN PROMOTING ETHICAL BEHAVIOR

Regardless of what work environment you choose in the fashion industry, you will encounter some type of unethical behavior during your career. One of the challenges you will likely face at the management level is how to handle employees who misbehave, treat others rudely, act disrespectfully, or who are quite simply "jerks." It is very important that these employees are handled in a way that is swift, compliant with policy, and legal. Ignoring just one employee's bad behavior can result in high turnover, low morale, and can even cost the company a lawsuit if the actions toward others become discriminatory. In his article *Jerks at Work*, Janove (2007) offers several useful suggestions for dealing with behavior issues (short of firing the employee who then, in turn, may sue the company for unjustified termination):

- The employee acting badly must be specifically told how his or her actions deviate from expected behavior, and what needs to be done to close that gap.
- The person must be given adequate time to change his or her behavior and also told what consequences will result (e.g., termination) if the behavior does not change.
- Last, each of these steps must be meticulously documented to protect the company from potential legal action by the employee who has disregarded the standards.

To avoid bad behavior in the first place, Janove suggests that job descriptions explicitly state what is expected in terms of getting along with others and how to appropriately respond to criticism from supervisors.

The importance of a strong leader cannot be minimized, and one of the most exciting things about a career in fashion is the pace at which hardworking people can be promoted into leadership roles. New college graduates often assume those roles immediately upon entering the career world. Of course, these positions include tremendous responsibility, not only for one's own actions, but also for the actions of subordinates. Your employees will look to you as a model for appropriate ethical behavior, and the actions of those who report to you will serve as reflections of your leadership and reputation. Your employees will also expect you to set the tone in creating a positive work environment. This is a key issue because a positive work environment not only helps to eliminate employee stress, but it also has a direct impact on employee retention. At companies with a strong ethical culture and "full formal programs," employees are 36 percent less likely to observe misconduct ("Unethical workplace," 2006) and more likely to report it when it does occur.

As a manager, the role of teaching and cultivating ethical behavior—honesty—in the workplace is one of the most important responsibilities you will undertake. Although written rules, regulations, and codes of ethics are essential, what employees want are leaders they can trust, who foster fairness, and who show concern for employees as individuals (Asacker, 2004). Furthermore, a key to success in today's businesses is the character and skill of leaders, managers, and employees who recognize their role in instilling their organization's ethical values and modeling the corresponding behaviors.

QUESTIONS FOR DISCUSSION

1. Thinking back on the managers you have worked for, what were some ethical behaviors they modeled? Were there any unethical behaviors?

2. What are some unethical behaviors you have witnessed at work or school? How were they handled?

3. Would you feel comfortable reporting unethical behavior to a teacher or manager? Why or why not?

4. Why do you think most people choose not to speak up when they witness unethical behavior?

5. Review the workplace values listed in Box 3.3. Give specific examples of how you practice at least three of these.

6. Have you ever witnessed—or been the victim of—bullying? Explain the circumstances and what was done (if anything) to correct the situation.

7. Aside from the reasons presented in the chapter, why do you think some people feel the need to bully others?

8. Review the suggestions provided for dealing with bullies. What other suggestions do you have?

9. Have you ever witnessed or been a victim of sexual harassment? Explain the circumstances and what was done to correct the situation.

10. Considering what you have read about American Apparel, would you want to work at this company? Explain your answer.

11. Why do you think people want to work for American Apparel?

12. Do you believe the fashion industry should dictate models' weight?

13. Why should the fashion industry be interested in the appearance and health of fashion models?

REFERENCES AND SUGGESTED READING

Amble, B. (July 5, 2007). Bullies blight U.S. workplaces. Retrieved on March 2008 from http://www.management-issues.com/2007/8/31/research/bullies-blight-us-workplaces.asp

Asacker, T. (2004). Ethics in the workplace: Start with honesty. T + D, 58(8), 42–44.

Brunner, P. and Costello, M. (2003). When the wrong woman wins: Building bullies and perpetuating patriarchy. *Advancing Women in Leadership.* Retrieved in March 2007 from http://www.advancingwomen.com/awl/spring2003/index.html

Christopher, B. (February 2007). Are we having fun yet? Attitude and peak performance in the workplace. *Business Credit, 109(2),* 63–64.

Clark, K. (June 2006). Who are you listening to? Exclusive survey of corporate ethics. *Chain Store Age Executive*, 33–35.

Critchell, S. (January 21, 2007a). U.S. fashion designers suggest healthy lifestyle for models. *The Athens [Ohio] Messenger*, p. B3.

Critchell, S. (January 13, 2007b). Fashion leaders draft guidelines for models. *The Columbus [Ohio] Dispatch*, p. B3.

Daniel, L. and Brandon, C. (March 2006). Finding the right job fit. *HRMagazine*, 51, 62–67.

Davis, G. L. (2004). Business ethics: It's all inside JCPenney grounded in golden rules of business conduct. *American Journal of Business*, 19, 7–10.

Dean, J. (September 2005). Dov Charney, like it or not. *Inc Magazine*, 124–131.

D'Innocenzio, A. and Kabel, M. (June 13, 2007). Wal-Mart struggling with rising loss from shoplifting and employee theft at its U.S. stores. Retrieved in March 2008 from http://biz.yahoo.com/ap/070613/wal_mart_theft.html

Elias, M. (July 28, 2004). Bullying crosses the line into workplace: Survey suggests many bosses unaware of verbal abuse in office. *USA Today*, p. D7.

Face value: Dov Charney, the hustler (January 6, 2007). *The Economist*, 382(8510), 55–56.

Giovis, J. (June 12, 2007). Theft at an all-time high $41.6 billion stolen or lost to error last year. *South Florida Sun-Sentinel*, p. D1.

Glenn, J. R., Jr. and Van Loo, M. F. (1993). Business students' and practitioners' ethical decisions over time. *Journal of Business Ethics*, 12(11), 835–847.

Gogoi, P. (June 22, 2007). The trouble with business ethics. *Business Week*, p. 1.

Gurchiek, K. (2006). U.S. workers unlikely to report office misconduct. *HRMagazine*, 51, 29, 38.

Hauck, W. E. and Leslie, C. A. (2005). Categories of sexual harassment: A preliminary analysis. *Kappa Omicron Nu Working Papers Archive*. Retrieved in March 2008 from http://www.kon.org/hswp/archive/leslie-hauck1.htm

Hisey, P. (May 2002). Retail: The state of ethics. *Retail Merchandiser*, 42(5), 17–18.

Hogsett, D. (May 23, 2005). Saks chargebacks may cause changes. *Home Textiles Today*, 26(36), 14.

How to: beat the bullies (June 7, 2007). *Caterer & Hotelkeeper*, 197(4479), 52.

James, M. S. (February 21, 2002). Are you ethical? The truth isn't exactly clear: Politics, circumstances, excuses can blur what is right. Retrieved on June 17, 2007 from http://abcnews.go.com/US/story?id=89985

Janove, J. (May 2007). Jerks at work. *HR Magazine*, 52(5), 111–114, 116–117.

Johnson, M. (February 1, 2007). New York considering weight regulations. *The Columbus [Ohio] Dispatch*, p. C9.

Johnson, P. and Indvik, J. (2006). Sticks and stones: Verbal abuse in the workplace. *Journal of Organizational Culture, Communication & Conflict*, 10(1), 121–126.

Kratz, E. (August 22, 2005). Marked down: How fashionable Saks Fifth Avenue swapped style for scandal—and turned into a bargain-priced takeover target. *Fortune*. Retrieved in March 2008 from http://money.cnn.com/magazines/fortune/fortune_archive/2005/08/22/8270030/index.htm

Kratz, E. (February 6, 2006). Can a new leader save scandal-plagued Saks? *Fortune*, 153(2), 31.

Kidwell, R. and Kochanowski, S. (2005). The morality of employee theft: Teaching about ethics and deviant behavior in the workplace. *Journal of Management Education*, 29, 135–152.

Lagan, A. (2006). Ethics at work. *Intheblack*, 76, 72–73.

Leonard, B. (2007). Study: Bully bosses prevalent in U.S. *HR Magazine*, 52(5), 22, 28.

Leslie, C. and Hauck, W. (2005). Extent and nature of sexual harassment in the fashion retail workplace: Ten years later. *Family and Consumer Sciences Research Journal*, 34(1), 7–33. Retrieved on March 17, 2008 from http://fcs.sagepub.com.cgi/content/abstract/34/1/7

Millage, A. (2005). Ethical misconduct prevalent in workplace. *Internal Auditor*, 62, pp. 13, 15.

Moin, D. and Young, V. (May 13, 2005). Saks Fifth Avenue fallout: Eight merchants said to be ousted. *Women's Wear Daily*, pp. 1, 13.

Norton, S. (2002). Women exposed: Sexual harassment and female vulnerability. In L. Diamant & J. A. Lee (Eds.), *The psychology of sex, gender, and jobs: Issues and solutions* (pp. 83–102). Westport, CT: Praeger.

Paulins, A. (2001). Student and supervisor perceptions of the ethical environment of retail merchandising internship sites. *Journal of Family and Consumer Sciences*, 93(4), 88–93.

Paulins, A. and Lombardy, L. (2005). Ethical dilemmas in retail merchandising: Student perceptions. *Journal of Family and Consumer Sciences*, 97(3), 56–62.

Pharmacists disciplined for not filling prescriptions for emergency contraception (December 1, 2005). *The Athens[Ohio] Messenger*, p. 2.

Ryan, L. (March 21, 2006). Taking a stand on ethics. *Business Week Online*. Retrieved on March 17, 2008 from http://www.businessweek.com/careers/content/mar2006/ca20060321_794407.htm

Schultz, D. P. (September 2007). 10 things you may have missed. *Stores*, 18.

Schwartz, M. (2004). Effective corporate codes of ethics: Perceptions of code users. *Journal of Business Ethics*, 55(4), 321–341.

Staff. (January 30, 2007). Skinny model furor: Not all fashion's fault, say designers, editors. *Women's Wear Daily*, pp. 1, 8–10.

Tanaka, R. (July 8, 2007). Bullying too common in U.S. workplace. Retrieved on March 17, 2008 from http://www.bullyinginstitute.org/education/bbstudies/def.html

Till, F. (1980). *Sexual harassment: A report on the sexual harassment of students*. Washington, DC: National Advisory Council on Women's Educational Programs.

Unethical workplace conduct continues, despite standards, surveys say (2006). *HR Focus*, 83, 8–9.

U.S. Department of Labor, Bureau of Labor Statistics (2006). Retrieved July 27, 2007 from http://www.bls.gov.html

Valenti, C. (February 21, 2002). Ethical culture: Is the Enron saga a sign that ethics in the workplace are disappearing? Retrieved on March 17, 2008 from http://abcnews.go.com/Business/story?id=87351

Verschoor, C. C. (2005). Ethical culture: Most important barrier to ethical misconduct. *Strategic Finance*, 87, 19–20.

Weinstein, M. (2006). Racism, sexism, ageism: Workplace not getting any friendlier. *Training*, 43, 11.

Whistleblowing workers: Becoming an endangered species? (2006). *HR Focus*, 83, 9.

Wolf, J. (April 23, 2006). And you thought Abercrombie and Fitch was pushing it? *New York Times Magazine*, Section 6, p. 58.

Workman, J. (1993). Extent and nature of sexual harassment in the fashion retail workplace. *Home Economics Research Journal*, 21(4), 358–380.

Young, V. M. (September 6, 2007). Saks settles with SEC. *Women's Wear Daily*, p. 10.

Zargani, L. (December 19, 2006). New rules for models: Milan to issue licenses verifying age, health. *Women's Wear Daily*, pp. 1, 10.

ENDNOTES

1. The Emperor's New Clothes [Danish: Keiserens nye Klæder (original spelling)] is a Danish fairy tale written by Hans Christian Andersen and first published in 1837, as part of Eventyr, fortalte for Børn (Fairy Tales, Told for Children).

It tells the tale of an emperor who was swindled by two weavers into believing that they were clothing him with the finest of costumes. They were so fine, in fact, that supposedly only the smartest of people could see and appreciate the clothes. However, when the emperor was paraded through town with his new clothes, he was actually naked, and at the risk of looking stupid, no one except for a small child would speak the truth.

2. Body Mass Index is a tool used to determine whether a person is healthy based on their weight and height. The standard accepted by The World Health Organization is that anyone with an index of less than 18.5 is underweight (Zargani, 2006).

Chapter 4

Processes and Pitfalls in Fashion Design and Product Development

---

THE OBJECTIVES OF THIS CHAPTER ARE TO:

- Understand the role of fashion in the design inspiration and development process

- Differentiate from among the methods used for design inspiration and selection, and explore the role of ethics for each

- Understand the definition and concept of intellectual property

- Explore the difference between design inspiration, creating knockoffs, and copyright infringement

- Compare and contrast the concepts of branding and brand representation with design and style

- Understand the relationship between developing intellectual property and participating in the fashion adoption process

- Examine the economic incentives for unethical behavior with respect to design and intellectual property

---

Fashion products are valued by consumers for their style to an extent that surpasses the item's ability to meet basic physiological needs. Fashions fulfill social and psychological needs rather than consumers' primary physiological needs of warmth, protection, and comfort. However, fashion apparel can meet these physiological needs as well. This functional element of fashion apparel introduces complications and controversy—ethical, artistic, and economic—with regard to owning and protecting design innovations.

FIGURE 4.1

Fashion exists when a critical mass of consumers select similar styles of apparel that fulfill desires to exhibit personal tastes, indicate membership in recognized groups, and/or demonstrate abilities to purchase exclusive or expensive merchandise. The fact that *fashion* is acquired out of desire, rather than necessity, lends conflict to the purpose of apparel and the role of design innovation presented through clothing. Fashion clothing, because of its functional body-covering role, is not protected by copyright law except in the case of specifically functional design features such as zippers, other fasteners, and unique patterns in fabrics and stitching (such as the Levi Strauss & Co. back pocket stitching). The roles of fashion apparel, footwear, and accessories as both functional and artistic items complicate the ethical perspectives of their fair use in the marketplace. Ongoing debates, often taking place in courtrooms, continually investigate whether design styles can or should be owned by copyright holders.

Design inspiration is complex, resulting from myriad influences. Completely new fashion products or styles are rare. Current fashions combine previous design ideas; they reflect historical, political, and technological influences and provide a combination of functional new style elements that generate consumer excitement while still exhibiting a certain level of comfort from familiarity. Essentially all "new" fashion styles are based on something that has been seen before. This concept was summarized by Donna Karan in the Foreword of Bonnie Young's (1998) *Colors of the Vanishing Tribes*: "As a designer, I am always asked where my inspiration comes from. The answer lies in the advice my mentor, Anne Klein, gave me: 'God gave you two eyes. Use them!'"

Fashion can apply to many categories, including home appliances, architectural structures, automobiles, literature, food, leisure activities, and hairstyles. Among the most obvious examples of fashion items are apparel, footwear, and accessories. The fashion aspect of these items are most easily recognizable by the styles depicted through silhouettes but can also be identified through branding, logos, signature colors, patterns or prints, and other distinctive design elements. For example, Tommy Hilfiger apparel, denoted with the distinct flag logo, may be a particularly fashionable item. A similar example is the Louis Vuitton handbag, recognized by its signature fabric; those who value fashion might consider this item to be desirable. Alternately, a classic-line short suit jacket without lapels, inspired by Coco Chanel, might be a popular style and therefore in fashion.

FIGURE 4.2   It is difficult to identify the originator and/or classic designs and styles that reappear on a seasonal basis. *Good Housekeeping* (October 2005) offers examples of how simple it is to find fashions of similar styles offered by a variety of designer brands and retailers at prices ranging from budget to better.

FASHION THEORIES ON ADOPTION AND DIFFUSION

The democratization of fashion was observed by Edward Sapir (1931), who noted that the Industrial Revolution permitted the spread of fashion diffusion by enabling a greater number of people to afford the fashions that could finally be mass-produced. Thorstein Veblen (1899) introduced the concept of conspicuous consumption in his book *The Theory of the Leisure Class*. He observed that fashion apparel, because of its highly visible nature, is a historically popular way for people to advertise their wealth and status—whether real or perceived. He stated that people are willing to forgo other, less visible, needs and comforts in order to support a certain amount of wasteful consumption, such as purchasing fashion items. He theorized that the social good and psychological satisfaction of portraying consumption activities made conspicuous consumption a rational choice. Veblen was also aware of the economic and social effects of copying original fashion items, when he commented that "the aesthetic value of a detected counterfeit in dress declines somewhat in the same proportion as the counterfeit is cheaper than its original. It loses caste aesthetically because it falls to a lower pecuniary grade" (p. 120). Thus, the role of copying has long been recognized and accepted in the fashion process. In fact, acceptance of copying in the fashion industry has historically been differentiated from copying of other creative products (such as book authorship), as evidenced by the following comment from Arnold Plant, a British professor of economics, in 1934:

> The leading twenty firms in the haute couture of Paris take elaborate precautions twice each year to prevent piracy; but most respectable "houses" throughout the world are quick in the market with their copies (not all made from a purchased original), and "Berwick Street" follows hot on their heels with copies a stage farther removed. And yet the Paris creators can and do secure special prices for their authentic reproductions of the original—for their "signed artist's copies," as it were (p. 172).

The fashion adoption process is familiar to apparel designers, product developers, sourcing specialists, and retailers. As styles go through a process of diffusion and are made readily available to consumers, fashion cycles, or trends, become established. Fashion is the prevailing style at the time. As previously mentioned, style can be depicted by silhouette, color, color combinations, print, fabric or other material, or specific design or pattern. Seasonal styles are conceived and presented by fashion designers who typically display their work through runway shows. These couture fashions are then worn by high-profile people who are often photographed for popular media outlets such as *Women's Wear Daily*, *People*, and *InStyle*.

After the styles gain credibility as being fashionable, mainstream manufacturers and retailers modify them for potential adoption by large numbers of people. Widespread adoption transforms a style into an accepted and recognized fashion.

George Simmel, a German sociologist, wrote in 1904 about the two contrasting forces of fashion—conformity and individuality. He observed that "the elite initiates a fashion and, when the mass imitates it in an effort to obliterate the external distinctions of class, abandons it for a newer mode" (p. 5). In his essay on fashion he emphasized the role of imitation in the adoption process. He noted that without broad acceptance of a prevailing style, fashion would not exist, and observed that "the very character of fashion demands that it should be exercised at one time only by a portion of the given group, the great majority being merely on the road to adopting it" (p. 9). How are the masses of consumers who eventually validate a style able to acquire the merchandise? Obviously, it must be made widely available at affordable prices. When the demand for merchandise similar to a desirable, but often limited, fashion item is established, the market for imitation items is born. With great insight, Simmel stated, "The more an article becomes subject to rapid changes of fashion, the greater the demand for *cheap* products of its kind, not only because the larger and therefore poorer classes nevertheless have enough purchasing power to regulate industry and demand objects . . . [and] even the higher circles of society could not afford to adopt the rapid changes in fashion forced upon them by the imitation of the lower circles if the objects were not relatively cheap" (p. 15).

Historic references to fashion adoption theorize a trickle-down process, where the upper class sets the prevailing style by wearing the latest expensive fashions shown in the couture houses. Current fashion is typically initiated by and associated with high-profile individuals, groups, or cultures. Rather than exclusively emanating from the upper class (such as haute couture runway items worn by socialites and celebrities), we also look to popular events, television shows, movies, athletes, subcultures, musicians, or other entertainers for influence. The grunge look of the 1990s and the sweat suits and leggings of the 1980s exemplify trickle-up fashion, where casual clothing of the masses found its way into designer collections. Cultural influences that become popular across a wider consumer audience, such as Sean John apparel (inspired by the youthful, inner-city population), demonstrate the trickle-across fashion theory.

Another way to explain fashion adoption is through role theory. In *The Presentation of Self in Everyday Life*, sociologist Ervin Goffman (1959) described the way that people perform in their life roles as if they were players on a stage. Visual cues such as clothing choices are components of the roles being played. Role theory suggests that our outward appearances (e.g., clothing choices) are selected to explain our

FIGURE 4.3   Doeringer and Crean's fashion pyramid

roles in society. In other words, we use fashions to express our place in the world. This concept is related to the concept of symbolic interaction, which was explored and presented by sociologist Herbert Blumer (1969) in his book *Symbolic Interactionism: Perspective and Method*. The theory of symbolic interaction expands on role theory to explain that the human process of social interaction creates meanings for the people involved through language and thought associated by and resulting from interactive communication. Role theory and the theory of symbolic interaction explain fashion adoption as a process of adapting one's appearance to better explain messages conveyed by the wearer.

The fashion pyramid (Doeringer and Crean, 2006) illustrates how fashion apparel typically originates in the elite setting of haute couture collections, where only a small group of consumers will adopt the items, and then increasingly greater volumes of apparel in fashionable styles are produced as the unique fashion content of the items are modified to reduce production costs, increase production speed, and yet still resemble the fashionable styles that consumers want. Generally, this "watering down" of fashion results in less distinguishing features in the apparel details (such as modified and diminished pockets, belts, and fasteners; finishing techniques, and fabrics) that enable production and retail costs to be reduced. These modifications can also change the new products enough from the originals to prevent lawsuits.

Because fashion evolves, generally building on recent trends rather than presenting entirely new style elements each season, merchandise for new lines and seasons rarely includes altogether unfamiliar styles. The "newness" of fashion often emerges by transforming familiar styles with new color combinations, hemlines, shoe heights, and silhouettes. Historic influences are incorporated along with new concepts as potential fashions are designed and introduced for consumer consideration. Director of Levi's brand presence, Amy Jasmer, described the typical process of fashion design when Victoria Lynford was tapped to serve as Designer for a Day with Levi's (Tucker, 2006b): "We told her to go out and see the denim trends, and then go to one of our stores and see what we do." Lynford reviewed the Levi's archives and discussed her design plans with a team. According to Jasmer, this helped lead to a "successful jean design" because Lynford was familiar with the styles of existing Levi's jeans and knew how she wanted to contribute to that. The new design was not created in a vacuum, nor did it differ substantially from the jean style familiar to Levi's customers.

FASHION BRANDS

The American Marketing Association (AMA) defines "brand" as a name, term, sign, symbol, or design, or a combination of them, intended to identify the goods or services of one seller or group of sellers and differentiate them from those of competitors (www.marketingpower.com). According to the AMA, the legal term for brand is "trademark." Copyrighted logos are also known as trademarks. A registered trademark (i.e., a trademark registered with the U.S Patent and Trademark Office) is denoted by the symbol ®. An unregistered trademark, or one in which the registration is pending must use the ™ symbol; likewise a claimed service mark, to indicate ownership of intellectual property designating a service may use the symbol ℠ prior to official registration. Although these informal trademark or service mark designations do provide some protection in the marketplace, official registration ensures that the claim for ownership will be legally recognized. To be successfully registered by the United States Patent and Trademark Office, the trademark or service mark must clearly distinguish the product or service from others in commerce. Registration is important for fashion trademark owners, particularly when they seek to register surnames, which require establishing a secondary meaning for consumers. For example, in order to successfully register the name "Zac Posen" as a trademark, Zac Posen must be linked to a secondary meaning beyond that of a personal name. The trademark registration may be approved when

> **Box 4.1**
>
> **GLOSSARY OF INTELLECTUAL PROPERTY TERMS**
>
> **Brand**—A name, term, sign, symbol, or design, or a combination of them, intended to identify the goods or services of one seller or group of sellers and differentiate them from those of competitors (www.marketingpower.com).
>
> **Copyright**—A registration of intellectual property ownership that protects artistic and literary work (www.uspto.gov).
>
> **Counterfeit**—A product that bears the label or distinct copyrighted design feature of another designer or brand without having paid licensing fees or obtaining permission to copy the trademark.
>
> **Knockoff**—A fashion item that is almost identical to a designer or brand name product in style, but does not bear false labeling to mislead the consumer into thinking that the garment is an object of the name brand itself.
>
> **Patent**—A property right granted by the government of the United States to an inventor to "exclude others from making, using, offering for sale, or selling the invention throughout the United States or importing the invention into the United States" for a limited time in exchange for public disclosure of the invention when the patent is granted (www.uspto.gov).
>
> **Piracy**—The act of illegally copying branded merchandise or protected intellectual property, named for the acts of maritime pirates who commit robbery for their own gains. Piracy in terms of intellectual property refers to the theft of copyrighted work, trademarks, service marks, and patents.

Zac Posen can establish that consumers recognize the name as a designer of fashion goods and not just the name of an individual person. Registered trademarks make it illegal for others to use or sell merchandise bearing the trademark without permission. Furthermore, trademarks are protected as part of the law prohibiting unfair competition.

Consumers often see a brand as a status symbol. Lack of possession or display of a certain brand may be seen by some as failure to achieve a desired status. For example, Lacoste is a longstanding brand with a recognizable logo—the crocodile—that has been a popular fashion item, especially among tennis players, since the 1930s. A polo shirt without a logo does not represent the level of prestige for its wearer that is associated with the Lacoste shirt. Other brands of similar shirts, such as Polo by

BOX 4.1 continued from page 84
GLOSSARY OF INTELLECTUAL PROPERTY TERMS

Service Mark—The same as a trademark, except that it identifies and distinguishes the source of a service rather than a product (www.uspto.gov).

Trade Dress—A product's design, product packaging, color, or other distinguishing nonfunctional element of appearance (www.uspto.gov). The Trademark Manual of Examination Procedures (TMEP) §1202.02 states that, in an application for trade dress, distinctiveness and functionality are two separate issues, both of which must be considered by the examining attorney. Trade dress is an extension of trademark law that extends when the product brand achieves secondary meaning for consumers insomuch that if it is copied, consumers will associate the copy mistakenly to be the original.

Trademark—A word, phrase, symbol, or design, or a combination of words, phrases, symbols, or designs, that identifies and distinguishes the source of the goods of one party from those of others. The owner of a registered trademark may pursue legal proceedings for trademark infringement to prevent unauthorized use of the trademark although registration is not required. Trademarks can be renewed forever as long as they are being used in commerce (www.uspto.gov).

Ralph Lauren (represented by a horse-riding polo player logo), are different from generic polo shirts and unique to their brand owners because their particular logos are copyrighted. Branded merchandise, evident by distinctive trademark features (such as the Nike "swoosh" or the word "PRADA" on a handbag), is often viewed as more desirable and more fashionable, than unbranded merchandise. Furthermore, branded merchandise is more expensive because (1) the law of supply and demand allows the market to bear higher prices associated with more desirable merchandise and (2) the costs associated with advertising brands and protecting copyrights are significant. Because logos are easy to recognize and potentially lucrative for anyone to sell, they are tempting to copy. Issues of ethics arise when those who do not own the trademarks are motivated to modify or copy popular logos, trademarks, or service marks and therefore benefit through sale of fake merchandise.

In addition to the concept of role theory previously discussed, Goffman (1959) also described the theory of symbolic interaction: a system where people portray behaviors and appearances that are interpreted by others as they negotiate social situations. Fashions, particularly those associated with explicit symbols such as logos or signature patterns, are easily recognized and widely used in social situations to both provide and interpret information about the wearers' taste, interests, rank or status, wealth, and personality. Consider the sports fan decked out in Dallas Cowboys merchandise—cap, jersey, sweatpants, jacket, etc. The message is clear. At a glance we know (or at least assume) about the wearers' interest in professional football, and his or her passion for the Cowboys. Furthermore, if the items feature the trademark logos, we assume that this consumer is willing to spend hundreds of dollars on trademarked merchandise that is only legally available from licensed producers and through specified retailers. The Dallas Cowboys and the National Football League (NFL) own the trademark and have the authority to determine what merchandise will display the copyrighted logo. The producers and sellers of the merchandise pay for licensing rights, and the economy of trademarked merchandise is built—along with the opportunity and market for copies.

Because logos and signature patterns, prints, and colors are highly visible and recognizable, they are easy to modify into new, similar styles and to copy outright. Modern technology (e.g., Internet access to high-resolution logo images) and high-performance embroidery machines that can produce thousands of copied logos per hour further motivate counterfeit production. Intellectual property ownership and copyrighting become important issues when a design or style is recognizable, associated with a certain status, and popular enough to be demanded by consumers.

WHAT IS INTELLECTUAL PROPERTY?

Intellectual property is an idea or invention, such as a particular fabric print, apparel detail such as a stitching design, or name. Intellectual property recognizes exclusive ownership through copyrights, trademarks, and patents. As its name implies, copyrighting offers the owner of original creative work the sole right to reproduce and distribute the work. Others who want to reproduce the work must seek permission, and generally pay a royalty to the owner to do so. Names, symbols, pictures or words, unique packaging, color combinations, product styles, and overall presentations that are associated with intellectual property may be granted trademark status. The words "trademark" and "brand" are used interchangeably to signify protected intellectual property.

Patents, which are associated with intellectual property of inventions, have virtually no application to fashion products for two reasons. First, patents are only granted to new ideas. As previously mentioned, most fashion products include some element of historic style. Second, the patent application process is prohibitively long. For a fashion style, the fashion window will have closed long before the patent has been granted. But patents do offer important protection for manufacturers with inventions related or contributing to the production of fashions. Patented fashion items include manufacturing processes to make pleats or other fabric variations, the manufacture of fibers, fabrics, and dye materials, and the processes to affix beads or sequins. Additionally, mechanical inventions, such as buckle and zipper fasteners, are often patented.

Brand owners create distinction for themselves in competitive markets when their advertising and other promotional techniques (coupled with customer experiences) lead consumers to associate status, success, prestige, improved quality of life, and other psychological and sociological benefits with the use of the particular branded product. Picture an image you associate with names such as Chanel, Nike, Calvin Klein, Sean John, Crocs, and Liz Claiborne. Chances are that you easily pictured images consistent with the advertisements and products of these brands because they are widely familiar to consumers, and distinctly different from one another. A brand that has built a strong association with a product category achieves great economic advantage in the marketplace. Consider the products associated with Kleenex, Xerox, Jell-O, iPod, Chapstick, and Under Armour. For these products, the brand defines the product. These products are so closely connected to their brand names that it is in the companies' best interests to spend significant time and money protecting their exclusive ownership. Tiffany spends over $1 million each year just on tracking and ceasing counterfeit online auctions (Casabona, 2006e). Lacoste spent $5 million in lawyer fees in 2006, which resulted in the confiscation of three million units in 4,000 different actions (Thomas, 2007). Companies often budget funds specifically to educate consumers, retailers, and other brand owners that their identities should not be used to generically define styles or product categories.

In many instances, the corporate reputation of a company that creates and sells goods is established through its products (Fan, 2005). When consumers mistake imitation merchandise for authentic goods, the reputation of the brand—and the business behind it—is compromised. For this reason, certain distinguishing fashion elements are protected by copyright law. Copyright law enables brand owners to recover financial damages when it is proven that sales of infringing merchandise have confused consumers to an extent that they mistake the copy for the real thing. As mentioned previously, fashion products themselves rarely receive copyright protection because of the functional nature of the creative work. But copyright law does cover artistic elements applied to clothing (e.g., the pattern designs

A NOTE OF INFORMATION AND ENTREATY TO FASHION EDITORS, ADVERTISERS, COPYWRITERS AND OTHER WELL-INTENTIONED MIS-USERS OF OUR **CHANEL** NAME.

CHANEL was a designer, an extraordinary woman who made a timeless contribution to fashion.

CHANEL is a perfume.

CHANEL is modern elegance in couture, ready-to-wear, accessories, watches and fine jewelry.

CHANEL is our registered trademark for fragrance, cosmetics, clothing, accessories and other lovely things.

Although our style is justly famous, a jacket is not 'a CHANEL jacket' unless it is ours, and somebody else's cardigans are not 'CHANEL for now.'

And even if we are flattered by such tributes to our fame as 'Chanel-issime, Chanel-ed, Chanels and Chanel-ized', PLEASE DON'T. Our lawyers positively detest them.

We take our trademark seriously.

Merci,

CHANEL, Inc.

FIGURE 4.4   Chanel ad that shows ownership of a name

of Burberry fabrics). Branding and logos offer additional economic advantages to producers of fashion merchandise, as discussed in the preceding section. It is also important to brand owners that their intended brand image is widely recognized by consumers. This secondary meaning is a recognized component in the registration of trademarks and plays an important role in the validity of competitor challenges in trademark law.

The nature of the fashion industry, where constant change is needed to ensure job security and to fuel commerce, presents challenges to brand owners who are torn between protecting their intellectual property and taking part in the industry's inherent "sharing and borrowing" that creates consumer demand and generates sales. Virtually no designer can create a completely unique line of fashion merchandise that will sell in the market, yet all would like the profits resulting from a hot fashion trend. This is a long-standing controversy in the field of fashion; designers have sought to protect the ownership of their creations for nearly 100 years. The Fashion Originators Guild was formed in 1932 by a group of designers who urged retailers to boycott manufacturers of copied designs. But trying to make retailers the responsible filter for ethics in the fashion industry was ill-founded because retailers had little motivation to increase their costs of merchandise and correspondingly decrease their sales volume and markup. Furthermore, it has been—and continues to be—difficult for original designers to identify a specific trade infringement for styles that do not have copyrighted items such as trademark logos, unique embroidery, and surface patterns on fabrics. And sometimes the very designers who indignantly complain about being copied are often targets of intellectual property complaints themselves.

Over the years, the Federal government has sought to bring a certain degree of ethics to the marketplace via legislation. The Tariff Act of 1930 offers protection of trademarks. The Landham Trademark Act of 1946 put the obligation of responsibility on producers and made it possible for trademark owners to sue to protect their work from being copied. The Trademark Law Revision Act of 1988 introduced protection for intellectual property owners at the Federal level in the United States. More recently, House of Representatives Bill 32, known as the "Stop Counterfeiting in Manufactured Goods Act," was signed into law by President George Bush in 2006. This law, the U.S. Federal Trademark Dilution Act, calls for prison terms of up to 20 years, fines up to $15 million, and mandatory forfeiture of merchandise, destruction of equipment used for manufacture, and restitution provisions to owners of intellectual property in response to counterfeiting. In addition to stiffer penalties, the new law criminalizes counterfeit trafficking regardless of whether the counterfeited products have counterfeit labels. This means that the styles themselves, whether or not they have been actually labeled with counterfeit logos or brand names, are subject to intellectual property protection. This is important because counterfeit goods can be manufactured in one location, imported, and then labeled in the final stages of distribution.

The Design Piracy Prohibition Act was introduced in the U.S. Senate in August 2007 after being presented to the House of Representatives in April 2007. At his press conference in New York City's fashion district to support the act, Sen. Charles Schumer (sponsor of the legislation) was accompanied by notable fashion designers including Jeffrey Banks, Narciso Rodriguez, Nicole Miller, Marc Bouwer, Richard Lambertson, Yeohlee Teng, Dana Foley, and Susan Posen (CEO of Zac Posen), as well as the past president and current executive director of the Council of Fashion Designers of America (CFDA), Stan Herman and Steven Kolb (Ellis, 2007). The proposed legislation calls for fashion designs, defined as "the appearance as a whole of an article of apparel, including ornamentation," to be subject to protection under the law. Among other things, the bill would protect original fashion designs for three years from their date of registration with the U.S. government. At the time of this writing, this act had not yet become law.

The Intellectual Property Owners Association (IPO) is a nonprofit trade group established in 1972 and based in Washington, D.C., that has traditionally focused on patent issues, but recently added trademark issues and counterfeiting to its agenda. The IPO has a Counterfeiting and Enforcement Committee, whose charge is to "develop materials and programs to educate intellectual property owners and other members of the public about legal and practical developments and strategies with respect to counterfeiting and piracy" (www.ipo.org). In the United Kingdom, the Quality Brand Protection Committee (QBPC) is the IPO equivalent (www.qbpc.org). A nonprofit trade group based in Washington, D.C., the International Anti-Counterfeiting Coalition (IACC), is comprised of trademark owners and exists for the purpose of identifying trademark infringements and seeking recourse from those manufacturers. This watchdog group compiles information about counterfeit activities and advocates for stronger anticounterfeiting legislation and greater consumer knowledge of the effects of counterfeits.

Fashion items are particularly difficult to protect using intellectual property laws for several reasons. As previously mentioned, the process of fashion creation, with tendencies to modify existing styles and reuse historical influences, contributes to the difficulty designers have in copyrighting and protecting their creations. Therefore, determining the specific design to be copyrighted is difficult. Another even more intrinsic barrier to protecting apparel fashion is that the fashion items themselves, clothing, have usefulness beyond the style designs. Historically, only

BOX 4.2

THE INTERNATIONAL ANTICOUNTERFEITING COALITION (IACC)

The IACC website presented the following in 2007:

- Counterfeiting costs U.S. businesses $200 billion to $250 billion annually.
- Since 1982, the global trade in illegitimate goods has increased from $5.5 billion to approximately $600 billion annually.
- Counterfeiting has increased over 10,000 percent in the last two decades in part due to consumer demand.
- The World Trade Organization estimates approximately 5 percent to 7 percent of the world trade is in counterfeit goods.
- U.S. companies suffer $9 billion in trade losses due to international copyright piracy.
- Counterfeit merchandise is directly responsible for the loss of more than 750,000 American jobs, according to the U.S. Customs and Border Protection (CPB).

Brand Owners That Are Members of the International AntiCounterfeiting Coalition (IACC)

Abercrombie & Fitch	Cisco Systems Inc.
Activision, Inc.	Coach
Adidas International Inc.	Columbia Sportswear Company
American Eagle Outfitters Inc.	Daimler Chrysler Corporation
Art In Motion	Deere & Company
Ashworth Inc.	Dickies© Brand Apparel
Batmark Limited	and Accessories
BeBe	Dolby Laboratories Inc.
Blueholdings Inc.	Electronic Arts Inc.
Burberry Ltd.	Energizer
Calvin Klein Inc.	Estee Lauder Companies
Chanel Inc.	Federal-Mogul Corporation
Chrome Hearts	Fila USA Inc.

Box 4.2 continued from page 91
THE INTERNATIONAL ANTICOUNTERFEITING COALITION (IACC)

FM Approvals LLC

Ford Motor Company

General Motors Corporation

Gucci America Inc.

Harley-Davidson

Harman International

Hit Entertainment

JT International SA

Johnson & Johnson Healthcare
     Systems

Kate Spade LLC

LaCoste USA Inc.

Levi Strauss & Co.

Lexmark International Inc.

Limited Brands

Liz Claiborne Inc.

Lorillard Tobacco Company

Louis Vuitton Malletier

Lucasfilm Ltd.

Mars Incorporated

Marvel Enterprises Inc.

MGA Entertainment

Microsoft Corporation

Nike Inc.

Nokia Inc.

Oakley Inc.

Orange County Choppers

Paul Frank Industries Inc.

Perry Ellis International Inc.

Pfizer Inc.

Philip Morris International Inc.

Philip Morris USA

Procter & Gamble

Puig USA

Quiksilver Inc.

Reebok International Ltd.

Richemont International Ltd.
     (Cartier)

Rolex Watch USA. Inc.

Seven For All Mankind LLC

The Collegiate Licensing Company

The Gillette Company

The Hearst Corporation/
     King Features

The Timberland Company

The Walt Disney Company

Tiffany & Company

Tommy Hilfiger USA Inc.

Underwriters Laboratories Inc.

VF Corporation

Viacom Inc.

Vivendi Universal Games Inc.

YKK Corporation of America

Zippo Manufacturing Company

creative designs that have no secondary utilitarian function have been subject to copyright. This means that specific stitching or appliqué patterns that are applied to apparel can be copyrighted, but the cut of the garment itself cannot be protected. Designers are debating this issue, but must continuously weigh the cost of fighting copyists with the need to move on and create the next season's fashions. Additionally, as has previously been mentioned, designers are apt to create rules that will actually target themselves as copyright offenders, as the inspiration for fashion styles and interpretation of trends is so vast, and the resulting fashion products often very similar.

Extent of Intellectual Property Dilemmas in the Fashion Industry

As the debate over knockoff styles and fashion copyrighting continues, the infringement of copyrighted and trademarked intellectual property is growing to unprecedented levels. Even with the legal protections offered to trademark holders (brand owners), the unlicensed production, distribution, and sale of branded products is rampant. Counterfeit merchandise is produced and sold worldwide. Why? Because these activities, seen by many as unethical, can nonetheless be profitable. But the greater the sale of counterfeits, the greater the loss for trademark owners. It is estimated that counterfeit goods cost U.S. companies $200 billion to $250 billion each year when consumers buy fake goods instead of the "real thing" (Clark, 2006b). Furthermore, the IACC estimates that more than 750,000 jobs in the United States are lost because of the counterfeit goods that are manufactured overseas. According to the IACC, estimated sales of counterfeit goods exceeded $600 billion in 2006, with $139 million worth of counterfeit goods seized by customs without reaching consumers. Counterfeit goods sold through unauthorized channels do not contribute taxes to the economy and as previously mentioned, jeopardize the product reputation of brand owners. This unethical practice is fueled by consumers' demands for branded and stylized merchandise coupled with their preferences for paying far-below-market prices. Liza Casabona (2006e) reported that Seven For All Mankind knocks 10,000 auctions off eBay every month using the Verified Owners Rights Program, an automated system (VERO) that enables brand owners to report suspected counterfeit auctions. Despite the vigilant monitoring, demand for the merchandise and potential for profit are so great that the number of reported and interrupted auctions does not decrease.

In his presentation to the IACC in October 2006, Ed Kelly, an intellectual property rights attorney, indicated that consumers are "partners in crime" with counterfeiters whenever they buy counterfeit goods. He noted that counterfeiters are often involved in drug trafficking, prostitution, and terrorism—activities that are supported by income generated through the sale of counterfeits. Designers of original merchandise and brands, many of whom are members of the IACC, claim that counterfeiting creates public health and safety hazards in addition to economic

BOX 4.3
FIVE REASONS YOU SHOULD NEVER FAKE IT

1. Counterfeiting is illegal and purchasing counterfeit products supports illegal activity.

2. Counterfeiters do not pay taxes meaning less money for your city's schools, hospitals, parks, and other social programs.

3. Counterfeiters do not pay their employees fair wages or benefits, have poor working conditions, and often use forced child labor.

4. The profits from counterfeiting have been linked to funding organized crime, drug trafficking, and terrorist activity.

5. When you purchase a fake, you become part of the cycle of counterfeiting and your money directly supports these things you would never want to support.

SOURCE: http://IACC.org, reprinted with permission.

harm. This is particularly true for industrial products such as bolts, screws, brake pads, and for pharmaceuticals. Susan Scafidi, a law and history faculty member at Southern Methodist University and author of *Who Owns Culture?* (2005), sponsors a blog that is dedicated to newsworthy counterfeit fashion activities (http://counter-feitchic.com). The volume of information on this blog alone offers testimony to the vast extent of the counterfeit fashion market.

THE FASHION DESIGN PROCESS: KNOCKOFFS VERSUS COUNTERFEITS. Copying in the fashion industry occurs over a wide spectrum—from deliberate deceit for illegal profit by counterfeiting trademarked logos, to deliberate style copying of runway garments for sale at moderate prices to mainstream customers, to unintentional or coincidental similarities in products that have been developed based on popular trends. Several authors (Green and Smith, 2002; Raustiala and Springman, 2006; Winograd and Tan, 2006) have contrasted the practice of design copying versus trademark counterfeiting and present arguments that support the legal freedom of designers to copy styles. For example, Kal Raustiala and Christopher Springman (2006) contend that without fashion copies, the fashion cycle would slow, prohibiting designers and retailers from reaping sales that currently result from quickly changing seasonal merchandise. Hilton, Choi, and Chen (2004) note that it is difficult to ascertain the quality or monetary worth of fashion items unless value, or credence, is applied to them by others. This phenomenon, known as "credence goods" is associated with luxury goods and exists when value is connected to the brand or reputation of a designer, manufacturer, or retailer. Because consumers see value in popular brands and styles, copyists have clear motivation to produce fashions that resemble or might be mistaken for items that are credence goods. This critical issue—whether the goods are actually confusing to the consumer and genuinely mistaken for authentic branded merchandise—is the underlying difference between copyright and trade infringements. Copyrights do not have to be proven to be confusing to consumers, whereas lawsuits based on trade dress (or style) infringements do. Consider the situation where a "Tiffany-inspired" lamp is made from plastic and designed as a furnishing for a child's doll house with a price of $1.99. This design is unlikely to be mistaken for a real Tiffany lamp, as would be necessary for a trade lawsuit, but if the style itself is copyrighted, the sale of toy lamps in the copied style could be legally halted.

Cathy Horyn (2002) described the discovery of Balenciaga designer Nicolas Ghesquiere's inspiration source for a vest presented in his 2002 spring collection: a little-known designer, Kaisik Wong, who had designed the original in 1973. The Balenciaga design offered identical patchwork shapes and placements and decorative tassels, admittedly copied from Wong by Ghesquiere. Horyn noted that "the freedom to copy is largely taken for granted at all levels of the fashion world," and quoted Stanford University law professor Lawrence Lessig's observation that "Copyright laws don't cover fashion as they do publishing and music—nor should they. We borrow and change—that's the creative process" (p. B10). Raustiala and Springman (2006) suggested that copying actually promotes innovation and enhances opportunities for the fashion design originator to offer new products to consumers, a phenomenon they refer to as the "piracy paradox." From this perspective, they explored and questioned the need for intellectual property protection in the fashion industry. Robert Green and Tasman Smith (2002) explored the measurement of the cost of counterfeit goods in the marketplace. They questioned whether copies really hurt the economy and brand owners. In their article, "Executive Insights: Countering Brand Counterfeiters," they noted that the following criteria must be considered when weighing the costs of counterfeit merchandise: production cost of counterfeit goods, sales lost (opportunity cost) by association for brand owners, damages to brand equity, and total sales volume of counterfeit goods.

The speed of fashion change, often due to the quick market saturation of fashion products resulting from widespread copies, strengthens the economic well-being of designers, manufacturers, and retailers. Traditionally fashions are introduced and trickle, and then flood, consumer venues at a pace that provides the design originator sufficient reward through sales and creative recognition. Technology complicates problems for design originators because others are able to reproduce the items and present them to consumers as fast as the original is rolled out. The extent to which the style of a fashion good is copied is an important distinction with respect to intellectual property rights. Intent to deceive either the wholesaler or the customer with a counterfeit is clearly an ethical violation, and in fact illegal. It is not as widely understood that creating an imitation, even if the intent of the manufacturer is clear, is also illegal. For example, in 2006, Burberry was awarded $100,000 in damages by the U.S. District Court in Manhattan from Marco Leather which, the court determined, had infringed on Burberry's trademark rights (Jones, 2006). Marco Leather had imported merchandise that included wallets and handbags with the widely familiar Burberry check design.

By contrast, creating merchandise that is similar in style to an original design, known as a knockoff, is an important economic contributor to the fashion adoption and diffusion process. However, the extent to which the knockoff resembles or is passed off as the "original" design determines the legality, and therefore the ethics, of the copy. The fashion innovation process obviously raises the question: Is imitation the highest form of flattery for designers, or does it cut into their bottom lines? In 2005, The Norman Lear Center held an event titled "Ready to Share: Fashion and the Ownership of Creativity," which explored these issues. The resulting book, *Ready to Share: Fashion and the Ownership of Creativity* (edited by David Bollier and Laurie Racine, 2006), and accompanying DVD provide insights and perspectives regarding fashion and design ownership and creative processes. The scope of the global fashion marketplace presents high stakes for creators who are cheated out of earnings and for thieves who will go to great lengths to reap illegal gains.

Even when market saturation of fashion products is attributed to a given designer or company, where is the legal line between what is a counterfeit copy and what is an acceptable knockoff? There is no clear-cut answer in this situation. The question of authenticity is important for items to be differentiated from others sufficiently to be protected by intellectual property laws. For example, Victoria's Secret has filed a legal request against Aspen Licensing International (Casabona, Jan. 2, 2007) asking the court to declare that the lingerie company's ski-themed merchandise with the word "Aspen" and imagery of the Aspen environment does not infringe on Aspen Licensing International's trademark.

Authenticity is related to the seller's intent to deceive consumers. If a consumer buys something believing that the item is an authentic representation of the brand, but later discovers it is a copy, the laws currently support removing that seller from the market. In their journal article on counterfeiting, Grossman and Shapiro (1998) discuss deceptive versus nondeceptive counterfeits, and note that both types of items can infringe on intellectual property rights to some degree. The authors also mention the fact that fashion items themselves are not protected. To win in court, brand owners must prove that their reputations are hurt as a result of fakes. For example, when a buyer on Canal Street in New York City knows the "Gucci"-looking watch is a fake, Gucci's reputation is not jeopardized, so there is no legal recourse against the style copier. Alternately, when the eBay buyer of a fake Louis Vuitton handbag—who believed the bag to be real—is disappointed with the poor quality, the brand reputation is put in jeopardy, supporting the legal right of Louis Vuitton to seek injunction against the manufacturer.

The range of intellectual property rights lawsuits is indicated by the news headlines shown in Box 4.4. Clearly, there is no simple solution to the intellectual property rights dilemma; companies must therefore consider ethical aspects of business decisions in addition to legal and reputation perspectives as designs are implemented.

Katherine Baumann, designer of high-end handbags, saw firsthand the effects of knockoffs, or imitations, on her business when her designs gained popularity among celebrities (Tucker, March 14, 2005). Frustrated by the copies of her intricate and expensive handbags, Baumann took it upon herself to interrupt her design and production time to investigate and track down copiers of her designs. Ross Tucker reported that Baumann spent over a year and a half canvassing stores, using shipping box labels and other investigative techniques to identify suppliers of her counterfeited merchandise. She even traveled to China to investigate a manufacturer, where she was able to buy copies of her own work! When she had gathered enough evidence, Baumann filed nearly a dozen lawsuits. Tucker quoted Baumann as saying, "You have to personalize this. The problem large corporations have is people look at them as a faceless entity that does not feel. We need people to understand this affects people's lives" (p. 19).

Most companies that rely on their brands for their existence employ firms specializing in the identification of counterfeit goods, or hire brand specialists within their companies for the same purpose. Brand specialists monitor the unauthorized use of a company's trademarks; the job entails reviewing Web sites, newspapers, magazines, and other media sources, even walking the streets of large cities such as New York, Chicago, and Los Angeles to locate and identify offenders. When identified, copyright offenders are told to cease their activities—and if they don't, they typically are turned over to litigation.

Box 4.4
EXAMPLES OF RECENT HEADLINES

Cartier Sues Amazon.com over Alleged Counterfeit Watches
SOURCE: Tucker, R. (November 5, 2004). *Women's Wear Daily*, p. 1, 18.

Nike Sues Adidas
SOURCE: (February 21, 2006). *Women's Wear Daily*, p. 5.

Burberry Files Federal Suit versus Burlington Coat Units
SOURCE: Casabona, L. (June 7, 2006). *Women's Wear Daily*, p. 10.

Fendi Sues Wal-Mart on Counterfeiting
SOURCE: Scoha, M. (June 13, 2006). *Women's Wear Daily*, p. 2.

Lucky Brand Sues Target
SOURCE: Casabona, L. (October 9, 2006). *Women's Wear Daily*, p. 2.

Diane von Furstenberg Sues Forever 21 over Copyright
SOURCE: Casabona, L. (March 28, 2007). *Women's Wear Daily*, p. 3.

Reebok Files Suit versus Nike Alleging Patent Infringement
SOURCE: Casabona, L. (April 5, 2007). *Women's Wear Daily*, p. 15.

Levi's Files Suit against Polo
SOURCE: Ramey, J. (July 23, 2007). *Women's Wear Daily*, p. 2.

Levi's Sues A&F over Trademark
SOURCE: Ramey, J. (July 26, 2007). *Women's Wear Daily*, p.10.

Aéropostale Files Trademark Suit
SOURCE: Casabona, L. (May 31, 2006). *Women's Wear Daily*, p. 13.

LVMH Files Suit against eBay Charging Counterfeit Sales
SOURCE: Marsh, E. (September 21, 2006). *Women's Wear Daily*, p. 3.

In some cases, powerful brands can leverage their resources to threaten smaller companies' existence when the issue of trademark infringement is murky. Raymond Flandez reported in the *Wall Street Journal* (November 28, 2006) that the U.S. Federal Trademark Dilution Act, passed in 1995, can create a barrier for companies that parody trademarks, citing Haute Diggity Dog's "Chewy Vuiton" dog toy as an example, because trademark owners need only to prove that there is a likelihood that their trademark has been diluted by the offending product, rather than that it actually has. In this situation, LVMH Moët Hennessy Louis Vuitton sued the five-employee company Haute Diggity Dog for use of the name "Chewy Vuiton" on a purse-shaped chew toy for dogs. After incurring legal fees of more than $200,000 and facing canceled orders by manufacturers that had been served cease-and-desist orders from LVMH, the owners of Haute Diggity Dog were exonerated when Judge James C. Cacheris wrote in his judgment, "The fact that the real Vuitton name, marks and dress are strong and recognizable makes it unlikely that a parody—particularly one involving a pet chew toy and bed—will be confused with the real product."

Similarly, Calvin Klein Inc. was the target of a complaint by Calvin Clothing Company Inc. in 2004 (Tucker, December 28 and January 3, 2005). The Calvin Clothing Company brand has manufactured boys' suits and tailored clothing since 1935. A mutual understanding between Calvin Klein and Calvin Clothing reportedly recognized that Calvin Clothing was distinct from the Calvin Klein label, which originated in the 1960s. The nature of the Calvin Clothing complaint emerged in 2002, when Phillips-Van Heusen purchased Calvin Klein and began opposing the Calvin Clothing Company's applications for certain Calvin trademarks. In response, Calvin Clothing sought a judicial declaration of its rights to the Calvin trademark and requested that all Calvin-branded merchandise manufactured for Calvin Klein be destroyed.

Trademark protection measures can also sometimes ensnare individual consumers. In 2006, crafters of embroidery products, who had purchased templates for their work, were informed that they would be sued for selling designs copyrighted by the distributors of the embroidery templates (Searcey, 2006). This has become such a rampant problem among embroidery hobbyists that the Embroidery Software Protection Coalition (ESPC), a nonprofit group of embroidery software and design manufacturers, was formed to defend the integrity and quality of embroidery products by promoting copyright compliance. Sara Meyer-Snuggerud, in a *Sew News* article (1998), presented a question-and-answer column about high-tech copyrights, with answers provided by the ESPC. One item noted that making unauthorized copies of intellectual property, even to share with friends, is akin to stealing. Sharing designs is not like loaning an object such as a car, which is not at your disposal if a friend is using it, but rather an act of piracy through duplication that results in both parties having the property at the same time.

DESIGNER AND MANUFACTURER RESPONSIBILITIES. Designers have an obligation to generate original work, and manufacturers have a responsibility to ensure that the items they produce are authentic and appropriately labeled.

The difficulty designers have in negotiating design inspiration and translating that into original designs is real, and will undoubtedly continue to be addressed by the industry.

The speed at which fashion changes in today's market—retailers strive to offer new merchandise on a continual basis rather than once a season—pressures designers to produce more new garments faster than ever before. Additionally, both vertical retailers and exclusive manufacturers want to reduce production costs in order to increase profit margins. This often means less investment in design teams and creative talent. Knocking off styles shown by fashion leaders enhances the bottom line by reducing design and development costs, and compressing the amount of time needed to bring items to the marketplace. Andrew Harmon and Brenner Thomas (2007) presented the following tips to help designers stay ahead of counterfeiters:

1. Register all brands and specific design motifs with the U.S. Patent and Trademark Office.

2. Work with U.S. Customs to counter foreign counterfeit shipments by showing officials where your goods are manufactured and what authentic products look like.

3. Register all trademarks in every country where business is conducted.

4. Select manufacturers that demonstrate tight control on inventory and manufacturing of hangtags, labels, and buttons.

5. Share services for intellectual property lawyers and private investigators with others in the marketplace, even your competitors.

6. Hire private investigators who are familiar with the territory under investigation.

7. Aggressively pursue counterfeiters. Brand owners who are vigilant about protecting their brands may be less likely to be counterfeited.

RETAILER RESPONSIBILITIES.   Retailers should ensure that only authorized vendors supply their products and portray them in an honest manner. Furthermore, as retailers offer branded items, they are often under contractual obligation to merchandise the goods according to the policies of the brand owners. Retailers must familiarize themselves with the policies of the brand owners they represent and promote and sell those goods accordingly. Additionally, as the "front line" between the brands and the customers, retailers have opportunities to educate consumers regarding brand details so that consumers are better able to make informed decisions.

Retailers should offer choices to consumers so that their needs and desires are met. While doing so, retailers are obligated—both ethically and legally—to offer full information to their customers regarding the origin and brands of their merchandise.

QUESTIONS FOR DISCUSSION

1. What is the difference between a knockoff and a counterfeit?

2. How would the economy be affected if fashion copies were eliminated from the marketplace?

3. How can a person tell the difference between copying that harms the fashion industry and copying that stimulates the economy of the fashion industry?

4. Who is responsible for product authenticity in the case of secondhand sales and online auctions such as eBay—the seller, the auction house, or the retailer? Why and how can that responsibility be enforced or monitored?

5. In your experience, how prevalent are counterfeit items in the marketplace? What are the environmental factors—cultural, economic, etc.—that support this level of availability?

6. Discuss the most prevalent sources of design inspiration for current fashions. Is there anything related to these fashion inspirations that enhance or detract from potential infringements on the intellectual property related to the designs?

7. Investigate the Design Piracy Prohibition Act. What is your view about it? Should designs of apparel be protected by copyright? Why or why not?

8. What steps can manufacturers and designers take to protect their original styles and designs from being copied?

REFERENCES AND SUGGESTED READING

American Marketing Association Web site: http://www.marketingpowercom

Bagwell, L. S. and Berneim, B. D. (1996). Veblen effects in a theory of conspicuous consumption. *American Economic Review*, 86(3), 349–373.

Barnett, J. M. (September 15, 2005). Shopping for Gucci on Canal Street: Reflections on status consumption, intellectual property, and the incentive thesis. *Virginia Law Review*, 91, 1381–1423.

Bloch, P. H., Bush, R. F., and Campbell, L. (1993). Consumer "accomplices" in product counterfeiting: A demand-side investigation. *Journal of Consumer Marketing*, 10(4), 27–36.

Blumer, H. (1969). *Symbolic interactionism: Perspective and method*. Englewood Cliffs, NJ: Prentice Hall.

Bollier, D. and Racine, L. (2006). *Ready to share: Fashion and the ownership of creativity*. Los Angeles: The Norman Lear Center.

Casabona, L. (July 7, 2005). Seven jeans resolves counterfeit suit. *Women's Wear Daily*, p. 8.

Casabona. L. (March 14, 2006a). Adidas, Nike awarded damages. *Women's Wear Daily*, p. 19.

Casabona, L. (May 31, 2006b). Aéropostale files trademark suit. *Women's Wear Daily*, p. 13.

Casabona, L. (June 7, 2006c). Burberry files federal suit versus Burlington coat units. *Women's Wear Daily*, p. 10.

Casabona, L. (June 14, 2006d). Miami pair convicted of counterfeiting. *Women's Wear Daily*, p. 2.

Casabona, L. (November 14, 2006e). Luxe brands fight online counterfeits. *Women's Wear Daily*, p. 5.

Casabona, L. (November 21, 2006f). Supply chain a key in counterfeit battle. *Women's Wear Daily*, p. 9.

Casabona, L. (July 23, 2007). Retailer Forever 21 facing a slew of design lawsuits. *Women's Wear Daily*, p 12.

Casabona, L. and Tucker, R. (October 22, 2007). The new counterfeit front. *Daily News Record*, p. 13.

Chaudhry, P. E. and Walsh, M. G. (1996). An assessment of the impact of counterfeiting in international markets: The piracy paradox persists. *Columbia Journal of World Business*, 31(3), 34–48.

Cholachatpinyo, A., Padgett, I., and Crocker, M. (2002a). A conceptual model of the fashion process – part 1: The fashion transformation process model. *Journal of Fashion Marketing and Management*, 6(1), 11–23.

Cholachatpinyo, A., Padgett, I., and Crocker, M. (2002b). A conceptual model of the fashion process – part 2: An empirical investigation of the micro-subjective level. *Journal of Fashion Marketing and Management*, 6(1), 24–34.

Clark, E. (March 16, 2006a). Fashion lobbies congress for tougher piracy stance. *Women's Wear Daily*, p. 3.

Clark, E. (October 3, 2006b). Global marketplace expands landscape of counterfeiting. *Women's Wear Daily*, p. 17.

Clark, E. (October 29, 2007). International anti-counterfeiting plan set. *Daily News Record*, p. 14.

A Comparative analysis of copyright laws applied to fashion works (1991). *Texas International Law Journal*. Retrieved on July 15, 2007 from http://www.utexas.edu/law/journal/

Derby, M., Tucker, R., and Rashid, F. (April 11, 2005). Vendors step up efforts in counterfeit war. *Women's Wear Daily*, p. 13.

Doeringer, P. and Crean, S. (2006). Can fast fashion save the US apparel industry? *Socio-Economic Review*, 4, 353–377.

Ekelund, R. B., Jr., Mixon, F. G., Jr., and Ressler, R. W. (1995). Advertising and information: An empirical study of search, experience and credence goods. *Journal of Economic Studies*, 22(2), 33–43.

Ellis, K. (March 2006). Thomas criticizes Bush on trade case. *Women's Wear Daily/Global*, p. 5.

Ellis, K. (March 17, 2006). Bush gets tough on counterfeiting. *Women's Wear Daily*, p. 13.

Ellis, K. (April 26, 2007). Copyrighting a dress: Congress mulling bill to protect designers. *Women's Wear Daily*, pp. 1, 13.

Emons, W. (1997). Credence goods and fraudulent experts. *RAND Journal of Economics*, 28(1), 107–119.

Faith in fashion. (January 25, 2007). *Women's Wear Daily*, pp. 1, 6–7.

Fan, Y. (2005). Ethical branding and corporate reputation. *Corporate Communications: An International Journal*, 10(4), 341–350.

Goffman, E. (1959). *The presentation of self in everyday life*. New York: Anchor Press.

Green, R. T. and Smith, T. (2002). Executive insights: Countering brand counterfeiters. *Journal of International Marketing*, 10(4), 89–106.

Grossman, G. M. and Shapiro, C. (1988). Counterfeit-product trade. *American Economic Review*, 78(1), 59–75.

Harmon, A. and Thomas, B. (October 22, 2007). 7 ways to stay one step ahead of the counterfeiters. *Daily News Record*, p. 17.

Hart, T. (February 2, 2005). Police raid store suspected of selling counterfeit items. *The Columbus [Ohio] Dispatch*, p. B7.

Hilfiger settles counterfeiting suit against retailer. (June 28, 2003). *New York Times*, p. C4.

Hilton, B., Choi, C. J., and Chen, S. (2004). The ethics of counterfeiting in the fashion industry: Quality, credence and profit issues. *Journal of Business Ethics*, 55, 345–354.

Horyn, C. (April 9, 2002). Is copying really a part of the creative process? *New York Times*, B10.

Jones, N. (July 21, 2006). Burberry gets 100K in trademark dispute. *Women's Wear Daily*, p. 2.

Jones, N. (July 27, 2007). Topshop to pay Chloé in dress settlement. *Women's Wear Daily*, p.15.

Kapferer, J. (2001). [Re]inventing the brand. Milford, CT: Kogan Page.

Malone, S. (March 4, 2005). Five cops arrested for fake bag bribes. *Women's Wear Daily*, p. 2.

Marsh, E. (September 21, 2006). LVMH files suit against eBay charging counterfeit sales. *Women's Wear Daily*, p. 3

Meyer-Snuggerud, S. (1998). High-tech copyrights. *Sew News*. Retrieved on September 20, 2006 from http://www.sewnews.com/library/sewnews/library/aamach20.htm

Miller, J. W. (December 14, 2006). Gumshoe's intuition: Spotting counterfeits at Port of Antwerp. *Wall Street Journal*, A1.

Nike sues Adidas. (February 21, 2006). *Women's Wear Daily*, p. 5.

OECD (Organization for Economic Co-Operation and Development) (1998). The Economic Impact of Counterfeiting. Retrieved on September 20, 2006 from http://www.oecd.org

Plant, A. (1934). The economic aspects of copyright in books. *Economica*, 1(2), 167–195.

Ramey, J. (July 23, 2007a). Levi's files suit against Polo. *Women's Wear Daily*, p. 2.

Ramey, J. (July 26, 2007b). Levi's sues A&F over trademark. *Women's Wear Daily*, p. 10.

Raustiala, K. and Springman, C. (December 2006). The piracy paradox: Innovation and intellectual property in fashion design. *Virginia Law Review*, 92, 1687–1748.

Sapir, E. (1931). Fashion. In R.A. Seligman (Ed.), *Encyclopedia of the Social Sciences*, 6. New York: Macmillan, pp. 139–144.

Scafidi, S. (2005). *Who owns culture?* New Brunswick, NJ: Rutgers University Press.

Searcey, D. (September 14, 2006). Sewing and suing aren't a happy mix for embroiderers. *Wall Street Journal*, pp. A1, A15.

Sheban, J. (May 17, 2006). Firms in Ohio hurt by illegal copying. *The Columbus [Ohio] Dispatch*, pp. D1, D2.

Shultz, C.J. II and Saporito, B. (1996). Protecting intellectual property: Strategies and recommendations to deter counterfeiting and brand piracy in global markets. *Journal of World Business*, 31(1), 18–28.

Simmel, G. (October 1904). Fashion. *International Quarterly*, 130–155. Reprinted in 1981: G. B. Sproles (ed.) *Perspectives of Fashion*. Minneapolis, MN: Burgess Publishing Co. pp. 5–16.

Socha, M. and Edelson, S. (June 13, 2006). Fendi sues Wal-Mart on counterfeiting. *Women's Wear Daily*, p. 2.

Trebay, G. (July 7, 2002). Imitation is the mother of invention. *New York Times*, p. C10.

Tschorn, A. (June 27, 2005). The wrath of True Religion. *Daily News Record*, p. 4.

Thomas, B. (October 22, 2007). Keeping it real. *Daily News Record*, pp. 16–17.

Tucker, R. (November 5, 2004a). Cartier sues Amazon.com over alleged counterfeit watches. *Women's Wear Daily*, pp. 1, 18.

Tucker, R. (December 22, 2004b). N.Y. counterfeit raid seizes record $12M in apparel. *Women's Wear Daily*, p. 2.

Tucker, R. (December 28, 2004c). Klein facing trademark suit. *Women's Wear Daily*, p. 2.

Tucker, R. (December 29, 2004d). Judge awards Polo subsidiary $1M. *Women's Wear Daily*, p. 10.

Tucker, R. (January 3, 2005a). Calvin label détente scuttled. *Daily News Record*, p. 10.

Tucker, R. (February 2, 2005b). Battling counterfeiters: Divulging the dangers of $500B global industry. *Women's Wear Daily*, pp. 2, 10.

Tucker, R. (March 14, 2005c). Designer Baumann's undercover war on knockoffs. *Women's Wear Daily*, pp. 18–19.

Tucker, R. (March 14, 2005d). Legal briefs. *Women's Wear Daily*, p. 14.

Tucker, R. (July 29, 2005e). North Face breaks up alleged counterfeiting ring. *Women's Wear Daily*, p. 4.

Tucker, R. (March 1, 2006a). Attacking counterfeits: Major ring broken up by Polo and North Face. *Women's Wear Daily*, pp. 1, 13.

Tucker, R. (October 19, 2006b). Levi's new cadence. *Women's Wear Daily*, p. 8.

Tucker, R. and Casabona, L. (October 3, 2007). Making fakes in the USA: Counterfeiters step up domestic manufacturing. *Women's Wear Daily*, pp. 1, 14.

Veblen, T. (1899). *The theory of the leisure class*, New York: The Macmillan Company, Mentor Edition, 1953.

Winograd, B. and Tan, C. L. (September 11, 2006). Can fashion be copyrighted? *Wall Street Journal*, pp. B1, B6.

Wristband fakes grabbed. (March 3, 2005). *Women's Wear Daily*, p. 2.

Young, B. (1988). *Colors of the vanishing tribes*. New York: Abbeville Press, Inc.

Young, V. (January 10, 2007). NYPD hits counterfeiting jackpot. *Women's Wear Daily*, p. 2.

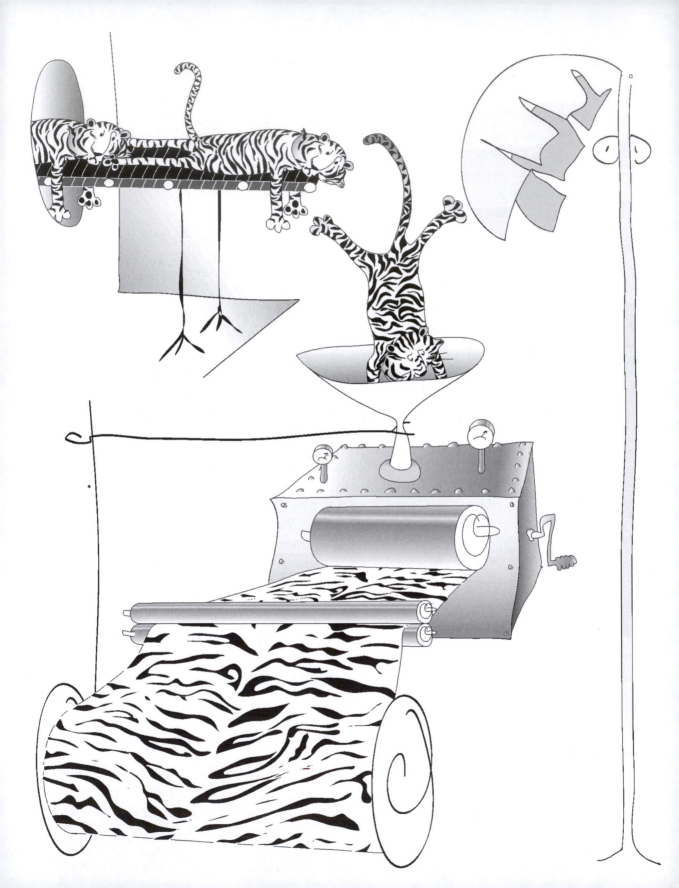

Chapter 5

Ethics in Manufacturing and Sourcing Fashion Products

THE OBJECTIVES OF THIS CHAPTER ARE TO:

- Identify a variety of manufacturing and sourcing issues presenting ethical dilemmas

- Address ethical decisions related to product identification and selection, and subsequently manufacturing and sourcing

- Identify the relationships that labeling and packaging have to manufacturing and sourcing in terms of ethics

- Explore various consumer and corporate perspectives that inform sourcing decisions

- Provide examples of manufacturing and sourcing practices where ethical dilemmas have developed

- Identify current and historical apparel, footwear, and accessory products that have introduced ethical controversies; investigate the nature of these ethical controversies and consider related manufacturing and sourcing decisions

Manufacturers and retailers of apparel items are challenged each season to determine what designs will be developed for production and offered to customers. After designs are selected the merchandise must be manufactured or sourced. Product design and development professionals engage in continual efforts to produce merchandise meeting customer needs, suiting customer tastes, fitting customer lifestyles, and reflecting current fashion trends. Businesses that design, manufacture, and retail their products using company resources are known as "vertically integrated retailers." Other retailers obtain their merchandise from manufacturers that specialize in the

FIGURE 5.1   A sourcing and manufacturing center in Singapore, China

design and development process, known as wholesalers. Some retailers supplement their in-house merchandise with brand-name products sourced from wholesalers. What types of ethical issues are considered when retailers and wholesalers decide what goods to produce and how the merchandise should be manufactured? In what way does the process of manufacturing—and the products themselves—involve ethics? This chapter addresses these questions and explores the relationship between ethics and manufacturing, sourcing, labeling, and packaging products.

Ethical considerations related to product selection and social responsibility are important to the decision-making process when manufacturing and sourcing goods. A company's reputation can depend on whether its products are safe for consumer use and the products it offers are consistent with the company's image and values. The concerns and preferences of some consumers today provide the incentive for companies to seriously consider the topic of social responsibility. Furthermore, for some companies, being socially responsible is the right thing to do because it demonstrates their corporate values. For others, being socially responsible may be important in terms of the company's image with its customers. Social responsibility is an important issue (as well as a buzzword) in the global manufacturing industry today. From a manufacturing perspective, "social responsibility" refers to:

- Producing merchandise in a way that contributes to the well-being of the environment, or at least does not harm environmental health
- Producing products that are safe to use, and even provide safety or well-being features for the consumer
- Using manufacturing processes that do not harm people, animals, or the environment

Socially responsible products can create goodwill between companies and brands and their customers, contributing to positive economic benefits. Merchandise associated with socially responsible production methods produce both physical and psychological benefits. The physical environment benefits from socially responsible practices that contribute to cleaner air and water, recycling, and the use of sustainable raw materials. The marketplace benefits from companies that provide positive work environments for their employees. Consumers who purchase and use merchandise associated with the philosophy and practice of social responsibility can enjoy the satisfaction of supporting a beneficial manufacturing process or company mission. Businesses that include social consciousness as part of their corporate culture span the gamut of industries, and include the realm of fashion. American Apparel and Nike were identified among the top ten most socially conscious brand names in a 2006 survey of college students conducted by Alloy Media + Marketing, placing fifth and eighth, respectively (Seckler, 2006). Other brands identified in the survey were (1) Ben and Jerry's, (2) Newman's Own, (3) Burt's Bees, (4) Yoplait, (6) Starbucks, (7) Seventh Generation, and (9) Body Shop and Coca-Cola (tie). The survey results also revealed that 24 percent of respondents indicated that they had bought something during that year because the product's brand was perceived to be socially aware.

The activities undertaken by companies to position themselves as socially responsible are typically promoted widely and conspicuously by these businesses, which often use their actions to shape their corporate and product images. Newman's Own salad dressings labels declare, "Paul Newman and the Newman's Own® Foundation have given over $200 million to thousands of charities since 1982." Burt's Bees products contain all-natural ingredients and are never tested on animals. Yoplait promotes its "Save lids to save lives" campaign, where consumers can save and mail in their pink yogurt carton lids to Yoplait, which then donates 10 cents per lid to the Susan G. Komen Foundation to help fund breast cancer awareness and research. Each year Ben and Jerry's publishes its Social and Environmental Assessment Report, which details how the year's practices reflect their mission toward social responsibility. Known for its nontoxic household products, Seventh Generation offers information on its Web site to help consumers save energy and other resources. Sales of the naturally inspired products offered by The Body Shop enable the company to participate in campaigns such as those benefiting endangered species and to fund The Body Shop Foundation, which in turn funds human rights and environmental protection groups. Despite some controversy related to monopolistic and discriminatory practices, The Coca-Cola Company has been recognized by *Fortune* as one of the "50 Best Companies for Minorities" and has been rated a top employer by *Black Collegian* and *Latina Style*.

Social responsibility is seen by many as a positive business philosophy, but some companies that seek to be socially responsible sometimes do so in response (sometimes court ordered) to negative publicity resulting from previous unethical or irresponsible practices. Thus, there is a "bigger picture" to consider when evaluating a given company's commitment to social responsibility. Because public perception of a business can affect the desirability of fashion brands, it is important for fashion businesses to protect their images and create positive publicity for their brands. Even companies that strive and intend to act ethically and positively can be associated with ethical dilemmas—and these companies are often scrutinized by competitors and watchdog groups. Retailers that source their products from wholesalers and both brand name as well as anonymous manufacturers similarly must monitor the practices of their suppliers to protect the quality of their products—and their reputation.

CONSUMER SOVEREIGNTY

The concept of consumer sovereignty refers to the power that consumers have in the marketplace to exercise choice and ultimately drive the production of goods. Economic theory (and common sense) holds that consumers will demand and purchase only those products that they find to be acceptable. Therefore manufacturers and retailers of substandard goods will fail in the marketplace because consumers will stop buying and using unsatisfactory products. According to the theory, this process of consumer-based regulation would consequently prevent unsafe or otherwise unacceptable products (such as foul-smelling bottled water or pants with uncomfortable waistbands) from existing in the market.

But the sovereign consumer is not necessarily an informed consumer. Subsequently, consumer rights advocates have brought issues of consumers' safety rights to a point where those rights are frequently valued more highly than consumers' rights to choose. In a market where many goods are available and consumers' knowledge of the goods, not to mention their time to learn about and experience goods, is limited, legislation has been introduced and governmental agencies and their representatives have been tasked with providing standards for product manufacture, product safety, and product availability to consumers. Furthermore, political and personal agendas of policy makers can influence marketplace freedom for both consumers and retailers. What consumers purchase and where they engage in consumption are regulated activities. Most cities have regulations about the types of businesses (e.g., businesses that serve alcohol) that may operate in certain areas. As a member of the fashion industry, you are encouraged to consider both present regulation policies and their applications to merchandising decisions, as well as potential future legislation that may develop in response to contemporary manufacturing, sourcing, and consumption issues.

In 2007, several types of products made in China were recalled in the United States because inappropriate and unsafe elements were used in their manufacture. These items ranged from toys and jewelry made with lead and lead paint to dog food that contained unsafe ingredients. Widespread media coverage alerted consumers to the potential dangers of products and in response, some consumers became more diligent about checking products for manufacture information. These incidents illustrate two points: (1) U.S. consumers generally think that what they buy will be safe, and (2) this assumption may be mistaken. Obviously, immediate, thorough communication is crucial when products causing grave illness or even death are found in the marketplace.

ISSUES

In fashion manufacturing and sourcing, two basic issues have ethical applications: safety and environmentalism. The term "safety," in this context, refers to the well-being of humans. Some would also include the well-being of animals in this category, with concerns about laboratory testing of animals for the development of personal care products or the use of animal skins for apparel products. Environmentalism is a topic of increasing interest worldwide. Ecological awareness began to take its place in the American consciousness during the 1970s; more recently special interest groups and scientists have called attention to environmental crises around the world. The 2006 documentary An Inconvenient Truth addressed the topic of climate change as a result of human activity and gave a credible and powerful voice to environmental concerns.

Environmentalism and safety issues are often related and arise in conjunction with each other. For example, the connection between the apparel and textile industries and dye factories; in the past, the waste products resulting from these manufacturing processes have contaminated nearby ponds and put exposed people—including those who played in the ponds as children—at risk for developing cancer ("Massachusetts town," 2006). Additionally, cancers related to occupational exposure have been identified among employees who work with solvents and dye products, natural fibers, and footwear manufacturing ("Fighting workplace," 2007).

Another issue related to ethics in manufacturing and sourcing is product selection itself, and the appropriateness of the product's role within the consumer target

FIGURE 5.2   Michael Stipes wearing Cartier's LOVE bracelet; a portion of the sales are donated to charities selected by various celebrities.

market, the company's value system, and the role the company seeks in terms of corporate social responsibility. Possible examples of controversial apparel products include thong underwear for preteens, T-shirts with offensive slogans, accessories that have dual purposes promoting or enhancing the use of drugs and alcohol (such as a shoe with a "secret" liquid reservoir), and as previously discussed, the use of fur or other materials that some might consider to be objectionable. Many companies will actively distance (or even sever) themselves from other types of ethically controversial associations as well. For example, shortly after Atlanta Falcons quarterback Michael Vick was indicted for sponsoring dog fighting in 2007, Nike Inc. suspended the release of a shoe that had been designed in conjunction with the football pro: Zoom Vick V (Beckett, 2007).

On the other hand, some companies actively seek or create opportunities to associate themselves with products that promote ethical behavior. The popular Anya Hindmarch "I'm Not a Plastic Bag" bag is an example of a fashion product developed to encourage responsible consumption that was met with high demand by consumers throughout the world (Iredale, 2007). A similar effort was that of high-end retailer Nordstrom, which sold T-shirts featuring the word "ONE" within a circle of people as a way to support the campaign to fighting poverty and AIDS in Africa (Moin, 2006). The T-shirts were made of 100 percent African cotton by Edun, a socially conscious clothing brand, and $10 from every shirt sold was donated by the company to the Apparel Lesotho Alliance to Fight AIDS. Donna Freydkin (2006) reported that $100 from the sale of each $475 Cartier LOVE bracelet was donated to charities selected by celebrities Scarlett Johansson (U.S.A. Harvest), Ashley Judd (YouthAIDS), Sarah Jessica Parker (UNICEF), and Spike Lee (NYU's Tisch School of the Arts).

Product Safety

American consumers are generally aware that certain product standards exist that protect them from unsafe foods, drugs, tools, electrical appliances, and automobiles; it is therefore common to see approval messages from the Food and Drug Administration (FDA), the Department of Transportation, and Underwriters Laboratory on a variety of consumer products. Additionally, consumers are familiar with processes such as recalls, which focus attention on products (such as babies' car seats, cookware, and automobiles) that have already made it to the marketplace and have been subsequently found to be unsafe. (Recalls are discussed in greater detail in the "Self-Regulation" section of this chapter.) When consumers purchase fashion goods, particularly from reputable retailers, it is generally assumed that these products are safe. In fact, basic ethical principles require that manufactured fashion products are safe for the wearer. Although it seems obvious that regulation is less necessary for apparel, footwear, and accessories than for products such as automobiles, lawn mowers, and chainsaws, merchandisers should nevertheless be aware that there are decisions related to manufacturing and sourcing with ethical implications related to the safety of fashion products. Occasionally, incidents of retailing unsafe fashion products threaten the reputations of retailers and brands. Company responses to these incidents as well as practices in place to prevent such incidents are closely related to—and demonstrate—corporate culture and ethical values.

Legislation

Prior to the 1950s, there was little regulation monitoring consumer product safety in the United States. Today, many products are subject to legislative regulation aimed at protecting the health and well-being of consumers, particularly children. Toys must meet safety standards to prevent choking hazards for children under age three, paint must be lead-free so that children do not ingest the deadly substance, and bicycle helmets are required to perform to a certain standard upon impact. The variety of materials used to manufacture apparel, footwear, and home furnishings introduces a range of potential dangers, therefore fashion products are not exempt from safety issues in their manufacture and in the standards set forth for their finished products. The Flammable Fabrics Act (FFA) was established in 1953 in response to manufactured fibers such as brushed rayon (popular at the time for sweaters) and children's wear (especially sleepwear) being so highly flammable that significant numbers of injuries were resulting from their use. The Consumer Products Safety Commission (CPSC) is charged with administration of the Flammable Fabrics Act (FFA) as well as maintaining and enforcing other standards for product safety. Standards for fabric flammability, and flammability of other materials used in wearing apparel and interior furnishings, have been established by the American Society for Testing and Materials (ASTM). Other safety standards include those regarding fabric toxicity (caused by gaseous emissions from dyes or finishing processes) and buttons and cords (which are prohibited from use in infant apparel because of the possibility of choking and strangulation). Product composition standards also exist for accessories, prohibiting such dangers as the presence of lead or mercury.

Self-Regulation

In addition to meeting legislative standards, manufacturers and retailers generally seek to offer safe products that perform well. Many companies test their merchandise in their own laboratories or subcontract their quality assurance processes to ensure that their merchandise reflects their quality and safety standards. In addition to toxicity and flammability standards, tests may be performed to determine whether children's apparel contains trims, such as buttons or zipper pulls, that would introduce choking hazards; fabrics hold their dyes; and garments stand up to repeated washings. Even garment comfort is evaluated through wear testing.

When products are discovered to be harmful, they are recalled. This means that they are voluntarily removed from retailers' shelves and consumers who have already purchased those products are notified and informed of how to return them for a refund, obtain repair kits to correcting the product defect, or have the product professionally repaired. When announcing recalls, retailers and brands have the opportunity to reinforce their position as ethical companies. The services offered and ease with which returns or repairs are made contribute to consumers' attitudes toward the companies. In 2006, Wal-Mart and Carrefour Group, along with several other retailers, found that skirts, blouses, and trousers they were selling, which had been manufactured in four Chinese factories, had failed inspections due to excessive levels of aromatic ammine or formaldehyde (both cancer-causing agents) emitted from the fabrics ("Toxic apparel," 2006). The retailers initiated recalls, once the problems were discovered, and customers were reassured that the companies were acting out of concern for their health. Similarly, children's toys were recalled by Mattel, Inc., when the company found that some of its toys (Big Bird, Dora the Explorer, and Elmo characters) contained unsafe levels of lead ("Parents," 2007). Mattel had previously recalled nearly 4.5 million Polly Pocket magnetic play sets after determining that the magnets could detach and pose a choking hazard for children ("4 million," 2006).

Good Housekeeping and *Consumer Reports* are two national magazines that regularly publish lists of recalled items in cooperation with the U.S. Consumer Product Safety Commission (CPSC); complete lists of recalled products can be found at the latter's Web site, http://www.cpsc.gov. Through that site, consumers can sign up for free e-mail lists of current recalls. Examples of recalled fashion items are presented in Box 5.1.

Retailers and manufacturers may strive to select and create products—particularly cosmetics—that are free of chemicals. This is a growing trend in the marketplace, as more and more consumers consider these types of products to be appealing. Groupe Clarins, a French cosmetics brand with research and development capabilities, and Kibio, an organic beauty brand, partnered to create a natural cosmetics line (Weil, 2006) to capitalize on consumer demand for organic cosmetics. The United States Department of Agriculture (USDA) offers its organic seal to beauty items as well as to food and apparel. Ellen Groves (2006a) reported in *Women's Wear Daily* that a variety of beauty products on the market (nail polish, hair spray, body scrub, moisturizer) include bamboo as an ingredient, which offers resilience, flexibility, a woodsy scent, and hydrating qualities, in addition to its ability to rapidly replenish itself in the environment.

But the retail success of organic fashion items does present a challenge. For example, organic cotton is one of the most widely recognized and sought after "eco-friendly" fashion fibers on the market. However, current production processes are more expensive than methods used to grow non-organic cotton, so the cost to consumers who want organic merchandise is higher than for traditional cotton goods. Similarly, other types of organic goods face competitive difficulties in the marketplace. Even though lotions, oils, and soaps are available in organic formulas, some consumers are unwilling to sacrifice performance of high-tech beauty formulas for organic alternatives (Nagel, 2007).

A component of the product development and evaluation process for many cosmetic and personal care companies is the use of animals for product testing. Animal testing is seen by some as a controversial practice because of the potential harm the testing introduces to the laboratory animals. Animal rights organizations, such as Animal Rights International (ARI), are concerned with animals' quality of life, safety, and health, and object to the practice of using animals in laboratory tests.

Likewise, the choice by apparel manufacturers and retailers to use controversial products such as fur, leather, and suede presents ethical issues and can make those companies vulnerable to consumer protest. Ultimately, designers and professionals involved in product development must make decisions about product components that are aligned with the company's values and ethics, as well as those of its current and future consumers. Apparel product developers can therefore be responsive to

BOX 5.1
RECALLS OF APPAREL, ACCESSORY, AND FOOTWEAR PRODUCTS

PRODUCT	PROBLEM
N-Kids girls' drawstring flannel pants and Pine Peak Blues boys' drawstring flannel pants sold for $12 to $18 at Nordstrom and through Nordstrom.com from July through December 2005.	The pants don't meet the standard for the flammability of children's sleepwear, posing the risk of a burn injury.
Cobmex youth jackets with drawstrings sold for about $30 at children's clothing and school uniform stores from January 2006 through February 2007.	The drawstrings can get entangled around a child's neck, posing risk of strangulation.
Really Useful Products Children's Mood necklaces and Diva Necklaces sold for about $1 at children's dollar, and discount stores throughout the U.S. from September 2004 through November 2006.	The jewelry contains high levels of lead, which is toxic if ingested.
Boys' heavyweight outer jackets manufactured by Samara Brothers that were sold from October 2006 through November 2006 for up to $50.	The snap closures on the jackets contain high levels of lead, which is toxic if ingested by young children.
Juicy Couture bracelets and necklaces sold in department stores between September 2005 and April 2006 for approximately $95.	The bracelets contain high levels of lead, which is toxic if ingested.

consumer demands, which reflect a wide variety of values and desires. The animal rights organization People for the Ethical Treatment of Animals (PETA) has success-fully lobbied apparel retailers and brands including Ralph Lauren, Martha Stewart, Ann Taylor, and Guess to discontinue the use of fur and other animal products in their merchandise. PETA's value for the well-being of all animals makes its actions ethically based (from Values Approach perspective). The goal of the organization is to transfer its values to retailers, manufacturers, scientists, and farmers through campaigns managed by its members (see Chapter 2 for more information about these campaigns). Protest rallies organized by PETA are disruptive to stores and influential with the general public—in addition, the resulting media attention and publicity can also reflect negatively on the retailers and brands. The group's efforts

Box 5.1 continued from page 116
RECALLS OF APPAREL, ACCESSORY, AND FOOTWEAR PRODUCTS

Rocky Shoes & Boots, Inc. recalled men's safety-toe hiker boots sold for $90–$100 under the Georgia Boot brand by independent shoe stores, Web sites, and other retail outlets between October 2005 and February 2006.

Product testing demonstrated that the boots may not comply with applicable safety standards for crush and impact resistance; consumers could suffer impact foot injuries.

Victoria's Secret Silk Kimono Tops sold through Victoria's Secret Direct catalogues and Web site from November 2005 through December 2005 for about $138.

Fabric fails to meet mandatory standards of fabric flammability in violation of the federal Flammable Fabrics Act. The sheer outer shell fabric of the kimono top can readily ignite and present a risk of burn injuries.

Cannondale C-Soles cycling shoes sold at Cannondale dealers between early 1997 through April 1997 for between $59.99 and $79.99.

The cleats could pull out of the sole, causing a cyclist's foot to slip off the pedal leading to an injury.

Levi Strauss & Co.'s fleece fabric shirts made from cotton-polyester blend material with a raised fiber surface; sold at retailers such as J.C. Penney, Levi's Only Store, and Levi's Outlet by Designs from October 1996 through February 1997 for about $30.

Garments were found to be highly flammable, failing to meet federal mandatory standards for fabric flammability and may ignite readily and present serious risk of burn injuries.

SOURCES: http://www.goodhousekeeping.com/recalls-childrens-products and http://www.cpsc.gov, Juicy recall, (2006)

are effective because designers and retailers do not want consumers boycotting their products and stores in sympathy with those who value animal rights and consider using animals for clothing to be unethical. Interestingly, the demand for fur has recently increased in the consumer marketplace (Scelfo, 2004; "Fur demands," 2007) and leather shoes, belts, handbags, and apparel products continue to be staples in the fashion arena (Tell, 2007). Animal protection can be seen both as a safety issue (with respect to the well-being of the living animals), and also an environmental issue (e.g., when demand for rare skins such as leopard and endangered materials, such as ivory, threaten not only the animals, but also vulnerable ecosystems and habitats).

ENVIRONMENTALISM

Environmentalism refers to both the health of Earth's resources and to the continued use and availability of resources that we consume. Product waste from textile factories that pollute water ways and consumption of crude oil to manufacture fibers, such as nylon and polyester, are examples of how the concerns of the product development industry overlap with environmentalism. Waste generation is a serious issue, particularly in the United States where, according to the Environmental Protection Agency (EPA), the average consumer generates 4.5 pounds of waste each day. In 2005, about 79 million tons of municipal waste products were recycled in the United States, accounting for 32 percent of all consumer waste. The percentage of waste recycled has increased from about 20 percent in 1992 and only about 7 percent in 1960. Waste disposal and environmental protection legislation in the United States has resulted in costs to businesses and consumers of more than $100 billion each year (Webber, 1995) but has resulted in a savings of resources, including landfill space. In 1971, Barry Commoner wrote *The Closing Circle*, which explored the relationships that increased industrialization and technology have to all aspects of life. He presented four Laws of Ecology that are related to recycling and conservation of resources:

1. Everything is connected to everything else (p. 33).

2. Everything must go somewhere (p. 39).

3. Nature knows best (p. 41).

4. There is no such thing as a free lunch (p. 45).

Commoner notes in his book that humans participate as members in Earth's environmental system, but paradoxically they exploit the environment in an effort to produce wealth for themselves. He advocates for awareness of the environment so this situation can be addressed through actions that will not harm the planet further.

According to the Secondary Materials and Recycled Textiles Association, approximately 4 percent of U.S. landfill space is consumed by textile waste. Tanya Domina and Kathy Koch (1997) studied the textile waste lifecycle in an effort to encourage dialogue among textile and clothing professionals, with the goals of reducing textile disposal in landfills and generating new or expanded recycling options for textile waste. They explored post-producer textile waste generated by manufacturers, preconsumer waste generated by retailers, and public generated post-consumer waste, such as used and discarded clothing, blankets, and rags.

The two reviewed literature and surveyed textile/apparel firms, retailers, trade associations, and nonprofit organizations, and based on that information, developed their Textile Waste Lifecycle model. The model meets Commoner's first two Laws of Ecology and reflects a growing interdependence between consumers and textile/apparel industries in textile waste disposal in an environmentally responsible manner. Domina and Koch note that recycling of post-consumer waste is a weak component of the textile waste lifecycle and encourage further development of programs and opportunities in this area.

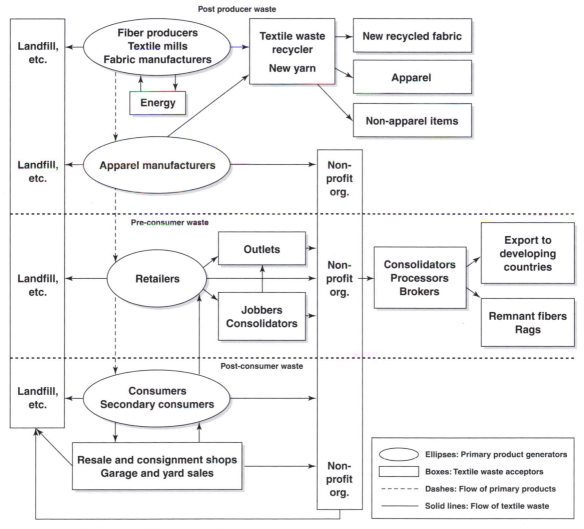

FIGURE 5.3   Textile waste lifecycle model

Sustainability

Sustainability is a concept that encompasses both social responsibility and environmentalism. According to the EPA, sustainability is "the ability to achieve continuing economic prosperity while protecting the natural systems of the planet and providing a high quality of life for its people." Sustainability requires that natural resources are renewed rather than depleted through the processes of production and consumption. "Green is the new black" is a familiar phrase in recent fashion publications, indicating that the notion of sustainability is seen as valuable. The April 2, 2007, issue of *Daily News Record* was labeled "The Green Issue," with the following statement printed on its cover:

> In this era of Whole Foods, Prius-driving starlets and Al "Oscar-winner" Gore, eco-fashion is ready for its moment in the sun. Companies from Levi's to LVMH, Gant to Gap, are aligning their products and brands with environmental concerns. Inside, an in-depth report on the trends, innovations and ideas shaping the greening of men's wear.

Similarly, a *Women's Wear Daily Intimates* article (Monget, 2007) proclaimed, "It's Not Easy Going Green" as benefits and challenges to producing eco-friendly merchandise were reviewed. Even general interest and news publications such as *Time* ("Apparel takes," 2007) have reported on the green clothing trend, noting a growing consumer market for eco-friendly apparel, as well as manufacturing and sourcing operations that accommodate eco-friendly processes.

As people become increasingly aware of environmental issues, manufacturers and retailers may find that their consumers will pay for more environmentally friendly products. Furthermore, the performance quality of fabrics and apparel made with eco-friendly fibers is high, helping motivate consumers' purchases in this category of merchandise. In addition to familiar natural fibers such as organic cotton, wool, and linen, new "green" fibers, now popular for apparel, include bamboo, soy, and hemp. Bamboo has good wicking properties and a soft hand. Hemp fibers are strong and durable. DuPont has developed a fiber with the trademark name Sorona® that is made from corn. Other manufactured fibers with environmentally friendly properties include Tencel® and Modal®, both manufactured from wood pulp (eucalyptus and beech, respectively) by the Austrian Lenzing Fibers Company, and Repreve® made by Unifi from recycled materials such as milk jugs and soda bottles.

Sustainable and renewable fashions are gaining in popularity; they're seen as "hip." Companies are more easily rewarded with sales and positive publicity when they produce merchandise, such as eco-friendly apparel, that is considered fashionable. The fashionability of these garments is largely due to their ethical ("it's the right thing to do") position in the marketplace. Ethics has obviously entered into the decision-making process for consumers who buy sustainable products. Because organic, fair trade, and fair labor products are more costly to produce than the typical merchandise manufactured throughout the world, the element of fashionability and appeal is a critical component because it makes the higher prices acceptable, particularly as producers seek to expand their markets. Despite a *Wall Street Journal* article (Binkley, 2007) blaming dowdy and otherwise unattractive fashions for the slow pace of eco-fashions attracting mainstream consumers, ethical fashion continues to grow both in popularity and as an economically viable segment of the industry. Ellen Groves (2006b) reported that ethical fashion designers have transitioned from focusing on distribution channels to the challenge of managing large orders.

Many observers have noted that historically, the fashionability or desirability of merchandise and its price are of greater importance to most consumers than the "ethicalness" of the products themselves (Boulstridge and Carrigan, 2000; Carrigan and Attalla, 2001; de Pelsmacker, Driesen, and Rayp, 2005; Dickson, 2001; Iwanow, McEachern, and Jeffrey, 2005; Loureiro, McCluskey, and Mittelhammer, 2002; Page and Fearn, 2005, Swinker and Hines, 1997; "Term Limits," 2007). That is, consumers are attracted to merchandise that is visually appealing and affordable. A growing, yet still relative, minority of consumers actively seek products due to their mode of manufacture; the number of consumers who report a willingness to purchase ecologically friendly apparel, footwear, and accessories has grown from 6 percent in 2001 to 18 percent in 2006 (Lipke, 2007). This trend is expected to continue as environmental issues are better understood and interest in restoring a healthy global environment increases.

Corporate response to environmental issues is reflected in Cotton Incorporated's Lifestyle Monitor™ report in the April 2, 2007, issue of *Daily News Record*. The report quoted Gap Inc.'s spokesperson Erica Archambault as saying, "Gap Inc. is always exploring innovative, socially responsible ways to make our products. We're exploring the use of sustainable fibers and products—whether that means new fabrics for our products, unusual materials for our packaging and store display fixtures, or new approaches to building construction" ("Term Limits," p. 5). Thus, the application of eco-friendly apparel product development and retailing can be extended beyond product manufacture to include fixtures in the store and store (or corporate headquarters, factory, warehouse, etc.) construction itself. The personal care brand Aveda, for example, switched its major manufacturing plant to wind energy in 2006 (Costello, 2007). Portland, Oregon-based activewear brand Nau plans

Box 5.2
GLOSSARY OF "GREEN"

Organic Cotton—Grown without the use of genetically modified seeds, synthetic fertilizers, or chemical herbicides and insecticides. Crops must be rotated to replenish the soil.

Organic Labeling—On apparel, it defines various levels of organic cotton usage. "100% Organic Cotton" must contain 100 percent organically produced cotton, including any sewing thread. "Organic Cotton" must contain at least 95 percent organically produced cotton; "Made with organic cotton" must contain at least 70 percent; and "Made with x percent Organic Cotton" must contain the percentage indicated.

Third Party Certification—It provides oversight of claims regarding organic attributes. There are a number of certifying bodies around the world, including the USDA, Demeter (Europe), SKAL (The Netherlands), the Soil Association (England), and The Japan Organic Cotton Association. The International federation of Organic Agriculture Movements creates international standards.

Sustainability—"The ability to achieve continuing economic prosperity while protecting the natural systems of the planet and providing a high quality of life for its people," according to the U.S. EPA. Alternatively, the British government defines sustainable development as "development which meets the needs of the present without compromising the ability of future generations to meet their own needs."

ecologically correct stores that offer customers charitable giving opportunities while they shop (Corcoran, 2006). Wal-Mart has reported a variety of initiatives to become more environmentally friendly, from increased recycling of its solid waste, to enhancing the efficiency of its truck fleet, to showing preference to suppliers that reduce their emissions (Zimmerman, 2006). Additionally, Wal-Mart president and CEO H. Lee Scott announced in 2005 the goal of developing a store that is 25 to 30 percent more energy efficient by 2009 (Bowers, 2007). These are examples of companies making business decisions that reflect a concern for the environment.

The Carrefour Group, the world's second largest retailer, publishes a Sustainability Report each year, which the company makes available online at http://www.carrefour.com/cdc/responsible-commerce/sustainability-report. In 2006, the report focused on six key issues: nutrition, sustainable/responsible products, diversity within the company, social audits, climate change, and sustainable construction. In the report the company emphasizes its commitment to sustainability and social responsibility,

BOX 5.2 continues from page 122
GLOSSARY OF "GREEN"

Carbon Footprint—"A measure of the impact human activities have on the environment in terms of the amount of greenhouse gases produced, measured in units of carbon dioxide," according to http://Carbonfootprint.com

Carbon Neutral—A state where a person or institution has reduced its carbon emissions where possible, and then purchased a carbon offset for its remaining emissions, bringing its carbon footprint down to zero.

Carbon Offset—The act of reducing net carbon emissions by allotting resources to practices that decrease pollutants. For example, emission credits can be purchased to lower pollutants from other sources, such as power plants, or to pay companies who emit less than the recommended amount. It can also be as simple as paying to have new trees planted, or investing in solar or wind power.

Fair Trade—According to Oxfam, "[It] is an alternative approach to conventional international trade. It is a trading partnership which aims at sustainable development for excluded and disadvantaged producers." The Fair Trade certification label allows consumers to endorse products that guarantee fair labor conditions are met.

SOURCE: Jenni Chang, The Glossary of "Green." *Daily News Record*, April 2, 2007, p. 14. Copyright © (2007) Conde Nast Publications. All rights reserved. Originally published in *DNR*. Reprinted with permission.

citing its core values: freedom, responsibility, sharing, respect, integrity, solidarity, and progress. The reports highlights activities such as offering environmentally friendly products, fair trade products, purchases from local suppliers, contributions to educational opportunities, and promotion of food safety. The 2007 report focuses on the following five key issues: balanced diet, sustainable consumption, manufacturing social conditions, being a responsible employer, and climate change.

Recycling

Recycling is important for its role in reducing landfill contents, renewing limited resources, and saving energy in the production processes. Greeting cards, office paper, and plastic products are often labeled "made from recycled materials." Recycling has become a way of life for many people, and many municipalities throughout the country now have separate facilities to accommodate recyclable

Box 5.3
IS RECYCLING WORTHWHILE?

Recycling is one of the best environmental success stories of the late twentieth century. Recycling, which includes composting, diverted over 72 million tons of material away from landfills and incinerators in 2003, up from 34 million tons in 1990—doubling in just 10 years. Recycling turns materials that would otherwise become waste into valuable resources. As a matter of fact, collecting recyclable materials is just the first step in a series of actions that generate a host of financial, environmental, and societal returns. There are several key benefits to recycling. Recycling:

- Protects and expands U.S. manufacturing jobs and increases U.S. competitiveness in the global marketplace
- Reduces the need for landfilling and incineration
- Saves energy and prevents pollution caused by the extraction and processing of virgin materials and the manufacture of products using virgin materials
- Decreases emissions of greenhouse gases that contribute to global climate change
- Conserves natural resources such as timber, water, and minerals
- Helps sustain the environment for future generations

SOURCE: United States Environmental Protection Agency (EPA), http://www.epa.gov/epaoswer/non-hw/muncpl/faq.htm

items. Recycling is a major industry in the United States, with thousands of companies employing millions of people. According to the Secondary Materials and Recycled Textiles Association (SMART; http://www.smartasn.org/), the textile recycling industry removes 2.5 billion pounds of post-consumer textile waste from the United States' solid waste stream, 35 percent of which is used clothing that is exported.

New apparel and home furnishings products made from recycled materials may be less familiar than some of the consumer items previously mentioned, but they are nevertheless available in products such as sweatshirts, jeans, underwear, blankets, hats, gloves, socks, luggage, and carpets. Mary Swinker and Jean Hines (1997) investigated whether consumers would willingly select apparel made from recycled fibers. Their study revealed that, when price was controlled, a majority of consumers selected sweatshirts made of recycled fibers over sweatshirts labeled with virgin fiber content. As would be expected, the researchers also found that consumers who selected sweatshirts made from recycled fibers were more familiar with recycling, were more ecologically conscious, and/or perceived that products made with recycled fibers were not inferior to products made with virgin materials.

A recent study was conducted to investigate the affinity of a specific target group of consumers to apparel made with previously used apparel components (Young, Jirousek, and Ashdown, 2004). This project incorporated William McDonough and Michael Braungart's (1998) philosophy, "waste equals food," by taking objects that would have been discarded and instead using them to produce re-created, useful objects. The targeted consumers, labeled "urban nomads" represented a demographic of "young professionals living in urban areas who commute using ecologically sensitive public and human-powered modes of transportation" (p. 61). The authors developed a design process, and then sourced materials by purchasing used jeans, sweatshirts, T-shirts, men's suits, button-down collar shirts, and wool sweaters in bulk from rag dealers. Their prototype garments were then "undesigned" and transformed into new apparel items. The line of products developed for wear testing and evaluation by a sample of urban nomads included a Denim Wave Skirt, a Pod Skirt, a Backpack Vest, a Decon Hoodie Cardigan, and a Reverse Reflect Vest. The authors noted that good design is a crucial first step for the environmental principles to be understood and accepted by consumers. They found that consumers were more willing to wear secondhand clothing that had been deconstructed and incorporated into new garments than normal used clothing.

Fair Trade

Fair Trade is a concept that mixes both ethics and business; it requires that producers of commodities such as cotton, wool, coffee, and apples be paid "fair" prices for their goods—rather than the minimum prices allowed in the marketplace. TransFair USA is a nonprofit organization that grants Fair Trade certification for goods that meet the Fairtrade Labeling Organization (FLO) International standards. Currently, Fair Trade certification is available in the United States for coffee, tea and herbs, cocoa and chocolate, fresh fruit, sugar, rice, and vanilla. TransFair USA evaluates and certifies products by working with importers and manufacturers to document trade practices associated with the specific goods. Apparel items are a more recent addition to this arena; however, they are difficult to certify because of the variety of labor contributions that go into garment components and assembly. Fair Indigo, established in 2006 offering a catalogue and Internet site, is a pioneering fashion apparel and accessories retailer that is promoting the

Box 5.4
THE FAIR TRADE FEDERATION

The Fair Trade Federation (FTF) is an association of fair trade wholesalers, retailers, and producers whose members are fully committed to providing fair wages and good employment opportunities to economically disadvantaged artisans and farmers worldwide.

FTF members link low-income producers with consumer markets and educate consumers about the importance of purchasing fairly traded products that support living wages and safe and healthy conditions for workers in the developing world. FTF provides resources and networking opportunities for its members and acts as a clearinghouse for information on fair trade. FTF membership is not a certification, but members are screened for their full commitment to fair trade.

By adhering to social criteria and environmental principles, fair trade organizations foster a more equitable and sustainable system of production and trade that benefits people and their communities.

SOURCE: http://www.fairtradefederation.com

concept in the operation of its business. Company founders plan to meet their goal of increasing wages for clothing laborers by sourcing products at worker co-ops and small family-owned factories that cooperate by paying their employees more than the prevailing wage (Chandler, 2006). As indicated, the scope of the Fair Trade concept also encompasses fair labor—the payment of living wages, availability of freedom of association, safe working conditions, and an absence of forced child labor. Fair labor is discussed in greater detail in Chapter 6.

Because of the guaranteed payment structure, certified Fair Trade products are typically associated with higher prices than products that aren't manufactured using Fair Trade guidelines, and are often sold with a certain percentage premium for the Fair Trade value. In order for these types of goods to be economically viable, consumers must be willing to pay premiums on prices beyond the market price to ensure that the producers receive the guaranteed fair price. The ethical results of Fair Trade products include improved quality of life for workers, enhanced working conditions and job security, and positive contributions to environmental sustainability. Critics of Fair Trade have expressed concerns that guaranteed pricing may artificially extend the life of some products beyond the time that their production is economically feasible, thus preventing farmers and manufacturers from seeking to produce newer, more sustainable crops and products.

MANUFACTURING PRODUCTS FOR TRADITIONALLY UNDERSERVED MARKETS

Ethical fashions include not only those products that are produced in ways that are safe and environmentally friendly, but also items that are available for a range of diverse consumers. As marketers have begun to realize, members of historically underserved populations such as Latinos and African Americans can bring significant spending power (and in some cases, influence) to the marketplace. As a result, both advertising and product development have become more targeted toward the unique consumer attributes of these populations in the past decade. Apparel that reflects cultural desires and shopping environments that appeal to members of specific market segments have become more widely available. As diversity is embraced and valued as a component of corporate social responsibility, additional consumer categories have developed; two notable examples are cosmetics for dark skin tones and plus-size women's apparel.

ADDITIONAL ETHICAL ISSUES IN PRODUCT DEVELOPMENT

Do retailers and product manufacturers have a *responsibility* to be "politically correct"? This is an issue that can ignite the ages-old profit versus ethics debate. Because making money is the major driver for so many businesses, decisions must be responsive to their bottom lines.

Target Market

Apparel product developers and retailers need to reference their corporate values and identify lucrative merchandise that appeals to their target market. But, obviously, products that appeal to one target market may potentially offend others. Trying to connect with the selected market may come at a cost of bad publicity, but many controversial retailers note that bad publicity from one group translates into free publicity in the broader market and increased sales from their target customers. Abercrombie & Fitch's controversial T-shirt slogans spawned protests that generated more free publicity than the company's advertising budget could have covered. The publicity surely prompted additional sales from consumers who were intrigued by the controversy and drawn to the company's edgy products.

Conversely, controversial products can detract from companies' sales when the target market is offended. This is particularly important when offering products or advertising in foreign countries or to unfamiliar cultures.

Manufacturing Authentic Merchandise

Although previously addressed in Chapter 4, the decision to produce authentic merchandise is worth briefly revisiting in the context of product manufacturing and sourcing. The authenticity of merchandise designs and logos is not only an ethical issue, it can also have legal consequences. Forever 21 was hard hit in 2007 by lawsuits from at least 20 designers and retailers including Anna Sui, Gwen Stefani, Diane von Furstenberg, Bebe, Tokidoki, and Anthropologie, which accused the company of copying their fabric patterns and/or designs. Lisa Casabona reported in *Women's Wear Daily* (2007) that "sources familiar with the cases say the retailer's actions and its responses to litigation seem indicative of a systematic approach to copying designers." Similarly, Levi Strauss & Company sued both Polo Ralph Lauren and Abercrombie & Fitch in 2007 citing trademark infringement for allegedly copying the famous blue jean pocket design. In addition to being costly, lawsuits create negative publicity for retailers and brands that can damage their reputations with members of the consuming public.

Labeling and Packaging

Merchandise must be labeled correctly so the customer can accurately determine what he or she is purchasing. A major responsibility of retailers is to ensure that the people manufacturing and sourcing goods produce appropriate labels. Most experienced consumers in the United States expect their apparel items to be manufactured with components that are listed in the labeling; retailers and brands that violate this expectation risk losing the trust of their customers. In early 2007, an investigation by the Humane Society of the United States revealed that fur products sold online by Nordstrom and Tommy Hilfiger contained pelts of domesticated dogs rather than synthetic fur as the labels had indicated ("Is your fur fake or is it Fido?" 2007). Although customers were notified and offered the opportunity to return the mislabeled merchandise, situations such as these leave retailers and brands vulnerable to consumer mistrust, particularly when buying products that may be selected as "ethical" substitutions for controversial fashion items. To strengthen goodwill between retailers and brands and their customers, labels should also comply with care labeling and country of origin requirements.

Merchandise should be packaged in a manner that ensures the integrity of the product, is not wasteful, and enables the intended use of the product to be clearly understood.

Decisions regarding materials and production processes have ethical implications, regardless of the present market demand. Companies that promote themselves as ethical must reinforce their image with action by offering authentic products that perform to the standards advertised. As professionals in a trend-driven industry, apparel merchandisers benefit from awareness of current marketplace issues and concerns that affect the products they design, produce, and sell.

QUESTIONS FOR DISCUSSION

1. Are you willing to pay more for environmentally friendly fashion products? Why or why not?

2. What steps do you take to reduce municipal product waste? What steps might you take in the future that would be a change from what you currently do? Describe and explain.

3. Identify the types of Fair Trade merchandise that is available at a store in your area. How is it promoted? What image do you associate with retailers who sell Fair Trade products? What is your opinion about the generally higher prices charged for fair trade merchandise?

4. Have you bought recycled apparel products? If so, what was your motivation for doing so? If not, why not? Explain.

5. What do you do with your apparel items when they are no longer useful to you? Explain. Can you think of other methods you might use in the future?

6. What "new" fibers have you seen on the market? Do you have any clothing manufactured with "new," sustainable fibers? If so, what are those fibers? Why did you purchase that particular item?

REFERENCES AND SUGGESTED READING

Four million toys recalled after kids swallow magnets. (November 22, 2006). *The Athens [Ohio] Messenger*, p. 2 [Associated Press; Washington, DC].

Abercrombie reacts to t-shirt protests. (April 20, 2002). *New York Times*, p. C2.

Apparel takes root. (March 1, 2007). *Time*, 20.

Bailey, J. (January 21, 1999). Walking on eggshells, polystyrene people make a comeback. *Wall Street Journal*, p. A1.

Beckett, W. (July 20, 2007). Nike suspends release of Vick shoe. *Women's Wear Daily*, p. 2.

Binkley, C. (April 19, 2007). Green jeans: Why designers are late to eco game. *Wall Street Journal*, pp. D1, D 10.

Boulstridge, E. and Carrigan, M. (2000). Do consumers really care about corporate responsibility? Highlighting the attitude-behaviour gap. *Journal of Communication Management*, 4(4), 355–368.

Bowers, K. (January 19, 2007). Wal-Mart prototype to use less energy, *Women's Wear Daily*, p. 2.

Carpenter, M. (March 12, 2006) Today's packaging can drive mild-mannered to 'wrap rage.' *The Athens [Ohio] Messenger*, p. B12 [*Pittsburgh Post Gazette*].

Carrefour Group 2006 Sustainability Report (2006). Retrieved on August 10, 2007 from http://www.carrefour.com/cdc/responsible-commerce/sustainibility-report

Carrefour Group 2007 Sustainability Report (2007). Retrieved on July 9, 2008 from http://www.carrefour.com/cdc/responsible-commerce/sustainibility-report

Carrigan, M. and Attalla, A. (2001). The myth of the ethical consumer—do ethics matter in purchase behavior? *Journal of Consumer Marketing*, 18(7), 560–577.

Carrillo, K. J. (October 11–17, 2001). Refashion network: Giving fashion an environmental conscience. *The New York Amsterdam News*, 92(41), p. 5.

Casabona, L. (July 23, 2007). Retailer Forever 21 facing a slew of design lawsuits. *Women's Wear Daily*, p. 12.

Chandler, S. (October 8, 2006). Fair-trade label reaches retail market. *Chicago Tribune*. Retrieved on October 15, 2006 from http://www.chicagotribune.com

Chang, J. (April 2, 2007a). Environmental friends: Eleven fabrics at the forefront of the eco-revolution. *Daily News Record*, pp. 26–28.

Chang, J. (April 2, 2007b). The glossary of 'green.' *Daily News Record*, p. 14.

Clark, E. and Tucker, R. (March 14, 2006). *Women's Wear Daily*, pp. 8–11.

Commoner, B. (1971). *The closing circle: Nature, man, and technology*. New York: Alfred A. Knopf.

Congress directs CPSC to review standard for children's sleepwear. (December 1998). *Fire Engineering*, 151(12), 1–3.

Corcoran, C. T. (September 1, 2006). Nau sets ecologically correct growth plan. *Women's Wear Daily*, p. 12.

Costello, B. (July 6, 2007). Beauty's business of going green. *Women's Wear Daily*, p. 10.

de Pelsmacker, P., Driesen, L., and Rayp, G. (2005). Do consumers care about ethics? Willingness to pay for fair-trade coffee. *The Journal of Consumer Affairs*, 39(2), 363–385.

Dickson, M. A. (2001). Utility of No Sweat labels for apparel consumers: Profiling label users and predicting their purchases. *Journal of Consumer Affairs*, 35(1), 96–119.

Domina, T. and Koch, K. (1997). The textile waste lifecycle. *Clothing and Textiles Research Journal*, 15(2), 96–102.

Ellis, K. (March 23, 2006). Customs seizes Chinese goods. *Women's Wear Daily*, p. 5.

Fighting workplace cancer. (March 28, 2007). *Women's Wear Daily*, p. 2.

Foreman, K. (August 9, 2006). Bamboo you. *Women's Wear Daily*, pp. 4–5.

Francis, S., Butler, S., McDonald, T., and Turnbow, H. R. (1991). Disposal of used clothing through charitable organizations. *Proceedings of the International Textiles and Apparel Association*, 58.

Freydkin, D. (June 27, 2006). Celebs share the 'LOVE' and proceeds. *USA Today*, p. 2D.

"Fur demand sends more Ohio trappers into woods." (February 25, 2007). *The Athens [Ohio] Messenger*, p. A6 [Associated Press: Berlin Center, OH].

Going green: Wal-Mart's move to organics could shake up retail world. [AP] *The Athens [Ohio] Messenger*, p. A7.

Groves, E. (August 9, 2006a). Green with beauty. *Women's Wear Daily*, p. 5.

Groves, E. (October 31, 2006b). Ethical fashion goes mainstream. *Women's Wear Daily*, p. 12.

Haggblade, S. (1990). The flip side of fashion: Used clothing exports to the Third World. *The Journal of Development Studies*, 26(3), 505–521.

Hirshlag, J. (May 23, 2006). Diamond politics usher in new era. *Women's Wear Daily*, p. 11.

Iredale, J. (July 19, 2007). Good things come to some who wait. *Women's Wear Daily*, p. 3.

Is your fur fake or is it Fido? (February 25, 2007). *The Athens [Ohio] Messenger*, p. A6 [Associated Press: Washington, DC].

Iwanow, H., McEachern, M. G., and Jeffrey, A. (2005). The influence of ethical trading policies on consumer apparel purchase decisions: A focus on The Gap, Inc. *International Journal of Retail and Distribution Management*, 33(5), 371–387.

Juicy recall. (May 16, 2006). *Women's Wear Daily*, p. 2.

Kalogeridis, C. (December 1990). Don't waste your waste: It's like burning dollars. *Textile World*, 140(12), 68–69.

Kalogeridis, C. (June 1992). Recycling should be your last resort, says EPA. *Textile World*, 142(6), 73–74.

Kron, P. (September 1992). Recycle—if you can! *Apparel Industry Magazine*, 53(9), 74–82.

Levi Strauss & Co. turns scrap denim into paper. (March 1994). *Apparel Industry Magazine*, 55(3), 13.

Lipke, D. (April 2, 2007). The greening of men's wear. *Daily News Record*, pp. 13–18.

Littrell, M. A., Ma, Y. J., and Halepete, J. (2005). Generation X, baby boomers, and swing: Marketing fair trade apparel. *Journal of Fashion Marketing and Management*, 9(4), 407–419.

Loureiro, M. L., McCluskey, J. J., and Mittelhammer, R. C. (2002). Will consumers pay a premium for eco-labeled apples? *The Journal of Consumer Affairs, 36*(2), 203–219.

Massachusetts town shudders after study details cancer risk. (May 12, 2006). *The Athens [Ohio] Messenger,* p. 2 [Associated Press: Ashland, Massachusetts].

McDonald's trims supersized portions. (April 2004). *Magazine of Physical Therapy, 12*(4), 11.

McDonough, W. and Braungart, M. (October 1998). The next industrial revolution. *The Atlantic Monthly, 202*(4), 82–91.

Mohr, L. A. and Webb, D. J. (2005). The effects of corporate social responsibility and price on consumer responses. *Journal of Consumer Affairs, 39*(1), 121–147.

Moin, D. (August 11, 2006). Nordstrom to sell ONE t-shirts. *Women's Wear Daily,* p. 12.

Monget, K. (May 8, 2006). Serving the needs of the well-endowed. *Women's Wear Daily,* p. 14.

Mognet, K. (July 2007). It's not easy going green: Intimate apparel manufacturers are discovering what it means to be eco-friendly. *Women's Wear Daily Intimates,* pp. 50–52.

Murray, A. (June 7, 2006). Frustrated 'greens' turn to boardrooms. *Wall Street Journal,* p. A2.

Nagel, A. (July 6, 2007). Naturals to see growth in 2008 with USDA seals. *Women's Wear Daily,* p. 10.

Newenhouse, S. (June 2000). Catalog company tackles textile recycling. *BioCycle, 41*(6), 50–51.

Page, G. and Fearn, H. (2005). Corporate reputation: What do consumers really care about? *Journal of Advertising Research, 45*(3), 305–313.

Parents, toy companies concerned about recall. (August 5, 2007). *The Athens [Ohio] Messenger,* p. D12 [Associated Press: New York].

Polo Ralph Lauren to stop using fur. (June 13, 2006). *The Columbus [Ohio] Dispatch,* p. E1.

Ramey, J. Child Cares (February 21, 2006). *Women's Wear Daily,* p. 42.

Ramey, J. (July 23, 2007). Levi's files suit against Polo. *Women's Wear Daily,* p. 2.

Ramey, J. (July 26, 2007). Levi's sues A&F over trademark. *Women's Wear Daily,* p. 10.

Rudie, R. (February 1994). How green is the future? *Bobbin, 35*(6), 16–20.

Scelfo, J. (October 11, 2004). Real fur is fun again. *Newsweek, 144*(15), 48.

Seckler, V. (July 12, 2006). A fashionable stamp of social consciousness. *Women's Wear Daily,* p. 12.

Swinker, M. E. and Hines, J. D. (1997). Consumers' selection of textile products made from recycled fibres. *Journal of Consumer Studies and Home Economics, 21,* 307–313.

Tell, C. (July 16, 2007). Exotics: Limited supplies get under designers' skin. *Women's Wear Daily*, p. 9.

Term Limits: Green is Apparel's Gray Area. (April 2, 2007). Cotton Incorporated's Lifestyle Monitor™ report in *Daily News Record*, p. 5.

Tesoriero, H. W. (April 22, 2006). Merck is handed another loss over Vioxx. *Wall Street Journal*, p. A3.

Toxic apparel discovered at retailers. (November 16, 2006). *China Daily*. Retrieved on August 9, 2007 from http://www.chinadaily.com

Toy safety warnings issued. (November 24, 2005). *The Athens [Ohio] Messenger*, p. 2 [Associated Press].

Webber, F. (1995). A watershed year in regulatory reform. *American Textile International*, 24(3), 56–61.

Weil, J. (October 6, 2006). Groupe Clarins, Kibio to do organic line. *Women's Wear Daily*, p. 13.

Young, C., Jirousek, C., and Ashdown, S. (2004). Undesigned: A study in sustainable design of apparel using post-consumer recycled clothing. *Clothing and Textiles Research Journal*, 22(1/2), 61–68.

Zimmerman, A. (December 20, 2005). Diamond industry rocked by allegations of bribery. *Wall Street Journal*, p. A1.

Zimmerman, A. (August 21, 2006). Wal-Mart sees profit in green. *Wall Street Journal*, p. B3.

Chapter 6

Responsibilities and Liabilities in a Complex Industry

THE OBJECTIVES OF THIS CHAPTER ARE TO:

- Understand the role of human labor and human capital in the production of apparel, textile, and other consumer products

- Define "sweatshop" and explore the concept of fair labor

- Identify government and non-government (NGO) regulation guidelines, offices, and organizations that pertain to apparel manufacturing

- Gain an awareness of cultural influences on labor practices and standards

- Explore the decision-making process as it relates to labor components and costing out of apparel products

After the decision to manufacture a product has been made, the process of manufacturing must be addressed. Product development includes design, sourcing of fabrics and other materials, and garment assembly. The process of distributing the merchandise to consumer outlets is something product developers must also consider. Obviously, nothing can be produced without the contributions of people. The people involved in manufacturing include creative and technical designers, sourcing specialists, plant managers, laborers in textile production, garment assembly, and packaging processes, and those who transport the merchandise to its destination.

In the 1960s about 6 percent of the textile industry was automated, compared to 40 percent by the 1980s (Pugatch, 1998). Although technology has automated many manufacturing procedures in the textile and apparel industry, displacing

FIGURE 6.1   Factory workers should be treated fairly and make appropriate wages.

workers in production areas such as weaving, knitting, cutting, and straight seam sewing, the human labor element of garment assembly continues to be among the most significant contributing cost of production for apparel products—or a significant area where production costs can be reduced, depending on the wage rate. In the book *A Stitch in Time*, Frederick Abernathy et al. (1999) describes the phenomena of lean retailing: the practice of continually evaluating and changing apparel forecasting, production, and distribution with the result being increasingly reduced costs. They note that the aspect of production in which apparel manufacturers have the greatest control is the employees and their labor wages contributing to garment costs.

The majority of apparel production cost is attributed to materials and labor. In 1995, it was estimated that, for men's shirts produced in the United States, the percent of cost attributed to labor was 25 percent (Abernathy et al., 1999). Even though apparel production is very labor-intensive, around the world the actual cost of labor to sew garments, relative to the final retail price, is often as low as only 1 percent (Adams, 2002; Hajewski, 2000; Robins and Humphrey, 2000). This is directly related to the wage paid to the people who sew and otherwise assemble the garments.

Retailers are often at odds with manufacturers. This situation is due to retailers' desire to appease their customers by selling merchandise at the lowest possible price (while still reaping a profit) and manufacturers' wish to be paid as much as possible for the merchandise they produce. Manufacturing companies, therefore, comply with retailers' needs for low wholesale prices by hiring a cheap labor force. Many complex ethical dilemmas result from this tenuous relationship.

The marketplace factors that are driving the need to reduce labor costs include the concentration of retailers and growing global competitiveness. Retailer mergers and acquisitions result in larger retail companies whose market power allows them to pressure manufacturing companies to contain production costs. Rather than the historical practice of manufacturers quoting their costs, retailers now demand that manufacturers meet their often-decreasing cost limits. When factories cannot comply with retailer demand, they are passed over as retailers find manufacturers willing to accept their orders. Increasing global competitiveness in retailing, which presents expanded consumer markets and labor pools, feeds initiatives to reduce product costs to improve margins (Barrett, 2007). Retailers and brand manufacturers have increasingly more options when seeking the least expensive labor cost possible. The growing global market for laborers further intensifies the competition for low wage rates. These situations present opportunities for ethical dilemmas because working conditions and employee compensation are directly related to the costs of apparel products. With relatively low labor costs in newly developing countries (see Table 6.1), the cost of labor is actually decreasing as a percentage of a garment's total cost. As apparel manufacturing has moved to predominately less developed countries, the price of apparel products has fallen and the products themselves have become more available to members of growing affluent and middle-class markets.

Consumers have high expectations for fashions to change; they also expect that desirable and affordable items will be available. This demand supports the continued exploitation of cheap laborers. Even in 1933, then U.S. Secretary of Labor Frances Perkins realized this relationship when she said, "The red silk bargain dress in the shop window is a danger signal. It is a warning of the return of the sweatshop, a challenge to us all to reinforce the gains we have made in our long and difficult progress toward a civilized industrial order" (Pugatch, 1998). Seventy-five years later, consumers' seemingly insatiable desire for fast fashion continues to fuel the practice of lowering garment costs. In fact, the fast fashion trend directly contributes to worker exploitation as factories are bound to meet retailers' shipment timelines, forcing their employees to work overtime that is often not adequately compensated.

TABLE 6.1

APPAREL MANUFACTURING LABOR COSTS IN U.S. DOLLARS IN 1998 OF THE WORLD'S 25 LEADING APPAREL EXPORTERS

COUNTRY	WAGE RATE
Indonesia	$0.16
Vietnam	$0.22
Pakistan	$0.24
Bangladesh	$0.30
India	$0.39
China	$0.43
Sri Lanka	$0.44
Philippines	$0.76
Thailand	$0.78
Tunisia	$0.98
Mauritius	$1.03
Romania	$1.04
Malaysia	$1.30
Morocco	$1.36
Dominican Republic	$1.48
Mexico	$1.51
Turkey	$1.84
Czech Republic	$1.85
Hungary	$2.12
Costa Rica	$2.52
Republic of Korea	$2.69
Poland	$2.77
Taiwan	$4.68
Hong Kong	$5.20
United States	$10.12

SOURCE: Gereffi, G., Memedovic, O. (2003). The global apparel value chain: What prospects for upgrading by developing countries? Vienna, Austria: United Nations Industrial Development Organization.

HISTORY OF FACTORIES AND INDUSTRIALIZATION

Industrialization occurs when historically agricultural communities move away from farming and seek employment in manufacturing, coupled with advances in technology that enable mechanized mass production. As economies shift away from agricultural foundations, consumer markets develop where demand for manufactured goods emerge. These goods are seen as affordable by consumers with incomes resulting from employment. In a domino-like manner, previously industrialized communities look to their less developed counterparts to provide labor and to manufacture goods in the lowest paying and least desirable employment sectors as employment options and market skills become increasingly sophisticated through industrialization.

Labor-intense manufacturing, such as apparel production, is traditionally an entry point into industrialized economic growth. Developing countries typically offer unskilled and low-wage labor forces who are eager to improve their economic situations. The relatively low-cost investment in sewing machines and the availability of low-wage workers allows easy entry into the garment assembly business. The easiest point of entry involves homework—with laborers sewing, knitting, embroidering, or doing other piecework in their own homes. Garment factories, often with poor working conditions that offer little attention to safety considerations or employee comfort, tend to proliferate as a much-needed source of income for impoverished communities. Among the people involved in various aspects of the apparel production process it is the laborers, who assemble garments either in factories or at home, who face the greatest challenge in regard to working conditions and fair wages. Although factory jobs are not desirable among the more affluent people of the world, those jobs do pave the way for individuals and communities to become more economically stable. In particular, women's labor roles have enabled them to seek better lives for themselves and their families. According to Karan Swaner of the Asia Foundation (Stier, 2001), "The [garment] industry has probably done more for Bangladeshi women in the last decade than all the [aid agencies] put together. First, it gets them out of the house, and then they come back with a paycheck. It gives them more power in families." These words offer a typical profile of the laborers who produce the bulk of the world's low to moderately priced fast fashion.

Sweatshops

Employees who earn the least in the world market are those people who are unskilled, uneducated, unorganized (in terms of labor and advocacy groups), and are the most easily exploited. Because apparel production is highly repetitive and does not require skilled labor, this industry employs among the world's least educated and skilled, and most unprotected people, who are primarily young and female. Garment assembly work is easily subcontracted for laborers to finish at home. Homework (also known as "outwork") is difficult to monitor, frequently involves child labor, and workers are frequently paid by the piece rather than paid an hourly wage. It is common for employees to be charged for the use of tools they need to do the work. Factories, where workers are employed together to engage in similar tasks, often offer deplorable work environments and frequently operate as sweatshops.

The term "sweatshop" originated in the late nineteenth century to describe a manufacturing facility where low-skilled workers performed piecework often under unacceptable conditions. Generally the laborers (often women) toiled in filthy conditions and for long (17 or more hours) workdays at pay rates less than a living wage, or "starvation wages," as they were called. These laborers were "sweated" by their employers, referred to as "sweaters," the middlemen between the workers and the manufacturers to whom work was subcontracted. Criticism of sweatshops, which reached a peak after the Triangle Shirtwaist Factory fire in New York City in 1911, helped spur passage of labor laws and workplace safety regulations.

In 1994, the U.S. Government Accountability Office (GAO) defined a sweatshop as "an employer that violates more than one federal or state labor law governing minimum wage and overtime, child labor, industrial homework, occupational safety and health, workers' compensation, or industry registration" (http://www. gao.gov). Two sources of recognized standards that are referenced widely as factory conditions are monitored are the U.S. Department of Labor's Fair Labor Standards Act (see Box 6.1) and The Apparel Industry Partnership's Workplace Code of Conduct (see Box 6.2). These standards address minimum wage, overtime, employee benefits, child labor, health and safety standards, and general work conditions. Box 6.3 presents a list of commonly observed violations that occur in sweatshops. In addition to the poor physical conditions that sweatshops provide their employees, those factories are also psychologically detrimental. In his book *Out of the Sweatshop* (1977), Leon Stein wrote,

> The sweatshop is a state of mind as well as a physical fact. Its work day is of no fixed length; it links pace of work to endurance. It demeans the spirit by denying workers any part in determining the conditions of the pay for their work. In the sweatshop, employers may discharge at will workers who protest against conditions or pay. The sweatshop, whether in a modern factory building or a dark slum cellar, exists where the employer controls the working conditions and the worker cannot protest. (p. xv)

Box 6.1

KEY ELEMENTS OF THE U.S. DEPARTMENT OF LABOR FAIR LABOR STANDARDS ACT

The Fair Labor Standards Act (FLSA) of 1938, as amended, is published in law in Sections 201–219 of Title 29, United States Code. The FLSA Act establishes standards for full-time and part-time workers in the areas of

- Minimum Wage
- Overtime
- Recordkeeping
- Youth Employment

The FLSA is enforced by the U.S. Office of Personnel Management.

SOURCE: http://www.opm.gov/flsa/overview.asp and http://www.dol.gov/esa/regs/compliance/whd/hrg.htm

Although much attention is given to factory conditions in developing nations, it is important to realize that poor conditions for textile and apparel workers are not limited to these countries. In 1996, the U.S. Department of Labor estimated that about 13,000 sweatshops employing approximately 300,000 people were operating in the United States. In fact, the agency estimates that half of the apparel factories in the United States are sweatshops. According to the labor union UNITE HERE's Web site (http://www.unitehere.org), 67 percent of the garment factories in Los Angeles and 63 percent of the garment factories in New York city operate with sweatshop conditions, specifically violating minimum wage, overtime, and Occupational Safety and Health Administration (OSHA) laws.

In the United States, illegal immigrants are easily exploited in sweatshop factories. Because they cannot legally seek protection under the Fair Labor Standards Act (FLSA) and fear being discovered and possibly deported, human rights violations against these workers go largely unreported. Furthermore, immigrants—particularly those entering the country illegally—are drawn to unskilled labor jobs in apparel factories or to piecework jobs done at home. The employees are paid cash "off the books," making records of their substandard pay difficult to produce. The Immigration Reform and Control Act of 1986 introduced employer sanctions that penalize companies hiring illegal immigrants, but strong demand for their

Box 6.2

FAIR LABOR ASSOCIATION (FLA) WORKPLACE CODE OF CONDUCT

The Fair Labor Association (FLA), which originated from the Apparel Industry Partnership (AIP), is a non-profit organization that combines the efforts of industry, civil society organizations, and colleges and universities to protect workers' rights and improve working conditions worldwide by promoting adherence to international labor standards. The FLA believes that consumers can have confidence that products that are manufactured in compliance with the standards embodied in the Workplace Code of Conduct are not produced under exploitative or inhumane conditions.

Forced Labor. There shall not be any use of forced labor, whether in the form of prison labor, indentured labor, bonded labor or otherwise.

Child Labor. No person shall be employed at an age younger than 15 (or 14 where the law of the country of manufacture[1] allows) or younger than the age for completing compulsory education in the country of manufacture where such age is higher than 15.

Harassment or Abuse. Every employee shall be treated with respect and dignity. No employee shall be subject to any physical, sexual, psychological or verbal harassment or abuse.

Nondiscrimination. No person shall be subject to any discrimination in employment, including hiring, salary, benefits, advancement, discipline, termination or retirement, on the basis of gender, race, religion, age, disability, sexual orientation, nationality, political opinion, social or ethnic origin.

Health and Safety. Employers shall provide a safe and healthy working environment to prevent accidents and injury to health arising out of, linked with, or occurring in the course of work or as a result of the operation of employer facilities.

Freedom of Association and Collective Bargaining. Employers shall recognize and respect the right of employees to freedom of association and collective bargaining.

Wages and Benefits. Employers recognize that wages are essential to meeting employees' basic needs. Employers shall pay employees, as a floor, at least the minimum wage required by local law or the prevailing industry wage, whichever is higher, and shall provide legally mandated benefits.

Box 6.2 continued from page 142
FAIR LABOR ASSOCIATION (FLA) WORKPLACE CODE OF CONDUCT

Hours of Work. Except in extraordinary business circumstances, employees shall (i) not be required to work more than the lesser of (a) 48 hours per week and 12 hours overtime or (b) the limits on regular and overtime hours allowed by the law of the country of manufacture or, where the laws of such country do not limit the hours of work, the regular work week in such country plus 12 hours overtime and (ii) be entitled to at least one day off in every seven day period.

Overtime Compensation. In addition to their compensation for regular hours of work, employees shall be compensated for overtime hours at such premium rate as is legally required in the country of manufacture or, in those countries where such laws do not exist, at a rate at least equal to their regular hourly compensation rate.

Any company that determines to adopt the Workplace Code of Conduct shall, in addition to complying with all applicable laws of the country of manufacture, comply with and support the Workplace Code of Conduct in accordance with the FLA's Principles of Monitoring and shall apply the higher standard in cases of differences or conflicts. Any company that determines to adopt the Workplace Code of Conduct also shall require its contractors and, in the case of a retailer, its suppliers to comply with applicable local laws and with this Code in accordance with the Principles of Monitoring and to apply the higher standard in cases of differences or conflicts.

SOURCE: http://www.fairlabor.org/conduct. Reprinted with permission of the Fair Labor Association.

labor continues. According to Alan Howard (1997), the legislation "actually makes it harder to enforce labor laws since employers have learned to use it as a threat against workers who dare to assert their rights" (p. 163). Workers in the United States who speak little or no English have difficulty navigating the bureaucratic system, and when they do file and persist with lawsuits, they find that the courts are often backlogged. Additionally, the small number of labor inspectors—just over 2,000 inspectors for over 130 million employees—reduces the likelihood that any given factory, particularly in New York and California, will be inspected.

BOX 6.3
COMMON FACTORY WORKPLACE VIOLATIONS

- Failure to pay overtime
- Coaching workers in anticipating of compliance audits
- Fraudulent wage and hour records
- Improperly positioned fire extinguishers
- Employing underage workers and child labor law violations
- Involuntary servitude (slavery)
- Confiscation of employee passports
- Overly long work shifts (as many as 20 hours)
- Corporal punishment, such as worker beatings
- Excessively low wages (as low as 65 cents per hour)
- No gloves and masks provided to workers (safety violation)
- No talking allowed in the workplace
- Firing pregnant women or requiring women to take birth control pills or undergo abortions
- Sexual harassment
- Termination for involvement in union activities
- No employee benefits
- Forced overtime
- Locked exit doors
- Poor ventilation, often accompanied by dangerous chemicals such as glue fumes

Kate Pagliaro, in her essay "Slavery and Sweatshops," revealed the 2004 personal account with sweatshops experienced by her mother, a former women's sportswear buyer, which summarizes the surprising existence of sweatshops in our midst:

During my many years as a buyer, I unfortunately came across some disturbing manufacturing practices in New York City that I never would believe still existed, had I not seen it with my own eyes. Some of the smaller sportswear firms had deplorable working conditions in their back rooms with illegal immigrants working the sewing machines. This all took place behind the façade of a beautiful showroom where buyers came to see the seasonal sportswear lines. I felt sorry for these young girls and they would never look up at anyone while they were working—I guess out of fear. (no page)

Although most consumers do not want to think that what they wear is made by children or mistreated employees who do not even earn a living wage, the fact is that this occurs regularly throughout the world (including the United States). Is it ethical to buy goods produced in a sweatshop? Does it make a difference if we know the origin of our purchases? Are sweatshop laborers better off working at the status quo than returning to their preemployment situations? Are retailers exploiting sweatshop employees or are they contributing to their improved futures? Does the existence of sweatshops undermine the efforts of companies whose factories provide good working conditions at fair wages? Should sweatshops be eliminated? If so, who should be responsible for doing this? You are encouraged to consider these ethically rooted questions and familiarize yourself with the issues so that you can make informed and ethical choices as both consumers and as representatives of apparel manufacturing and retailing companies.

The Role of Unions in the Textile and Apparel Industry

Exploitation of laborers is common when employees have little negotiating power in the employer–employee relationship. Unbearable sweatshop conditions inevitably lead to unrest among laborers and desperate measures to bring about change. Unions have emerged from the efforts of laborers to collectively demand improvements in their working conditions. Unions seek to establish conditions of fair labor; that is to say that laborers should be fairly and legally compensated for the work they do and they should be provided clean and safe environments in which to work.

Historically, women have been the largest labor force in the apparel manufacturing industry, and have faced more abusive work environments and situations than their male counterparts. Women, as a group, have been viewed as temporary laborers until marriage takes them out of the workforce, whereas men have been viewed as breadwinners who need a good salary to support their families. These conflicting perspectives have resulted in wage disparities between female and male employees. Women have also historically faced workplace harassment, sexual and otherwise, to a greater extent than men. To provide support and representation to women in response to their marginalized position, the Women's Trade Union League (WTUL) was founded in Great Britain in 1873 by Emma Ann Patterson, a suffragette who was also concerned with labor issues. William English Walling introduced the concept of the WTUL to Mary Kenney O'Sullivan, who in 1903 established the Women's National Trade Union League in the United States during the American Federation of Labor (AFL) annual convention.

But the most widely recognized early union to represent American apparel laborers was the International Ladies' Garment Workers Union (ILGWU), established in 1900 and originally representing about 2,000 workers, mostly Jewish and Italian immigrants who produced women's clothing. Two early strikes organized by the ILGWU established the union as a major force in the apparel industry and contributed to its membership. "The Uprising" was a strike in 1909 of 20,000 New York shirtwaist makers that lasted 14 weeks. Shortly after that strike, 60,000 cloak-makers went on strike in 1910. The strikes established unions as a powerful force in labor relations and negotiations within the garment industry. The "Protocol of Peace" that resulted after the cloakmakers' strike is considered a turning point in the evolution of American industrial labor relations, associated with introducing the concept of democracy into the workplace (Greenwald, 1998). The Protocol became a model of modern union negotiations for all industries; laborers received increased wages and new benefits, including health exams.

The power of textile and apparel unions was solidified in the United States after the infamous Triangle Shirtwaist Factory fire of 1911. As a result of this inferno, 146 workers, primarily young women, died. Most of the deaths occurred because the employees, working on the eighth, ninth, and tenth floors of the factory building, could not escape the flames, which were fueled by scraps of fabric and paper patterns strewn throughout the factory. Many employees jumped to their deaths; others died of smoke inhalation and burns. The public outrage that emerged after the news of the fire spread (many New Yorkers observed the horror firsthand) lent support to the garment workers' efforts to unionize. In addition to the continued presence of the ILGWU, the Amalgamated Clothing Workers of America (ACWA) formed in 1914, representing workers in the men's clothing industry. And in 1939, the Textile Workers Union of America (TWUA) was founded to represent laborers in that industry. The various unions were strong and their oversight of labor conditions throughout most U.S. factories was effective until the late 1960s.

Union memberships dwindled when imports began to play a significant role in American consumption, labor laws advocated by unions grew increasingly restrictive, and American manufacturing jobs were displaced by foreign manufacture. In 1976, the ACWA and the TWUA merged to form the Amalgamated Clothing and Textile Workers Union (ACTWU). Similarly, the Union of Needletrades, Industrial and Textile Employees (UNITE) was formed in 1995 when the ILGWU and

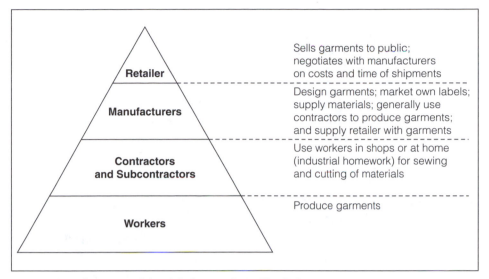

FIGURE 6.2   Structure of the global apparel retailing industry

the ACTWU merged. And the Hotel Employees and Restaurant Employees (HERE) merged with UNITE in 2004, forming the UNITE HERE union. UNITE HERE currently represents almost half a million employees in the apparel, hotel, and restaurant industries. About one-quarter of the textile and apparel workers in the United States are currently represented by a union.

The Shift of Labor to Low-Wage Manufacturing Venues

Until fairly recently, almost all apparel products sold in the United States were manufactured domestically. Manufacturing, including apparel and textile products, was a key industry in this country during most of the twentieth century, and garment factory employees, although relatively low paid, were mostly earning legal wages and working in factories where health, safety, and work standards were enforced.

Apparel and fashion retailing exceeds $200 billion annually in sales as an industry in the United States. Imported merchandise, with its low product cost as a result of decreased cost of labor, has introduced and increased competition with higher priced, domestically produced apparel, footwear, and accessories. According to the U.S. Bureau of Economic Analysis, in 2006, the United States imported almost $90 billion of apparel, footwear, and household textile goods, accounting for about half of the total consumption of these products. Meanwhile,

Box 6.4

UNITE HERE HISTORICAL TIMELINE

1891   Hotel Employees & Restaurant Employees International Union forms.

1900   Workers making women's clothes form the International Ladies' Garment Workers' Union (ILGWU).

1906   The San Francisco earthquake nearly wipes out the hospitality industry for months.

1909   A winning strike of 20,000 garment workers, mostly teenage girls, in New York City truly launches the ILGWU.

1911   A fire at the Triangle Shirtwaist Factory in New York City kills 146 workers, leading to the first workplace health and safety laws.

1914   Men's clothing workers form the Amalgamated Clothing Workers of America (ACWA).

1923   The ACWA opens the Amalgamated Bank for workers and unions.

1939   New York City Hotel Trades Council forms and signs first contract with the Hotel Association.

1939   Southern textile workers found the Textile Workers Union of America (TWUA).

1941   ACWA begins employer-paid health and life insurance.

1947   Strike at the Brass Rail ends victoriously after six years.

1958   100,000 striking ILGWU members in eight states win the required use of the union label.

1963   The TWUA begins organizing at textile giant JP Stevens.

1960s New York's HERE locals march to support the lunch counter sit-ins to end segregation in the South.

the level of apparel and accessories exported was only $7 billion. Clearly, the American consumer market for imported apparel and footwear continues to be strong.

Though controversial, the ability to manufacture apparel in the United States at low wage rates continues to make domestic apparel and accessories viable at moderate-priced retail outlets. As marginalized workers, such as illegal immigrants or immigrants with limited literacy skills, are increasingly seeking employment, there is strong motivation to operate factories that offer highly competitive products sought by price-conscious retailers. However, retailers or brand manufacturers operating in this manner run the risk of being publicly associated with illegal and unethical labor practices—which would be detrimental to the company's image.

Box 6.4 continued from page 148
UNITE HERE HISTORICAL TIMELINE

1976   ACWA and TWUA merge and create the Amalgamated Clothing & Textile Workers Union (ACTWU).

1980   After 17 years, 4,000 workers at JP Stevens win a contract.

1984   HERE organizes Yale University's support staff.

1995   UNITE is formed out of the ILGWU and ACTWU.

1998   Strikers at the Las Vegas Frontier Hotel & Casino win after nearly 7 years. UNITE begins major organizing campaigns in laundries, coming to represent 40,000 within 5 years.

1999   5,000 workers at Fieldcrest Cannon textile mills join UNITE after 25-year struggle.

2001   The attack on the World Trade Center kills 43 HERE members; the resulting economic downturn costs thousands of HERE and UNITE members their jobs.

2002   Workers at the Marriott Hotel in San Francisco negotiate first contract after a 22-year fight.
       UNITE forms partnerships with the NAACP and the Sierra Club to further civil and workers' rights and bring the environmental and labor movements together.

2003   HERE & UNITE work together on the Immigrant Workers Freedom Ride, the Yale strike, and H&M organizing campaign.

SOURCE: http://www.unitehere.org/about/history.php. Reprinted with permission of UNITE HERE.

When the California Labor Commission (CLC) discovered illegal labor conditions of workers manufacturing Guess apparel in El Monte, California, in 1996, the company faced the expensive tasks of complying with labor laws as well as damage control and restoration of its image with the public. In 1997, Guess moved its manufacturing to Mexico, citing new North American Free Trade Agreement (NAFTA) regulations that enabled the company to take advantage of free trade, thus cutting costs. The move enabled compliance with labor laws while maintaining a low cost of production, but effectively eliminated jobs for the California workers the business had previously employed. Similar competitive issues have faced European manufacturers and markets. Companies with vertical operations have shifted away

TABLE 6.2

VALUE OF U.S. APPAREL IMPORTS OVER TIME

1970	1980	1990	1998	2006
$1.05 billion[1]	$5.7 billion[a]	$24.7 billion[2]	$50.4 billion[b]	$71.2 billion[3]

1. Ghadar, F., Davidson, W. H., and Feigenoff, C. S. (1987). *U.S. Industrial Competitiveness: The Case of the Textile and Apparel Industries.* Lexington, MA: D. C. Heath and Company.

2. Gereffi, G. (2001). Global Sourcing in the U.S. Apparel Industry. *Journal of Textile and Apparel Technology and Management, 2*(1), 1–5.

3. "U.S. Apparel Imports Increase" (February 2007). *Apparel Magazine, 48*(6).

from company-owned factories in favor of subcontracting, or outsourcing, the work to factories located in less developed countries where labor costs are exponentially lower. Carrefour Group, the European-based giant retailer with over 12,000 stores and operations in 29 countries, subcontracts its manufacturing throughout the world. The tradeoffs that accompany decisions about factory location and labor pool are fraught with ethical implications.

The additional incentive for retailers and manufacturers to reduce lead times in production—the time it takes for a design concept to reach the consumer—influences the location of factories because the cost of transportation is also considered in the manufacturing and distribution process. In the fashion industry, the concept of product lifecycle management is important when making decisions about production processes and locations. Managing the amount of time it takes to roll out new products to replace previous styles, determining the length of production time for merchandise, and adopting efficient time-to-market strategies are important factors for economic reasons and for presence in the marketplace. Both retailers and manufacturers want a short time to market, and the location of the labor force plays a role in the transportation and logistic issues related to moving merchandise and influences the labor rate. Companies must therefore consider a manufacturer's ability to produce goods quickly, cheaply, and to transport them to the retail marketplace. The U.S. retail market obviously has significant power, prompting factories to be built in places where trade barriers and travel time have historically been low such as the Caribbean basin and Mexico. This has, in turn, created a demand for domestic sweatshop labor in those regions.

With the 2005 expiration of the Multifiber Arrangement (MFA), which had placed quotas on certain garments and were particularly restrictive for Taiwan, Hong Kong, South Korea, and China, trade barriers have been eliminated with these countries, some of whom offer among the lowest wage rates and therefore garment costs. Ironically, lifting quotas from low-wage countries with huge labor pools, notably China, has threatened the existence of garment factories in other countries such as Honduras, Guatemala, Bangladesh, and Nicaragua.

Furthermore, retailers are price driven, with leading companies such as Wal-Mart seeking to decrease product costs each year—which they strive to pass on to the consumer. Sharon Edelson (2007) quoted Bill Simon, Wal-Mart's executive vice president and chief operating officer, discussing the company's back-to-school pricing strategy: "Americans are looking to us to provide the best value, and we will. Let there be no doubt [that] we mean business when it comes to price leadership." Virtually the only way retailers can reduce the costs of the products they sell in today's competitive market is to subcontract with manufacturers offering the lowest wholesale costs. Manufacturers obtain those wholesale cost reductions by reducing the contribution of the labor cost. Consumers eagerly respond to low retail prices, therefore rewarding retailers that can source the lowest cost goods. The current barrier-free trade conditions that pit impoverished countries against each other to win bids for garment factories has been coined as a global "race to the bottom"—where ethical practice is not encouraged as a business strategy. Because of the never-ending cycle of underbidding, this situation ultimately produces a world economy that cannot sustain itself.

In January 2007, the Decent Working Conditions (DWC) and Fair Competition Act (FCA) was introduced in the U.S. Senate. This act, a form of protectionist legislation targeted at imported merchandise, proposed prohibiting sweatshop-produced goods from entering the United States. Interestingly, although the act was designed to protect the jobs of American laborers, garments made in U.S. sweatshops would not face the same scrutiny entering the U.S. consumer market as their imported counterparts. Introduced in the California Senate in 2007, the Worker Assistance Bill proposed an amendment to the Trade Adjustment Assistance Program (TAAP) to provide automatic eligibility for textile and apparel workers who lose their jobs when companies close because of foreign trade. Again, this measure reflects Americans' concern about the influx of imports that threaten U.S. jobs, but is unlikely to become law because of its economic implications to American consumers and the elusive burden of proof that specific jobs would be lost primarily because of foreign trade.

BENEFITS OF SOCIALLY CONSCIOUS MANUFACTURING

Social consciousness is not only an ethical response to business practices, it is also good for business. In today's world of instant news and public awareness, a company's ability to conform to the public's expectations of appropriate behavior is directly related to its image, which can be translated into fiscal performance. Apparel producers and retailers seeking to be socially conscious have an advantage in the court of public opinion. It is worth noting that companies that have been early adopters of ethical sourcing and labor guidelines have typically done so in response to controversial and inappropriate practices in which they had participated. Often watchdog groups or government regulation organizations impose remedial steps for companies that ultimately improve their images and position them as industry leaders in the area of corporate social responsibility.

In 1991, Levi Strauss & Co. established its Global Sourcing and Operating Guidelines, which describe the company's ethical standards. According to the U.S. Department of Labor, the guidelines state,

> Levi Strauss & Co. is committed to continuous improvement in the implementation of its Global Sourcing & Operating Guidelines. As we apply these standards throughout the world, we will acquire greater experience, As has always been our practice, we will continue to take into consideration all pertinent information that helps us better address issues of concern, meet new challenges and update our guidelines.
>
> Business partners are contractors and subcontractors who manufacture or finish our products and suppliers who provide raw materials used in the production of our products. We have begun applying the Terms of Engagement to business partners involved in manufacturing and finishing and plan to extend their application to suppliers.

For many years Levi's operated U.S.–based factories even though many U.S. apparel manufacturers had already relocated overseas. The company has historically been viewed as iconic of American culture and has been regarded with respect in terms of its employment and operation practices. In 2004, Levi's closed the last of its U.S. factories, moving to production facilities located abroad, where labor costs were lower. Despite the negative result of lost jobs, the company has continued to promote its image as a U.S. brand, which remains an American icon.

Box 6.5

C&A STATEMENT ON ETHICAL RESPONSIBILITY

In today's world there is more requested from a company than just doing daily business. Although successful financial performance is essential, not only to sustain the future of the business, but also to contribute to the prosperity of society as a whole, companies are expected to do more.

This is particularly the case for a company that is present in European retail markets—and world-wide supply markets—and where expectations are different from area to area.

As a company we want to be a good corporate citizen.

The philosophy that underpins our approach to our social responsibilities can best be described as follows:

Our strategy is to earn and retain the trust of our stakeholders by accepting our responsibility to:

- Provide best value, safe, quality products
- Act responsibly in the communities where we operate
- Support the development of improved employment/working conditions in our supplier markets—particularly the developing countries
- Play our role in building and serving a more sustainable society

SOURCE: http://www.c-og-a.dk/aboutUs/socialResponsibility/ethics/, reprinted with permission of C&A.

The Gap Inc., another company highly publicized for its early response to social accountability, developed its Sourcing Guidelines in 1992 (later replaced by its Code of Vendor Conduct in 1996). Throughout the 1990s The Gap implemented compliance processes to oversee the activities in its production facilities. Chelan David (2007), in an interview with Dan Hekle, The Gap's senior vice president of social responsibility, reported that the company's success in ethical sourcing begins with connections to local stakeholders where factories are located. Support for self-monitoring is essential to the achieving appropriate factory conditions.

The European fashion retail company C&A created its Code of Conduct for the Supply of Merchandise in 1996 (Graafland, 2000) and established the Service Organisation for Compliance Audit Management (SOCAM) to monitor its manufacturing facilities. SOCAM functions as an independent monitoring agency that conducts social accountability audits. According to C&A, SOCAM inspections (there were more than 1,400 factory visits in 2005) are never announced in advance and detected breaches between C&A's Code of Conduct and the supplier will result in the suspension of business (with a corrective plan required before business can resume).

American Apparel touts its role as a socially conscious manufacturer and appeals to consumers who are willing to pay for the fashion image American Apparel projects. The company promotes itself as "sweatshop free," "brand free," and "made in downtown L.A." (Graham, 2005); these elements appeal to some socially conscious consumers. Among the benefits offered to American Apparel factory employees are high wages (twice the minimum wage), health insurance, subsidized lunches, and paid time off to take English classes on site (Palmeri, 2005). (See Chapter 2 for information about the company's corporate culture.)

Perspectives on Ethics in Apparel Product Development

A variety of perspectives can be considered relating to ethics in the global apparel product development, manufacturing, and distribution arenas. As with most ethical dilemmas, right and wrong decisions are not always clearly evident. The interpretation of "the best course of action" depends on one's perspective. Doris Hajewski (2000) noted in her article describing the job of a Nicaraguan garment laborer, "what the economists and activists disagree on is whether the piles of denim around his sewing machine represent the fabric of exploitation or the material from which workers can weave a better existence." The environmental conditions in which apparel is manufactured have become also important to retailers and brand owners whose products are associated with the laborers' working conditions. Company and brand image are open to scrutiny by numerous groups whose agendas support social consciousness as well as individual consumers. Consumer apathy is a phenomenon that intensifies retailers' dilemmas with ethical decisions. Apparel manufacturers and retailers are competing in a worldwide market for the spending of consumers who expect quality fashions at low prices. Therefore, apparel manufacturing has become a global issue and a social consciousness issue that continually presents ethical dilemmas for industry decision makers.

Cultural Perspectives

Culture, simplified as "the way we do things," differs significantly among countries and even among geographic regions within a given country. Certain practices that some cultures might view with indifference other cultures might respond to with varying levels of condemnation (Pitta, Fung, and Isberg, 1999). Engaging in global trade and contracting work for a company from one country with a manufacturer from another introduces the potential for ethical conflicts arising from differences in culturally acceptable workplace norms. Robert K. Dowling (2001), managing editor for *Business Week*, noted that a growing world economy is the best way to improve lives, but those economic improvements must be balanced against the high costs of laborer abuses.

Two of the most widely cited problem areas for global labor are low wages and unionization (Bernstein, 2004). Depending on one's perspective, low wages may be an advantage or an abuse. Similarly, unionization may be seen as either a threat (by the factory owner) or an advantage (by the worker). Cultural approaches to wage issues, enforcement of guidelines and standards, and labor relationships vary worldwide and complicate interactions between vendors, buyers, and laborers in a global market.

Cultural approaches to rule enforcement has resulted in an entirely new industry in China—consultants who assist factories in passing certification audits. Reports indicate that many of these consultants actually assist factories in producing fake documents and coaching workers to respond to questions with prepared speeches so that factories will pass inspections (Roberts et al., 2006). Global companies have begin investigating their factory conditions and seeking certification of sweatshop-free labor, but Chinese factories cannot afford to take steps to fix their shortcomings, which would force them to increase production costs—resulting in the loss of contracts. Thus, Chinese factory managers claim that U.S. price pressure motivates them to falsify their records so that they only appear to meet the labor standards valued by American companies and consumers (Roberts et al., 2006). The manager of a Chinese audit team responded in the following manner to the allegations of Roberts et al., in a feedback blog (Engardio, 2006) using the screen name "Mr. Wong":

> . . . to expect [Chinese factories] to meet the ideal is impractical, unrealistic, and naively Western. When the local government sets the minimum wage at $75 per month, it doesn't expect the factories to comply. They expect the factories will make an effort to stop paying $50 and get closer to $60. American companies must understand this process and allow for continuous improvement.

Further complicating the multicultural complexities between Chinese facto-ries and American companies, the Chinese government itself is not particularly effective, nor necessarily motivated, in enforcing labor laws.

Consider the following questions: What does it mean to enforce rules? What is the proper relationship between an employee and his or her supervisor? What type of discipline is appropriate at work? What level of financial contribution to the family (and extended family) and household is appropriate for members of various ages and genders? What are the most important life values? Responses to these questions differ depending on cultural context. An understanding of cultural influences, as well as a clear definition of universal and absolute values, is impor-tant when making ethical decisions with cross-cultural implications.

Business and Profitability Perspectives

Companies benefit through participation in activities that encourage and ensure fair labor practices. Their associations with socially conscious endeavors that promote posi-tive public perceptions enhance the images of their brands. Boulstridge and Carrigan (2000) noted that recent poor corporate behavior has led companies to give attention to corporate reputation management. The position of "chief reputation officer" has emerged as a recognized corporate leader who is charged with managing the firm's image (Saxton, 1998). In addition, non-governmental organizations (NGOs) have been formed and, through members' self-regulation, provide systems where companies can improve employee work environments without government intervention (which is seen by some as expensive and ineffective). Aaron Bernstein (1999) observed that ". . . outside monitoring by human-rights groups can work, even if the results are painful or embarrassing" (p. 106). In his *Business Week* article, Bernstein quoted Roberta S. Karp, the Senior Vice President of Business Development in Legal and Corporate Affairs at Liz Claiborne Inc., who indicated that although violations are identified, the companies are then able to investigate the problems and implement solutions.

Savvy consumers understand that retailers have control over the merchandise they carry and are reminded of this by a multitude of campaigns waged by special interest groups seeking improved working conditions worldwide. Both retailers and manufacturers stand to benefit by giving attention to their corporate values and making appropriate ethical choices with respect to sourcing their merchandise.

Ronald Adams, in his 2002 article in the *Journal of Retailing and Consumer Services,* "Retail Profitability and Sweatshops: A Global Dilemma," noted that corporate codes of conduct can help improve sweatshop conditions by setting standards for factory operations. Retailers, because of the fiscal power they hold in the market and their high visibility with consumers, have the opportunity to publicize their role in manufacturing and enforce factory standards. Unfortunately, if conflict is observed between stated company values and corporate behavior, corporate reputation is jeopardized. Companies who are performing well, such as American Eagle Outfitters (AE) and Wal-Mart, are particularly scrutinized. As research shows (Adams, 2002; Graafland, 2002), there is a strong correlation between low merchandise prices and financial performance, lending credence to the strategy of watchdog groups to closely monitor the world's most successful retailers.

The extent to which companies' stated standards match their behaviors is an important criterion that has ethical implications. The 2007 boycott UNITE led against American Eagle Outfitters was a result of the company's use of the National Logistics Services' distribution center while employees at NLS faced harassment and intimidation in response to their request to join UNITE HERE. UNITE HERE notes that these negative actions were a direct contradiction of AE's Code of Conduct, which states, "Vendors and contractors must respect the rights of employees to associate freely, join organizations of their choice and bargain collectively without unlawful interference" (http://phx.corporate-ir.net/phoenix. zhtml?c=81256&p=irol-VendorConduct). Thus, establishing a standards code is simply the first step in ethical decision making. Carrying out the code's standards is the measure of ethical success.

Business competitors can also be an important factor in a given company's ethical decisions. Some consumers and employees will compare one company to another, and then choose to associate (whether through patronage or employment) with the business offering a better philosophical fit. When leading companies such as Levi's, The Gap, and Starbucks are seen as socially conscious entities, it behooves other businesses to follow suit in order to keep their images competitive in the marketplace.

Employee Perspectives

Information regarding substandard working conditions comes from a variety of sources, including the firsthand reports from those who actually produce the world's apparel. These accounts provide powerful and disturbing perspectives about the workplace environments. Wendy Diaz, a then-teenage Honduran employee of Global Fashion, lent insight into factory conditions where she worked in the following description (Krupat 1997):

At Global Fashion, there are about 100 minors like me—13, 14 years old, some even 12. I started working at Global Fashion when I was 13 years old. We were forced to work, almost every day, from 8:00 a.m. to 9:00 p.m. Sometimes they kept us all night long, working until 6:30 a.m. I made at most 240 lempiras which I am told is about $2.61. No one can survive on these wages. The supervisors insult us and yell at us to work faster. Sometimes they throw the garment in your face, or grab and shove at you. The plant is hot like an oven. The bathroom is locked and you need permission and can use it twice a day. Even the pregnant women they abuse. Sometimes the managers touch the girls, our legs or buttocks. Many of us would like to go to night school but we can't because they always force us to work overtime. We have no health care, sick days, or vacation. Most of the girls are afraid. They fired a number [of workers] and said they would fire all of us if we tried to organize.

Kim Saxton (1998) noted in her article "Where Do Reputations Come From?" that employees provide both opportunities and threats to businesses by virtue of their roles representing the company, both on and off the job. Their satisfaction (or lack of) with their employer is reflected in workplace interactions, social situations, and general everyday behaviors. Thus, ethical decisions of companies not only affect the well-being of their employees, but also shape the manner in which employees interact with clients and customers.

Some employees want to work as many hours as possible, even for very low wages, because they see the income as a way out of the unbearable poverty of their current situations. Such workers consider factory closings—even for violations of their safety and human rights—as impediments to improved lives. This raises another ethical dilemma: At what expense to individuals should improvements in general working conditions be made? Many people would respond that basic human rights are paramount to the well-being of people and need to be protected at all costs. But the perspective of the worker seeking to improve her life should not be discounted.

Consumer Perspectives

Consumers who become advocates for fair labor have the potential to exert powerful influences over manufacturing decisions and organizations. In the 1990s, consumer activism in response to apparel production factories gained momentum as practices and workplace conditions were made public through television shows such as *Dateline* and news publications including *Newsweek* and *Time*. Similar to the public outcry after the Triangle Shirtwaist Factory fire of 1911, the formation of consumer advocacy groups provided incentive for apparel manufacturers and retailers to improve the workplace conditions of their factory employees.

The No Sweat campaign orchestrated by UNITE in 1996 appealed to consumers' sense of fairness. This campaign brought to light the fact that many apparel production facilities were in fact sweatshops and encouraged consumers to buy only garments that were certified to be manufactured in sweatshop-free, or "no sweat," conditions.

In 1997, the National Labor Committee prepared a letter to the Walt Disney Company that consumers were encouraged to duplicate and send. The letter appealed to consumers' sense of compassion for people and their familiarity with the Disney brand as a wholesome and ethical entity. The letter highlighted the workplace conditions of a Haitian factory and therefore educated consumers while advocating on their behalf.

Kathie Lee Gifford was among the first celebrities to be publicly humiliated in connection with the use of child laborers working in sweatshop conditions. This was the manufacturing system that was producing the apparel for Gifford's brand of a Wal-Mart clothing line, and was discovered and publicized by the National Labor Committee in 1996. Similarly Mary-Kate and Ashley Olsen's Wal-Mart apparel was criticized for its manufacture in Bangladesh factories with poor working conditions, and Sean Combs' Sean John merchandise has come under fire for being produced in Honduran sweatshops. Consumers' recognition of these brands and association of the brand image with the individuals for whom they are named strengthens the need for ethical considerations, and if needed, damage control.

Anti-sweatshop advocacy has been gaining strength on college campuses ("New Student Activism," 1999). United Students Against Sweatshops (USAS) formed in 1997 in response to the anti-sweatshop movement. A well-organized, international organization, USAS has led successful campaigns to remove Coca-Cola from college campuses, due to its allegedly pressuring union members in Columbia to sign letters of resignation using Coca-Cola letterhead, and has addressed collegiate licensing of sweatshop-manufactured merchandise. USAS founded the Worker Rights Consortium (WRC), an independent fair labor monitoring organization, in 2000. Campuses including Duke, the University of Wisconsin, Georgetown, Boston College, Michigan State University, Pennsylvania State University, and Stanford

Box 6.6

MODEL LETTER FOR THE WALT DISNEY COMPANY

Date

Michael Eisner, CEO
Walt Disney Company
500 South Buena Vista Street
Burbank, CA 91512

Dear Mr. Eisner:

We support Walt Disney's decision to produce in Haiti. The Haitian people need jobs. However, we hope that the high level of unemployment and poverty is not used to exploit the workers.

Walt Disney Company has licensing agreements with two U.S. companies—L.V. Myles and H.H. Cutler—who in turn contract with several companies in Haiti to produce Mickey Mouse and Pocahontas pajamas. Three of these companies—Quality Garments, National Sewing Contractors, and N.S. Mart manufacturing—are openly violating Haiti's wage laws, paying their employees as little as 12 cents per hour.

We ask that you translate Walt Disney Company's corporate code of conduct into Creole, to post it in your contractors' plants, and distribute it to the workers. We ask you to agree that independent human rights observers will have access to your contractors' plants to monitor compliance with your stated human rights concerns. Also, we know that Haitian women are being paid 7 cents for each pair of $11.97 Disney pajamas they make. This seems unjust—even criminal—to us. Is there any reason Walt Disney cannot work with your contractors to double, triple, or even quadruple the wages these women are being paid in Haiti? If you were to quadruple the wage, the women would still be earning 28 cents for every pair of $11.97 Disney pajamas they produced. Disney and the other companies involved would still keep $11.69—or 98 percent of the sales price. Couldn't the Walt Disney Company afford this? Wouldn't the $11.69 provide plenty of room for an adequate profit?

Lastly, can you explain to us how the U.S. people can trade with Haitian people earning 30 cents an hour? Of course, it is impossible. What do the U.S. people gain when U.S. companies pay such starvation wages in Haiti? Without fair social standards in international trade—linked to sustainable wages and human rights

Box 6.6 continued from page 160
MODEL LETTER FOR THE WALT DISNEY COMPANY

protections—the North American people cannot prosper, as we will be forced to compete for jobs in a race to the bottom over who will accept the lowest wages and the most miserable working conditions.

As we are sure Walt Disney Company stands by its human rights principles and has nothing to hide, we look forward to your company's promptly signing the attached Pledge. We await your response. Thank you.

Sincerely,

Attachment: Pledge

Walt Disney Company: Please Sign the Pledge

The Pledge

We, Walt Disney Company, pledge to immediately comply with all Haitian labor laws concerning all employees producing goods for our company, especially:

- To pay at least the legal minimum wage of 30 cents an hour, including proper overtime rates;
- To pay all legal benefits, such as health, pension, sick days, and 7th day bonus pay;
- To end sexual harassment;
- To respect the workers' right to organize and the right to collective contract;
- To improve working conditions and to cease arbitrary and unfair production speedups;
- To translate our code of conduct into Creole, post it in our contractors' plants, and distribute it to all employees; and
- To allow independent human right observers to monitor our contractors' compliance with our corporate code of conduct.

SOURCE: National Labor Committee (1997). An appeal to Walt Disney. In A. Ross, ed. *No Sweat: Fashion, Free Trade, and the Rights of Garment Workers*. New York: Verso, pp. 95–112. Reprinted with permission, courtesy of the National Labor Committee.

have made national news for their students' activities protesting sweatshops. In 2007, nearly a dozen Stanford students conducted a sit-in at the president's office demanding that the university join the WRC ("No-Sweat," 2007). James Keady, former assistant soccer coach at St. John's University, quit his job in protest over the university's contract with Nike, citing Nike's use of contractors that failed to meet international standards for workers' rights ("New Student," 1999). Nike's co-founder and president, Philip Knight, has been publicly at odds with his alma mater, the University of Oregon, after UO relented to student demands to join the WRC. Knight claimed that the WRC was a less desirable labor monitoring organization than the Fair Labor Association (FLA), an organization to which Nike belongs. The extent of this conflict led to Knight revoking a $30 million pledge to the University of Oregon, and demonstrates that ethical positions can have significant financial repercussions.

WHO IS RESPONSIBLE FOR ETHICAL MANUFACTURING AND SOURCING?

Both retailers and manufacturers must be accountable for sourcing their products. Because of the potential for high visibility and the general understanding that conditions of garment factories throughout the world are well known, every business involved in the merchandising process has responsibilities regarding fair labor practices.

The question of knowledge introduces an interesting angle into the discussion of ethical decision making. Prashad (1997) described the concept of "structural exploitation" as a way that responsibility is shifted away from financial investors and company representatives when unethical practices occur, with the claim that actions were not intended by the group bearing responsibility and were also not brought to their attention. Is it ethical to be involved in business practices when you don't know the employment conditions throughout the business? In 1996, Kathie Lee Gifford's claim of ignorance regarding the manufacture of her brand was a wake-up call for the industry and for the world. Information and documented facts are widely available and accessible, so virtually no businessperson (or celebrity brand namesake) can claim unawareness today. During the 1990s, brand owners such as Nike, Reebok, and Liz Claiborne resisted identification of their factories, citing that doing so would violate the confidentiality of their subcontractors and result in competitive disadvantages. Protests, largely by college students, pressured the companies to release factory information, which opened the door to scrutiny regarding the working conditions there. Although this was a painful process for the brand owners, the reforms resulting from public awareness have improved labor conditions on a global scale and strengthened the trust of labor rights activists and consumers.

Social compliance audits have emerged as the favored method to monitor factory conditions for most manufacturer and retail brands, which will generally subcontract with a company specializing in Social Compliance Audits. Audit teams then investigate the labor conditions of the client factories, noting such things as wage and overtime practices, workplace conditions, adherence to local laws and industry labor standards, employee freedoms to associate with collective bargaining groups, and compliance with safety regulations.

In its 2005 Report on Ethical Sourcing, Wal-Mart reported finding, through compliance audits, serious violations at 52.3 percent of the factories producing its apparel (Bowers, 2006). Audit processes for Wal-Mart and other companies have evolved and improved as a result of scrutiny into the procedures by both trade organizations and human rights groups. Some of the controversial practices that have surfaced include coaching employees with "appropriate" responses to auditors' questions and giving factory staff advance notice of upcoming audits. Companies are self-reporting and self-monitoring to a great extent, due largely to publicity and the scrutiny of competitors, consumers, and human rights activists. Amy Wyatt, spokesperson for Wal-Mart, indicated in 2006 that Wal-Mart's increase in cited violations from the number in 2005 have resulted from changes in audit criteria and greater frequency of unannounced inspections (Bowers, 2006). Industry leaders claim that the increased occurrences of documented sweatshop violations indicate improvements in monitoring systems rather than a growing number of incidents of human rights violations in factories.

Legislation

The U.S. Department of Labor enforces the Fair Labor Standards Act (FLSA), which was originally established in 1938. The FLSA covers wage regulations, child labor, and general workplace conditions. The FLSA continues to be the most widely referenced labor guideline in the United States.

Additionally, state legislators have developed specific standards in response to labor issues that have emerged in their local workforces. The state of New York, where about one-quarter of the apparel made in the United States is manufactured, has recently led an effort to crack down on sweatshops by passing legislation requiring manufacturers or businesses in New York to pay a surety bond based on their record of labor law violations (Morrow and Pensiero, 2006). Governor George Pataki signed the bill into law in 2007. In California, labor activists, garment industry leaders, and retailers collaborated to reach an agreement that resulted in Assembly Bill 633. The California legislation, signed into law by Governor Gray Davis in 1999, provides wage guarantees for minimum wage and overtime and a process for workers to recover unpaid wages. The bill authorizes the Labor Commissioner to revoke registrations of garment manufacturers that fail to pay wages owed; increases registration fees for garment manufacturers to fund enforcement efforts; establishes successor employer liability to ensure that factories do not close down, and then reopen to avoid paying wages owed; and allows garment workers employed by unregistered factories to take court action to recover wages.

Although laws have been enacted as a method of addressing labor problems and enforcing factory condition standards, retailers and manufacturers alike still benefit from self-regulated, socially conscious business practices.

Regulation and Support of Ethical Practices

Self-regulation, as opposed to government oversight, is preferable in many industries because it provides more direct oversight, less punitive consequences, and opportunities for businesses to improve their public image. The absence of legal censure lends credibility to businesses seeking enforcement of standards. Because the U.S. Department of Labor employs fewer than 800 factory investigators to oversee 6.5 million workplaces in the United States, governmental enforcement alone is not sufficient to ensure safe and fair wage factories. A variety of organizations, some of which are described below, have been established to improve workplace conditions throughout the world by advocating for ethical treatment of factory employees.

A variety of non-governmental organizations (NGOs) and high-profile campaigns have emerged to address workplace issues, oversee compliance, seek solutions to fair labor violations, and educate the public. NGOs are member-funded, typically composed of businesses, and are established by partners with common goals but limited individual resources. Campaigns are sponsored by government organizations, NGOs, unions, or consumer activist groups. NGOs such as the National Labor Committee (NLC) and the Ethical Trading Initiative (ETI) work on behalf of laborers worldwide as watchdogs to protect human rights and improve workplace and living conditions. Campaigns, regardless of the sponsoring agencies, generally use high-profile media outlets to communicate their goals and persuade businesses and consumers to support their efforts. Through campaigns, businesses are urged to change their operating practices and consumers are encouraged to boycott companies' products or to contact the CEOs and urge reform.

The wide variety of NGOs that currently exist emerged to meet a growing demand from human rights activists, brand owners, and retailers for inspections of factories so that sweatshops could be identified and reformed. While the increasing frequency of factory audits is a positive step in sweatshop eradication, the number of different inspection and certification organizations is burdensome to the factories. The labor standards that are identified by each NGO, while all similar in nature, are each slightly different. A condition of certification for each NGO is that the labor standards are clearly posted in the factory in languages native to the workers. Large factories contracting with multiple brands and retailers often need to post numerous labor standards and comply with audit procedures (such as work log documents) that are each unique to the certification agency.

The International Labor Organization (ILO) was founded in 1919 as part of the Treaty of Versailles, which ended World War I, with a vision that "universal and lasting peace can be established only if it is based on social justice." It became the first specialized agency of the United Nations in 1946. The ILO has 181 member states and is responsible, on a global scale, for establishing and overseeing international labor standards. According to the ILO Web site, the organization is devoted to advancing opportunities for women and men to obtain decent and productive work in conditions of freedom, equity, security, and human dignity. Relevant to the apparel manufacturing industry, its conventions have addressed child labor issues, producing documents that prescribe guidelines and restrictions for the use of child labor.

The National Labor Committee (NLC) was founded as a nonprofit NGO in 1981. This organization often partners with labor unions and other human rights groups to effect change with regard to labor standards. It was the NLC that implicated Kathie Lee Gifford in 1996 in connection to the plight of sweatshop workers, tarnishing her public image and ultimately spawning change in the accountability of retailers for the sourcing of their garments. In 2007, the NLC advocated on behalf of workers at the Fashion Curve factory in Jordan when it was discovered that young women were routinely physically abused, forced to work 13- or 14-hour days, and denied overtime pay. A few weeks after publicizing the situation, the NLC announced that the labor law violations had been resolved and the factory had met compliance with Jordanian labor laws.

The Asian Immigrant Women Advocates (AIWA) was founded in 1983 in response to the emerging labor force in the San Francisco and Silicon Valley areas of low-income Asian immigrant women, most of whom possessed limited English speaking skills, and who were quickly becoming the major pool of laborers in the garment, hotel, restaurant, and electronics assembly factories in California. The AIWA's mission is to empower women through education, leadership development, and collective action so that they experience dignity and justice in their workplaces and lives. The AIWA garment workers led the Garment Workers Justice Campaign against Jessica McClintock in the mid 1990s, agitating for wages due workers after one of the company's subcontractors went bankrupt, which culminated in an agreement in 1996 for worker protections for thousands of garment laborers in the San Francisco Bay Area. Esprit de Corp., Byer California, and Fritzi of California entered labor agreements with AIWA in 1997.

The U.S. government's interest in reducing sweatshop labor throughout the world began to gain momentum in the early 1990s. Under the Clinton administration, the No Sweat Initiative (NSI) was established and enjoyed support not only from government officials such as then-Secretary of Labor Robert B. Reich, but also from high-profile individuals including Kathy Lee Gifford. The No Sweat Initiative is perhaps the most widely recognized campaign to date that educates consumers about sweatshop-produced garments and encourages retailers to reward manufacturers that provide fair labor environments while punishing those that do not. Sponsored by the U.S. Department of Labor and endorsed by the National Labor Committee, UNITE (now UNITE HERE), and other activist groups throughout the world, its goal is to eradicate sweatshop labor. The Apparel Industry Partnership (AIP), composed of industry, labor, and human rights leaders, was formed as a result of the Clinton administration facilitating a series of meetings between a diverse group of leaders in their respective fields at the White House to discuss industry conditions. In 1997, AIP developed a Workplace Code of Conduct that is used as a standard for fair labor throughout the world. The Fair Labor Association (FLA), which grew out of the Apparel Industry Partnership, was formed in 1998. The FLA is a nonprofit organization whose mission is to complement international and national (U.S.) efforts to promote respect for labor rights. At the time of this writing, its members comprised 194 colleges and universities, NGOs, and brand-name companies including Adidas, Eddie Bauer, GEAR for Sports, H&H, Liz Claiborne, New Era Cap, Nordstrom, Nike, Patagonia, Phillips-Van Heusen, PUMA, Reebok, Top of the World, and Zephyr Graf-X. Factories that are compliant with FLA guidelines are eligible for accreditation through a process of inspection and auditing.

Colleges and universities that are members require their licensees to participate in the FLA licensee program. Like the FLA, the Worker Rights Consortium (WRC) is a nonprofit organization comprised of member colleges and universities formed for the purpose of monitoring and advocating for the labor rights of factory workers worldwide—particularly those in the textile and apparel industry who labor in sweatshop conditions. Colleges and universities have been particularly

Box 6.7

HOW DO COLLEGES AND UNIVERSITIES BECOME AFFILIATED WITH THE WRC AND FLA?

How does a college or university become affiliated with the WRC?

When a college or university decides to affiliate with the WRC, this affiliation is expressed in the form of a letter from the school's President or Chancellor, or other official designated by the school, to the WRC stating the institution's decision to affiliate and its recognition of the three obligations of affiliation: maintaining a manufacturing code of conduct, providing the WRC with factory disclosure information, and paying affiliation fees. A sample letter to express membership interest is available at http://www.workersrights.org/model_letter.asp. Annual affiliations fees are either $1,000 or 1 percent of gross licensing revenues, whichever is greater. Each college and university also designates a contact person from the administration to serve as the main liaison to the WRC.

How does a college or university become a member of the FLA?

The FLA membership form is available at http://www.fairlabor.org/all/colleges/univregistrationform07.doc. Dues for membership in the FLA are based on a school's licensing revenues. For schools with licensing programs, dues are 1 percent of the previous year's gross licensing revenue. For schools with no licensing programs, the dues are currently $100 per year.

active in this cause; licensing has provided money to the schools but have exploited the workers who are paid fractions of pennies for each product they produce. Ironically, the WRC and the FLA are seen as competing organizations, vying for membership (whose dues fund their activities) from the same pool.

The Fair Factories Clearinghouse (FFC), founded in 2004, is a nonprofit industry partnership based in New York whose purpose is to facilitate responsible sourcing among apparel, footwear, and other manufacturers. Its activities are funded by member companies as well as a grant from the U.S. Department of State's, Bureau of Democracy, Human Rights, and Labor. The FFC's goal is to form a collaborative effort among companies to compile a database with information about factory conditions throughout the world. This database provides a system by which social compliance audits can be monitored in a noncompetitive environment.

Box 6.8

FAIR FACTORIES CLEARINGHOUSE

Retailers, consumer brands, trading agents, and other buyers face the challenge of ensuring that factory workplace standards are properly integrated into their supply chain and sourcing operations.

A key tool in assessing factory workplace conditions is the use of social compliance audits. Buyers also use audits to assess security and environmental conditions in factories. Nevertheless, there is no comprehensive process for managing or sharing social compliance audit information. Many laudable efforts to create a widespread process have resulted in multiple, duplicative systems.

To help address this challenge, Federated Merchandising Group, Hudson's Bay Company, Mark's Work Wearhouse Ltd., Reebok International Ltd., The Wet Seal, the National Retail Federation, the Retail Council of Canada, and World Monitors Inc. have jointly organized the Fair Factories Clearinghouse (FFC), a collaborative industry effort involving retail and consumer brands and retail trade associations to create a system for managing and sharing audit information.

The FFC will house a global database of factory information and social compliance audit reports for the purpose of managing and sharing non-competitive information about workplace conditions in a manner that is cost-effective, can inform sourcing decisions by retailers and brands, and help improve factory workplace conditions around the world.

The FFC is a New York non-profit corporation founded in 2004 and funded by member contributions and a grant from the U.S. Department of State's, Bureau of Democracy, Human Rights, and Labor.

SOURCE: http://www.fairfactories.org/. Copyright © Fair Factories Clearinghouse, 2007. Reprinted with permission.

Social Accountability International (SAI) was established in 1997 under the name Council on Economic Priorities Accreditation Agency (CEPAA). SAI is an international nonprofit human rights organization dedicated to the ethical treatment of workers. SAI developed an auditing certification standard known as SA8000, which is a system for ensuring compliance with ethical sourcing standards established by the ILO conventions, the Universal Declaration of Human Rights, and the United Nations Convention on the Rights of the Child. The certification audits, evaluates and accredits manufacturers with respect to the workplace

BOX 6.9

PRINCIPLES INCLUDED IN THE ETHICAL TRADING INITIATIVE (ETI) BASE CODE

- No one should be forced to work
- Workers should be able to join and form trade Unions
- Working conditions should be safe and healthy
- Child labour shall not be used
- Working hours should not be excessive
- Wages should be enough to live on and provide some discretionary income
- Workers should be treated equally, regardless of their sex, ethnic group, religion, or political opinions
- Regular employment is provided
- No harsh or inhumane treatment is allowed

SOURCE: Reprinted with permission of the Ethical Trading Initiative.

issues of child labor, forced labor, health and safety, freedom of association and right to collective bargaining, discrimination, discipline, work hours, compensation, and management systems. Factories that are SA8000 certified must meet the minimum standards in each of these areas.

Special-interest activities sponsored by businesses or NGOs are offered with growing frequency for the purpose of better education on the topic of labor issues and to develop strategies for implementation of improved ethical practices. The "Making it Right: Lessons and Solutions in Global Sourcing and Labor Issues" conference held in November 2002 focused on the power that U.S. companies have over the conditions of apparel employees in developing countries and how to implement social responsibility and eliminate sweatshops (Clark, 2002).

IMPLICATIONS FOR THE APPAREL PRODUCT DEVELOPMENT AND RETAILING INDUSTRIES

Companies that discover factories with significant workplace violations are faced with the dilemma of whether or not to continue to do business with those factories. Although the simple solution would seem to be ceasing the relationship with the offending factory, the situation of the workers and compassion for their well-being must also be considered. If the factory closes, those workers will be unemployed. Is their continued employment in a sweatshop factory more desirable than unemployment? If a particular company abandons a factory because of its labor practices, it is likely that another company will contract with that factory with its same sweatshop policies. Many reputable companies, therefore, have embarked on troubleshooting and reform procedures with factories associated with high-risk violations in an effort to improve the lives of the employees, to maintain a source of income and improved standard of living for those in the factory communities, and to prevent other companies from moving in to perpetuate the sweatshop problems.

Wal-Mart reported completing 13,600 reviews of 7,200 factories in 2005, more than any other company (Roberts et al., 2006). As a result of these audits, Wal-Mart ceased doing business with 141 factories due to serious infractions such as child labor. The company's policy allows three audits with infractions, with the fourth as cause for ending the business relationship. Maria S. Eitel, Nike's vice president for corporate responsibility, observed that participating in factory audits is progress because it results in a system for identifying and dealing with labor issues (Bernstein, 2004).

Economists Robert Pollin, Justine Burns, and James Heitz (2004) conducted a study to determine whether raising retail prices could effectively improve the wage rates of apparel laborers. They determined that wage increases could be financed through retail price increases that would not exceed the level American consumers indicate they would be willing to pay to ensure good working conditions for garment laborers. Although they appear to be promising, these findings contrast with a variety of other studies (Boulstridge and Carrigan, 2000; Carrigan and Attalla, 2001; de Pelsmacker, Driesen, and Rayp, 2005; Iwanow, McEachern, and Jeffrey, 2005; Loureiro, McCluskey, Mittelhammer, 2002; Page and Fearn, 2005) that indicate consumers' foremost considerations regarding apparel purchases are price and style, even when informed that garment laborers are mistreated and underpaid. Marsha Dickson (2001) investigated the appeal of a No Sweat label or hangtag in apparel, indicating compliance to certain working conditions for the clothing bearing the tag. In a sample of consumers, only 16 percent indicated that they would use a No Sweat label to influence their purchase decisions.

Johan Graafland (2002) conducted a case study of the C&A company, a European retailer, to investigate its application of ethical values regarding sourcing and that relationship to profit. Specifically, Graafland explored whether a recent downturn in profitability affected C&A's implementation of its ethical standards. He interviewed C&A managers and their Asian suppliers and used newspaper articles to gather data which indicated that, although C&A's SOCAM has contributed positively to the company's reputation, customers seem unwilling to pay higher prices for clothes produced in ethical environments. Graafland concluded that the financial risks of social responsibility strategies need to be considered as companies gauge marketplace demand for ethically produced apparel.

Opportunities for education and improvement are great for worldwide labor conditions of apparel, textile, and footwear manufacturers. The cultural influences that introduce unique interpretations of ethical behaviors complicate the global issues. Furthermore, the paradox between opportunities for income and improved lives and the horrors of exploitation and abuses of human dignity are vast and not easily resolved. As Graafland (2002) suggests, dialogue is needed to increase awareness of labor issues as well as to propose and consider practical solutions to ethical dilemmas in business situations.

QUESTIONS FOR DISCUSSION

1. Should companies seek the lowest cost for apparel production, regardless of working conditions and other environmental issues? Why or why not?

2. Do you think the choice of production method or facility should be influenced by consumer opinion? Explain.

3. What level of responsibility do apparel product developers and brand owners have in overseeing the factories that subcontract the manufacture of their products?

4. What do you think about the role of garment assembly factories as a means for empowerment of women in underdeveloped communities?

5. Are laborers in developing countries better off with the income that sweatshops provide, or should the factories be closed? Provide the ethical perspective for your answer.

6. Is your college or university a member of the WRC or FLA? If so, how do you see the influence of this membership on your campus? If not, describe how your school could benefit from this association.

REFERENCES AND SUGGESTED READING

Abernathy, F. H., Dunlop, J. T., Hammond, J. H., and Weil, D. (1999). *A Stitch in time: Lean retailing and the transformation of manufacturing—Lessons from the apparel and textile industries.* New York: Oxford University Press.

Adams, R. J. (2002). Retail profit and sweatshops: A global dilemma. *Journal of Retailing and Consumer Services, 9*(3), 147–153.

American Eagle Outfitters (n.d.) Vendor code of conduct. Retrieved on August 1, 2007 from http://phx.corporate-ir.net/phoenix.zhtml?c=81256&p=irol-VendorConduct

Barrett, M. (January 2007). Tracking apparel technology trends. *Apparel Magazine, 48*(5). Retrieved on July 20, 2007 from Business Source Complete.

Bender, D. E. (2004). *Sweated work, weak bodies: Anti-sweatshop campaigns and languages of labor.* New Brunswick, NJ: Rutgers University Press.

Bernstein, A. (November 8, 1999). Sweatshops: No more excuses. *Business Week,* 104–106.

Bernstein, A. (September 20, 2004). Online extra: Nike's new game plan for sweatshops. *Business Week.* Retrieved on August 1, 2007 from http://www.businessweek.com

Blumenstyk, G. (April 21, 2006). U. of Michigan to buy Coke again. *The Chronicle of Higher Education,* A38–A39.

Boulstridge, E. and Carrigan, M. (2000). Do consumers really care about corporate responsibility? Highlighting the attitude—behaviour gap. *Journal of Communication, 4*(4), 355–368.

Bowers, K. (September 29, 2006). Wal-Mart factories cited for 'high risk' violations. *Women's Wear Daily,* p. 17.

Carrigan, M. and Attalla, A. (2001). The myth of the ethical consumer—do ethics matter in purchase behavior? *Journal of Consumer Marketing, 18*(7), 560–577.

Clark, E. (May 5, 2006a). ILO report cites decline in child labor. *Women's Wear Daily,* p.11.

Clark, E. (October 10, 2006b). Jordan takes steps to improve worker conditions. *Women's Wear Daily,* p. 11.

Clark, E. (October 26, 2007). Advocacy group finds violations at Bangladesh apparel factory. *Women's Wear Daily,* p. 14.

Clark, K. (December 2002). Making global sourcing right: An urgent call for smarter collaboration. *Chain Store Age*, 78(12), 122–124.

David, C. (January 2007). How Gap manages social compliance. *Apparel Magazine*, 48(5). Retrieved on July 20, 2007 from http://www.apparelmag.com

de Pelsmacker, P., Driesen, L., and Rayp, G. (2005). Do consumers care about ethics? Willingness to pay for fair-trade coffee. *The Journal of Consumer Affairs*, 39(2), 363–385.

Dickson, M. (2001). Utility of No Sweat labels for apparel consumers: Profiling label users and predicting their purchases. *The Journal of Consumer Affairs*, 35(1), 96–119.

Dowling, R. K. (June 11, 2001). The price of globalization. *Business Week*. Retrieved on August 1, 2007 from http://www.businessweek.com

Edelson, S. (July 24, 2007). UNITE calls for American Eagle boycott. *Women's Wear Daily*, p. 11.

Edelson, S. (July 24, 2007). Wal-Mart cuts b-t-s prices. *Women's Wear Daily*, p.2.

Ellis, K. (June 21, 2005). Wal-Mart rebuts 'Dateline' flap. *Women's Wear Daily*, p. 12.

Ellis, K. (May 16, 2006). The politics of port security. *Women's Wear Daily*, p. 14.

Ellis, K. (January 24, 2007). Senators push law banning sale of "sweatshop" imports. *Women's Wear Daily*, p. 13.

Ellis, K. (July 6, 2007). Fuentes line factory to comply with labor laws. *Women's Wear Daily*, p. 18.

Engardio, P. (December 18, 2006). Steamed over sweatshops. *Business Week*. Retrieved on August 1, 2007 from http://www.businessweek.com

Firoz, N. M. and Ammaturo, C. R. (2002). Sweatshop labour practices: The bottom line to bring change to the new millennium case of the apparel industry. *Humanomics*, 18(1/2), 29–45.

Govekar, P. L. and Govekar, M. A. (2006). A tale of two fires: Igniting social expectations for managers' responsibility. *Journal of Management History*, 12(1), 90–99.

Gereffi, G. (2001). Global sourcing in the U.S. apparel industry. *Journal of Textile and Apparel Technology and Management*, 2(1), 1–5.

Gereffi, G., Memedovic, O. (2003). The global apparel value chain: What prospects for upgrading by developing countries? Vienna, Austria: United Nations Industrial Development Organization.

Glazer, S. (May 18, 2007). Fair trade labeling. *CQ Researcher*, 17, 433–456. Retrieved on August 1, 2007 from http://library.cqpress.com/cqresearcher/cqresrre2007051800

Graafland, J. J. (July 2002). Sourcing ethics in the textile sector: The case of C&A. *Business Ethics: A European Review*, 11(3), 282–294.

Graham, A. H. (July 20, 2005). Is Dov-y too lovey? A look at American Apparel's CEO. *The Black Table*. Retrieved on March 17, 2008 from http://blacktable.com/graham050720.htm

Greenwald, R. A. (1998). More than a strike: Ethnicity, labor relations, and the origins of the Protocol of Peace in the New York ladies' garment industry. *Business and Economic History*, 27(2), 318–329.

Hajewski, D. (December 29, 2000). The unsettling price of low-cost clothes. *Milwaukee Journal Sentinel* (online). Retrieved on March 17, 2008 from http://www.jsonline.com

Howard, A. (1997). Labor, history, and sweatshops in the new global economy. In A. Ross, ed. *No sweat: Fashion, free trade, and the rights of garment workers*. New York: Verso, 151–172.

Iwanow, H., McEachern, M. G., and Jeffrey, A. (2005). The influence of ethical trading policies on consumer apparel purchase decisions: A focus on The Gap Inc. *International Journal of Retail and Distribution Management*, 33(5), 371–387.

June, A. W. (January 13, 2006). U. of Wisconsin will require a quarter of its apparel factories to allow unions. *The Chronicle of Higher Education*, 52(19), A30.

Krupat, K. (1997). From war zone to free trade zone: A history of the National Labor Committee. In A. Ross, ed. *No sweat: Fashion, free trade, and the rights of garment workers*. New York: Verso, 51–78.

Loureiro, M. L., McCluskey, J. J., and Mittelhammer, R. C. (2002). Will consumers pay a premium for eco-labeled apples? *The Journal of Consumer Affairs*, 36(2), 203–219.

Massachusetts town shudders after study details cancer risk. (May 12, 2006). *The Athens [Ohio] Messenger*, p. 2 [Associated Press].

McDonald, J. (August 10, 2006). Wal-Mart seeks talks with Chinese after unionization votes. *The Columbus Dispatch*, p. F3 [Associated Press].

McLaughlin, K. E. (July 3, 2007). Cost impact of China labor law tough to assess. *Women's Wear Daily*, p. 3.

Morrow, E. and Pensiero, C. (April 24, 2006). New York state legislature gets tough on sweatshops. *Women's Wear Daily*, p. 20.

Nearly nude Penn Staters protest sweatshop labor. (March 28, 2006). *The Chronicle of Higher Education*. News Blog; Retrieved on March 17, 2008 from http://chronicle.com/news/article/176/nearly-nude-penn-staters-protest-sweatshop-labor

"New student activism takes on sweatshop" (February 27, 1999). *America*, 180 (6), 4.

Nike opens its books on sweatshop audits. (April 27, 2000). *Business Week*. Retrieved on August 1, 2007 from http://www.businessweek.com

No-sweat sit-ins hit academe. (June 11, 2007). *The Nation*, p.8.

O'Donnell, J. (May 25, 2001). Agency sues Wal-Mart for not reporting 41 injuries. *USA Today*, p. B1.

Page, G. and Fearn, H. (2005). Corporate reputation: What do consumers really care about? *Journal of Advertising Research*, 45(3), 305–313.

Pagliaro, K. (n. d.). Slavery and Sweatshops. *Marist College Writing Center*. Retrieved on July 29, 2007 from http://www.marist.edu/writingcenter/escript04_13.html

Palmeri, C. (June 27, 2005). Living on the edge at American Apparel. *Business Week*. Retrieved on March 17, 2008 from http://www.businessweek.com

Pitta, D. A., Fung, H., and Isberg.S. (1999). Ethical issues across cultures: Managing the differing perspectives of China and the USA. *Journal of Consumer Marketing*, 16(3), 240–256.

Pollin, R., Burns, J., and Heintz, J. (2004). Global apparel production and sweatshop labour: Can raising retail prices finance living wages? *Cambridge Journal of Economics*, 28(2), 153–171.

Prashad, V. (1997). No sweat. *Public Culture*, 10(1), 193–199.

Pugatch, T. (April 30, 1998). Historical development of the sweatshop. INTS 92: The Nike Seminar. Retrieved on March 17, 2008 from http://www.unc.edu/ffiandrewsr/ints092/sweat.html

Roberts, D., Engardio, P., Bernstein, A., Holmes, S., and Ji, X. (November 27, 2006). *Business Week*. Retrieved on August 1, 2007 from http://www.businessweek.com

Robins, N. and Humphrey, L. (2000). *Sustaining the rag trade: A review of the social and environmental trends in the UK clothing retail sector and the implications for developing country producers*. Hertfordshire, England: The International Institute for Environment and Development, EarthPrint Ltd.

Saxton, M. K. (1998). Where do reputations come from? *Corporate Reputation Review*, 1(4), 393–399.

Selingo, J. (May 27, 2005). Anti-sweatshop group accredits 6 companies. *The Chronicle of Higher Education*, 51(38), A30.

Stamping out sweatshops. (May 23, 2005). *Business Week*. Retrieved on August 1, 2007 from http://www.businessweek.com

Stein, L. (1977). *Out of sweatshops: The struggle for industrial democracy*. New York: The New York Times Book Co.

Stier, K. (June 4, 2001). The garment trade may unravel...but a new port would help. *Business Week*. Retrieved on August 1, 2007 from http://www.businessweek.com

Sweating for fashion. (March 6, 2004). *Economist*, 370(8365), 14–15.

Tran, K. T. L. (April 19, 2007). California workers win on back pay. *Women's Wear Daily*, p. 16.

Tucker, R. (May 16, 2006). The next level of corporate responsibility. *Women's Wear Daily*, pp. 12–13.

Upadhyay, R. (May 16, 2006). India seeks edge with full-package approach. *Women's Wear Daily*, p. 6.

U.S. apparel imports increase. (February 2007). *Apparel Magazine*, 48(6).

United States General Accounting Office (September 2004). Fact Sheet for the Chairman, Commerce, Consumer, and Monetary Affairs Subcommittee, Committee on Government Operations, and House of Representatives. Tax Administration: Data on the Tax Compliance of Sweatshops. Retrieved on July 9, 2008 from http://archive.gao.gov/t2pbat2/152819.pdf

Walters, W. K. (April 14, 2006). Soft drinks, hard feelings. *The Chronicle of Higher Education*, 52(32), A30–A32.

ENDNOTE

1. All references to local law throughout this Code shall include regulations implemented in accordance with applicable local law.

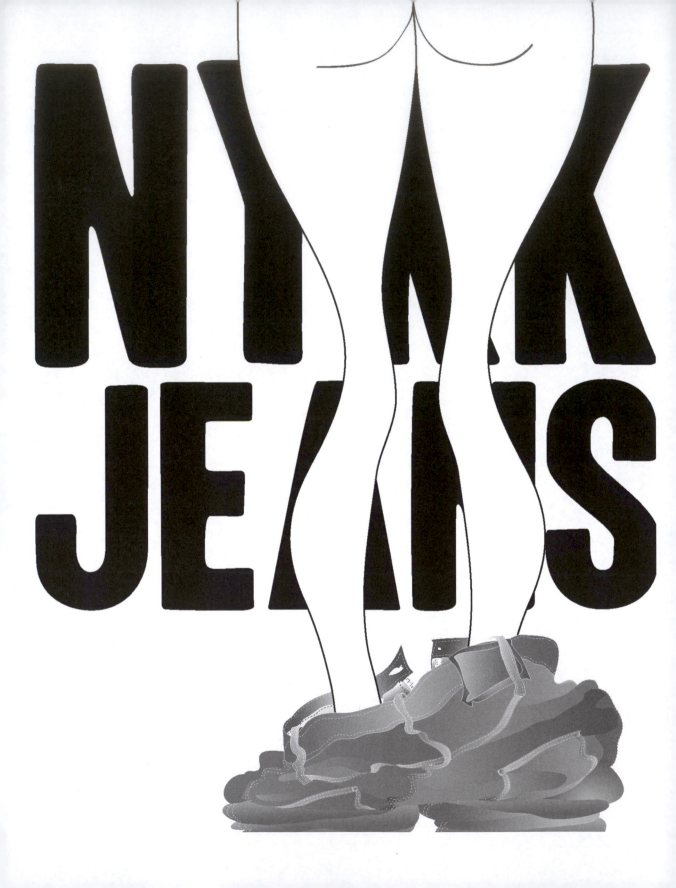

Advertising and Promotion

Perhaps one of the most visible ways for observing the ethics of a company is through its advertising and promotional campaigns. Historically, the focus on ethics with regard to advertising has primarily been concerned with pricing strategies and advertising misrepresentation. In fact, numerous consumer laws have been enacted over the years in order to better protect the public against such deceptive practices.

UNETHICAL ADVERTISING

Examples of unethical (and sometimes illegal) practices include "bait-and-switch" pricing, advertising an item as having a false "regular price," and placing limiting conditions of a sale price in the fine print of an ad.

Bait-and-Switch Advertising

This practice is not only unethical but also illegal in many states. The well-known advertised product, usually in short supply at the retailer's location, is advertised at a very low price to bring customers into the store. Once the customers arrive, they

FIGURE 7.1

find the product "out of stock" with store personnel then offering to sell them a similar product that allows a better profit margin for the retailer.

Regular Price as Promotional (Sale) Price

Many retailers offer continuous promotional pricing, so much so that consumers are aware that they should never expect to pay the "regular" price. This is a common advertising practice. The issue of ethics is raised when the advertisements lead customers to believe they are getting a better price than if they do not act on the current promotion.

Conditions in Fine Print

A third practice that is not illegal but that can certainly be questioned from an ethical perspective is the conditions placed on sale items in the fine print of an ad. Customers are sometimes drawn to the store for the low advertised price of the merchandise only to find that the fine print eliminates their favorite brands from the promotion. This is quite common for cosmetic and jewelry products. For example, a store may advertise "Everything is on Sale" only to include in the fine print that certain brand-name cosmetics and jewelry are excluded.

In 2006, Federated Department Stores was fined $725,000 in civil penalties for engaging in misleading advertising practices, which included the following:

- Using small print to exclude a significant number of items from a savings coupon that promised discounts on every item in the store
- Using photographs of merchandise on savings coupons that were not eligible for the extra discounts
- Using vague terms to describe the items ineligible for the sale events
- Misleading sale signs in its stores

In 2005, Federated had agreed to stop promoting fraudulent sales, but subsequent allegations revealed that the store had not done so. The company continued to use promotional lines such as "Lowest Prices of the Season," "Lowest Prices of the Year," and "One Day Only Super Sale" to create the idea that the prices were for a limited time. In fact, the items continued to be sold at the discounted price after the advertised sale period ended. Federated agreed that all of their stores in New York, including Macy's and Filene's, would comply with the terms of the $725,000 settlement even though the false advertising only occurred in their Kaufmann's division (Bucciferro and Morrow, 2006).

CONTROVERSIAL ADVERTISING

Although the previously discussed advertising practices reflect important ethical considerations in the communication between businesses and consumers, attention has recently been focused on the visual messages of advertisements themselves. Therefore, the attendant ethical issues in these situations concern underlying messages that can possibly be read into the advertisement. Obviously, this is content that is not easily regulated. There is often a fine line between allowing images to capture the attention of consumers, and misleading or offending them. Consider some examples:

- An H&M campaign that featured a picture of Claudia Shiffer modeling nude-colored underwear on the side of NYC busses was pulled due to consumer complaints.
- In 2000, Sears stopped selling Benetton products due to the latter's "Looking Death in the Face" campaign, in which convicted murderers on death row were profiled.
- Dolce & Gabbana's ad depicting what critics say is a gang rape ran in several magazines, including *Esquire* in March 2007, but was subsequently pulled from publication in the United States as well as Italy and Spain, among other countries. (See http://loveyourbody.nowfoundation.org/offensiveads.html and http://www.about-face.org/ for specific images),

Companies have also quickly dropped celebrities endorsing their products if the celebrity commits an ethical violation and there is a chance that customers will associate the bad behavior with the company. The adage "innocent until proven guilty" may work in a court of law but advertisers cannot necessarily wait for legal resolutions regarding celebrity and spokesperson behavior. Even when no legal wrongdoing is found, companies typically cannot afford aligning themselves with controversial people because of the possible negative association in the mind of the public—their customers. Therefore businesses generally distance themselves from troubled celebrities to protect their own reputations in the marketplace. Examples of these situations include:

- Pepsi cancelled its planned ad campaign with Madonna after her *Like a Prayer* video aired showing burning crosses, which was offensive to many Christians.
- Dell quietly let spokesman Benjamin Curtis's (the Dell "dude") contract expire after he was arrested for allegedly trying to buy marijuana.
- Sears and Federal Express pulled their sponsorships of *Politically Incorrect* after host Bill Maher called Americans "cowards" for "lobbing cruise missiles from 2,000 miles away" after September 11, 2001.
- Nike suspended the release of its product line named after Atlanta Falcons quarterback Michael Vick after he was indicted for and subsequently found guilty of operating a dog-fighting ring on his property.

From an ethical perspective, problems commonly arise when there are inconsistencies between the advertised message and the product itself. In other words, "taboo" advertising would be least likely to offend the established target market of a "taboo" product. But the same advertising campaign would likely be considered offensive if it were advertising a product such as children's clothing. The promotional campaigns of Calvin Klein and Abercrombie & Fitch provide examples of ads that people some consider to be inappropriate and others, offensive.

Calvin Klein

Calvin Klein has continued to create controversy over the years by pushing the advertising envelope in product promotion. His company's controversial ads began in the 1980s with an adolescent Brooke Shields modeling Calvin Klein jeans and declaring the provocative line "Nothing comes between me and my Calvins." In the 1990s, the controversy continued as he used waif-like Kate Moss for his *Ck One* and lingerie lines. The suggestive ads for his fragrances were one of the first linking sex and sexuality to fragrances; this has made the company's fragrance line somewhat of a phenomenon.

Calvin Klein has built his empire with ads notorious for blatant sexuality, nudity, and the use of children and adolescent models. For example, he promoted his underwear line by mounting a giant billboard in Times Square featuring a chiseled male model wearing only white briefs. He also stirred major controversy and debate in 1995 by using pubescent models in provocative poses to promote his Calvin Klein jeans. Many critics believe the ads crossed the line from fashion into pornography. The photos used in the ad were shot in a sleazy suburban "rec room," complete with cheap paneling and brightly colored shag carpeting and were inspired by pornography from the 1960s. This campaign stirred so much controversy that it eventually led to the U.S. Justice Department launching an investigation into whether or not the ads violated child pornography laws. Under increasing scrutiny, Klein finally withdrew the ads, but only after his jeans had become the "must-have" item of the season.

In 1999, Klein found himself and his company embroiled in yet another heated controversy concerning an advertising campaign designed to promote his children's underwear line. On February 17, 1999, a full-page ad appeared in the *New York Times* featuring pictures of toddlers and small children playing on a sofa wearing only CK underwear. Simultaneously, the same three pictures were featured on a huge billboard in Times Square. The backlash from this ad campaign was so intense that the company pulled the ads just 24 hours later. Critics cited Klein's track record of exploitative advertising to make their case that the ads were pornographic although Klein argued that he was simply mimicking the home pictures that parents often take of their children (Peters, n.d.).

Abercrombie & Fitch

Another example of a company creating ethical controversy is the promotional campaigns of Abercrombie & Fitch, a clothing company whose stores include abercrombie, Abercrombie & Fitch, Hollister, and its newest store, Ruehl. Collectively, the first three stores target pre-teens to college students; Ruehl seeks to cater to the post-collegiate young adult. In general, the company has used "lifestyle marketing" to promote its fashions. Although the promotion of this lifestyle is paying off in large sales gains, the strategy is not without controversy, especially from parents and various watchdog organizations. This is particularly true of the *A&F Quarterly*. Controversy has surrounded not only the company's advertising but has also carried over into its products, T-shirts in particular, and its hiring practices (the latter is discussed in Chapter 2).

The *A&F Quarterly* was a magalog (a magazine-catalog hybrid) sold by Abercrombie & Fitch from 1997–2003 that featured articles about college life, photo essays, and advertisements for the company's clothing. The circulation reached as high as 1.2 million during the late 1990s. The controversies surrounding the publication are highlighted below in chronological order:

- In 1998, MADD (Mothers Against Drunk Driving) and The Center for Science in the Public Interest spoke out against the publication's *Drinking 101* promotion, which included recipes for mixed drinks, instructions and props for a drinking game, and a campaign encouraging readers to be creative in their drinking binges. Due to public pressure, the company did pull the drinking game pages from the catalogues being sold in stores and also sent a letter of apology to its subscribers.

- In 1999, a consumer boycott was launched against the "Naughty or Nice" holiday issue, which included an interview with a well-know porn star and images of a celebrity in sadomasochistic poses with Santa Claus. The boycott was led by Illinois Lt. Governor Carrine Wood and was joined by Michigan Attorney General (now Governor) Jennifer Granholm. Granholm charged that the magalog could not be distributed to minors due to its pornographic content—which included advice on how to have sex with three people. In total, four states threatened legal action against the publication.

- In summer 2001, the *A&F Quarterly* included pictures showing naked or nearly naked young adults cavorting on the beach. Groups such as Concerned Christians of America and the National Organization for Women criticized the publication for promoting unrealistic body images for young women and for promoting group sex. Again the publication included an interview with a porn star discussing various sex acts, which many people found offensive.

- During the 2003 holiday season, the publication was once again criticized by religious and women's groups for its content, forcing the publication to be removed from stores. The issue, which proved to be the demise of the publication, contained articles about oral sex, men kissing, group sex, and images of young, nude adults in a river.

Abercrombie & Fitch said its decision to cease publishing the magalog was to free up space in its stores for a new fragrance line but consumer watchdog groups credited the demise of the *Quarterly* to their pressure on the company. Today it publishes A&F *magazine* and has managed to do so with little controversy.

Despite the controversy surrounding Abercrombie & Fitch's promotional activities, the company's stores have continued to be the destination stores of choice for its target market. In 2005, it reported a December sales increase of 29 percent, which capped off a year of double-digit increases. Many industry experts believe that A&F has been successful because it has done a good job of differentiating itself in an overcrowded marketplace, and by creating a lifestyle and a look consistent with an iconic brand. It also has been quite successful in convincing its customers to buy at full price, a feat the majority of retailers cannot accomplish. Not only has A&F built its brand by promoting the clothing, but the company also has been successful creating and promoting the "Abercrombie experience" for customers in its stores through the unique ambience including the staff, merchandising, music, lighting, and even smell (Podmolik, 2006).

Use of Models

As discussed in Chapter 3, one of the most pervasive controversies in fashion advertising surrounds the depiction of an ultra-thin beauty ideal. Such advertising has been blamed for eating disorders such as anorexia and bulimia, increased dieting among pre-teens, and for women striving to achieve an unrealistic body. In reaction to these criticisms, many fashion-related companies are reexamining the types of models used in their marketing campaigns, including print advertisements and fashion shows. In 2007, consumer-product group Unilever NV/Plc (one of their product lines is Dove) adopted a new global guideline banning from their advertising and marketing communications super-slim models, or ones who promote an "unhealthy slimness." In enforcing this ban, Unilever expects all of its brand directors and agencies to use a Body Mass Index of 18.5 to 25 as a guideline when selecting advertising models ("Unilever bans super slim models from advertising," 2007). Along similar lines, Israeli fashion photographer Adi Barkan has spent the last several years trying to raise awareness in the modeling community about the problems of eating disorders. Through his work, including legislation and public relations, this renowned owner of a Tel Aviv modeling agency successfully submitted legislation to Israel's Parliament requiring all Israeli modeling agencies use the Body Mass Index as a prerequisite for employment. To date, over 30 Israeli CEOs have joined Barkan's campaign and agreed to hire models for their advertisements only after they pass a health exam. Barkan and his supporters hope that such changes in the industry, which promote a healthier appearance, will help to change how young women view themselves in terms of their body image (Lovitt, 2007). Box 7.1 provides a timeline of the controversy surrounding the use of thin models.

In addition to being criticized for the use of ultra-thin models, a recent controversy involves the lack of diversity found in fashion advertisements and on the catwalks. Critics believe this promotes a blond-haired, blue-eyed ideal; some consider it to be racist. Critics also say this makes for very boring and monotonous fashion shows and advertising campaigns. Bethann Hardusin, a former model who now runs a successful modeling agency promoting racial diversity, recently convened a panel of fashion experts in New York City to discuss "The Lack of the Black Image in Fashion Today." Although black women spend more than $20 billion on apparel each year, black faces on the runway and in print, are noticeably absent. For example, the March 2008 issue of *Vogue*, which has more than 400 pages of advertising and copy, included only 14 shots of black or Asian women, two of which were Naomi Campbell (Sharp, 2008). Although the Council of Fashion Designers of America (CFDA) has adopted a formal position regarding the use of thin models (see Chapter 3), thus far the organization has declined to become directly involved in the controversy surrounding the lack of racial diversity in fashion advertisements.

Academic research studies have also addressed the depiction of women in fashion advertisements. For example, one study compared Asian and Western models in women's magazine advertisements in Singapore, Taiwan, and the United States. The findings suggested that Western models were used more in advertisements that were more "body" oriented (e.g., clothing advertisements) and also were used in advertisements in Asia when the underlying marketing strategy was "sex sells." Furthermore, the study found that Asian models were used more frequently in advertisements for hair and skin beauty products. Overall, Western models were put forward in the advertisements as being the "seductive beauty type" (Frith, Cheng, and Shaw, 2004).

Box 7.1

A TIMELINE FOR BANNING THIN MODELS

- **August 2, 2006:** Brazilian model Luisel Ramos, age 22, dies of anorexia nervosa–related causes.
- **September 9, 2006:** Madrid fashion show (Pasarela Cibeles) says models with body mass index ratings under 18 will not be allowed to work in the event.
- **September 18, 2006:** Tessa Jowell, British Culture Secretary, applauds Madrid show's decision. London Fashion Week show ignores Jowell's recommendation to do the same. The British Fashion Council says that it "does not comment or interfere in the aesthetic of any designer's show."
- **September 21, 2006:** Giorgio Armani comments on the models he prefers to employ: "I have never wanted to use girls that are too skinny. I prefer girls that show off my clothes in the best way."
- **November 17, 2006:** Brazilian model Ana Carolina Reston dies of anorexia at age 21.
- **December 1, 2006:** Brazilian modeling agencies begin to require prospective models to have medical certificates saying they are healthy. Those who wish to be models will have to take blood tests to get their certificates.
- **December 18, 2006:** Milan fashion show bans models with BMI under 18.5 and models under age 16.
- **January 9, 2007:** The Academy for Eating Disorders (AED) suggests guidelines for the fashion industry, including requiring models to be at least 16 years old, promoting the use of models of all sizes in fashion shows, and eliminating digital enhancements to make models in photos look slimmer.
- **January 25, 2007:** Organizers of London Fashion Week take a different approach than fashion shows in Madrid and Milan, choosing not to ban very thin models. Officials stress that they had asked designers to use only "healthy" models. The British Fashion Council argues that barring too-thin models "is neither desirable nor enforceable."
- **January 25, 2007:** Spain's government reaches agreement with major fashion designers to create standards for women's clothing sizes. The stated goal is to promote a healthier image.
- **February 12, 2007:** Pasarela Cibeles show in Madrid follows through on its promise, banning five models from participating.
- **February 13, 2007:** Brazilian model Eliana Ramos, age 18, dies of heart failure due to anorexia.

Box 7.1 continued from page 187

A TIMELINE FOR BANNING THIN MODELS

- **May 2, 2007:** International model Marvy Rieder meets with the Academy of Eating Disorders (AED) to discuss interventions for models in danger of developing eating disorders.
- **May 9, 2007:** Amsterdam-based Unilever, a consumer products group, eliminates models with BMI under 18 and over 25 from their advertising.
- **June 15, 2007:** English model Rosanna Carr Taylor wins the Miss East Anglia pageant and endorses *beat*, formerly known as the Eating Disorders Association. Ms. Carr Taylor speaks of pressure to lose weight in the industry.
- **July 11, 2007:** Independent panel logs preliminary report suggesting that London Fashion Week ban models under age 16, and that a "rigorous" study be conducted to determine the prevalence of eating disorders among models. The panel also suggested regular medical checks for models to screen for eating disorders.
- **September 15, 2007:** New model Maddison Gabriel dominates headlines at Australia's Gold Coast Fashion Week—a day before her 13th birthday.
- **November 14, 2007:** Israeli model Hila Elmalich dies from complications of self-starvation. Photographer Adi Barkan ramps up his campaign for healthier models: Modeling agency Elite International holds auditions at which prospective Israeli models are told that the agency is committed to hiring those with healthy BMIs.

SOURCES: Associated Press. (September 21, 2006). London rejects thin model ban. *International Herald Tribune*. Retrieved on May 16, 2007 from http://www.iht.com/articles/2006/09/18/business/rthin.php

Booth, Jenny. (July 11, 2007). Models under 16 to be banned from London fashion week under new proposal. FOXNews.com. Retrieved on July 11, 2007 from http://www.foxnews.com/story/0,2933,288951,00.html

Heath, Mark. (June 15, 2007). Model joins battle against fashion waifs. *EADT 24*. Retrieved on June 24, 2007 from http://www.eadt.co.uk/content/eadt/news/story.aspx?brand=EADOnline&category=News&tBrand=EADOnline&tCategory=News&itemid=IPED14+Jun+2007+23%3A53%3A43%3A270

Lovitt, Benji. (November 23, 2007) Israeli fashion photographer leads worldwide campaign for healthier models. *Israel21c*. Retrieved on December 3, 2007 from http://www.israel21c.org/bin/en.jsp?enDispWho=Articles^l1860&enSearchQueryID=24&enPage=BlankPage&enDisplay=view&enDispWhat=object&enVersion=0&enZone=Culture&

Parker, Eloise. (September 19, 2007). 13-year-old Maddison Gabriel is the kitten of the catwalk. *NYDailyNews.com*. Retrieved on September 22, 2007 from http://www.nydailynews.com/lifestyle/2007/09/19/2007-09-19_13yearold_maddison_gabriel_is_the_kitten-1.html

Reuters.com. (September 22, 2006). Armani: anorexia isn't fashionable. *People*. Retrieved on May 16, 2007 from http://www.people.com/people/article/0,26334,1537967,00.html

Reuters, Inc. (May 9, 2007). Skinny types need not apply for Unilever ads. Retrieved on January 28, 2008 from http://www.reuters.com

Available: http://eatingdisorders.about.com/od/anorexianervosa/a/bantimeline.htm

SOCIAL COMMENTARY ADVERTISING

While Calvin Klein and Abercrombie & Fitch have built retailing empires with the help of controversial ads, other retailers have stirred discussion through promoting their own beliefs in their advertising campaigns. Kenneth Cole is an example of a manufacturer whose own ethical beliefs appear in the advertising campaigns for his product lines. Cole has definitely sparked discussion among conservatives and has found himself in the middle of political controversy because of the social commentary featured in his company's ads. His advertisements, which often include a play on words, have in the past addressed gun control, abortion, gay rights, same-sex marriage, AIDS, human rights, and homelessness. Some examples include:

- The September 12 (2001) campaign reminded Americans that "on September 12, 14,000 people still got HIV. . ."
- His statement concerning safe sex (when advertising condoms was illegal) included a pair of his shoes and showed a condom with the message "Our shoes aren't the only thing we encourage you to wear."
- His views on gun control with an open letter to the president of the National Rifle Association, the state of Texas, K-Mart shoppers, and gun manufacturers, which read, "Congratulations. We hear your product is really making a killing."
- His shoe campaign, which read, "We condemn the right to bear arms and bare feet."

While conservatives criticize such slogans, Cole has openly stated that he does not want these people as his customers anyway and believes that his sales do not suffer because his critics were never his customers to begin with (Keane, 2004; Kenneth Cole pours heart and sole, 2004).

In addition to messages included in his advertising campaigns, Cole's business has a segment of its Web site devoted to organizations that his company supports. Entitled "Just Causes," the tagline reads, "We at Kenneth Cole think that being aware is more important than what you wear."

In a similar spirit, Robert Duffy, the president and CEO of Marc Jacobs International, and fashion designer Marc Jacobs convinced over a dozen fashion celebrities (e.g., Wynona Ryder, Christy Turlington, Hillary Swank, Carolyn Murphy) to pose nude for a fund-raiser benefit for the New York University School of Medicine's Interdisciplinary Melanoma Cooperative Group. According to *Women's Wear Daily*, the idea for the project came after Duffy was diagnosed with skin cancer in 2003, a result of spending his summers on the beach and tanning during his high school years. Plans for the event were finalized when Duffy ran into a deeply tanned Murphy and learned that her tan was out of a cosmetic bottle. The resulting photographs, from which six-foot-tall prints were made, were displayed at the benefit (held during the 2007 NYC Fall Fashion week at Marc Jacob's after-show party). For the fund-raiser, the six-foot prints were auctioned to guests. In addition, the prints appeared on T-shirts and were sold in Marc Jacob's retail stores for $20. The T-shirts were displayed in the store windows along with huge banners warning of the dangers of skin cancer. Accompanying the pictures on the T-shirts were catchy slogans like "Protect Your Largest Organ" on the men's shirts and "Protect the Skin You're In" on the women's shirts (Berman, 2006; Iredale, 2006). (Figure 7.2 features an example of the T-shirts.)

FIGURE 7.2   Designer Marc Jacob's T-shirt features Helena Christensen, one of many models who posed to help fight skin cancer.

RESPONSIBLE ADVERTISING

While some companies have built their businesses through the use of controversial advertising, others have chosen to focus their efforts on what is called "responsible advertising." From an ethical standpoint, their advertising is aimed at reflecting society's views of what is morally right.

One such ad campaign that has received a lot of attention is from Unilever promoting its Dove products. Positioning itself apart from the conventional approach to advertising (i.e., using ultra-beautiful female models) Dove decided to show "real" women as part of its 2004 "Real Beauty" campaign. The women of various shapes and sizes were shown modestly posing in their underwear with the slogan "Real women have curves." The women in the ads were not professional models and were selected to challenge society's view on age, body shape, race, and beauty. The ads were featured in magazines, television ads, billboards, and print ads. Reactions to the ads were mixed. Although most people found the ads favorable, some found them to be "offensive" precisely because the women featured were not within the parameters of society's definition of beauty. Because the reactions to the ad sparked such a debate, Dove created a public forum for discussion about the issue of beauty through a line in its ads directing consumers to www.campaignforrealbeauty.com. The campaign has been expanded to include "The Dove Self-Esteem Fund" in partnership with the Girl Scouts of America; this initiative is aimed at improving the self-esteem of young girls (Prior, 2005).

Prior to launching the campaign, Dove partnered with Massachusetts General Hospital/Harvard University Program in Aesthetics and Well Being and the London School of Economics to survey 3,200 women from 10 countries concerning their feelings about beauty and their opinions concerning the impact of mass media and culture. Highlights of the results are in Box 7.2.

As previously mentioned, the ad campaign was not without controversy. Some people didn't like the ads because the women in the ads were not the "typical" size 2 supermodel. However, others questioned the motives of Dove because the ad campaign was used to sell products like "firming lotion" aimed at reducing cellulite. Critics believed this sent a mixed message: you should love your hips the way they are—but you should still erase the cellulite underneath. Furthermore, the critics pointed out that there is no scientific proof that the Dove firming cream works (Traister, 2005). Regardless, analysts forecasted Dove's entire hand and body lotions line to bring in $60 million to $70 million in 2005 (Prior, 2005), and overall the ad campaign has been received favorably by Dove customers.

Another company that has also begun a campaign aimed at "real beauty" is Bath and Body Works. In conjunction with American Girl dolls, the retailer

BOX 7.2

DOVE'S *CAMPAIGN FOR REAL BEAUTY* SURVEY RESULTS

Results of a study conducted by Unilever used to launch Dove's *Campaign for Real Beauty* included the following:

- Only 2 percent of respondents described themselves as beautiful.
- Sixty-three percent strongly agree that women today are expected to be more attractive than their mother's generation.
- Sixty percent strongly agree that society expects women to enhance their physical attractiveness.
- Forty-five percent of women feel women who are more beautiful have greater opportunities in life.
- More than half (59 percent) strongly agree that physically attractive women are more valued by men.

Concerning the degree to which mass media has perpetuated an unrealistic view of beauty, findings indicated:

- More than two-thirds (68 percent) of women strongly agree that "the media and advertising set an unrealistic standard of beauty that most women can't ever achieve."
- Well over half of all women (57 percent) strongly agree that "the attributes of female beauty have become very narrowly defined in today's world."
- The majority of women (76 percent) indicated their wish that female beauty be portrayed as being made up of more than just physical attractiveness.
- Seventy-five percent of the respondents wanted the media to do a better job of portraying women of diverse physical attractiveness, including size, shape, and age.

SOURCE: Only 2 percent of women describe themselves as beautiful: New global study uncovers desire for broader definition of beauty. (September 29, 2004). Retrieved on March 17, 2008 from http://www.campaignforrealbeauty.com/press .asp?section=news&id=110

launched a product line aimed at "tween" girls (ages 9–12). Similar to Dove's self-esteem campaign, the product line and advertising materials promote the idea that real beauty comes from the inside. The line includes items as *Truly Me* sparkling powder puff. In addition to the personal care items, accessories include self-help books aimed at building confidence and answering questions concerning adolescent issues like body changes, healthy eating, and strategies for feeling good about themselves.

The use of models who look more like the "average" consumer is definitely gaining popularity. According to Marti Barletta, author of *Marketing to Women* and the president of TrendSight Group, clothing companies such as Eileen Fisher, Nordstrom, and J. Jill are examples of businesses that are moving forward with this idea. Additionally, Soma, an intimate apparel and loungewear store that targets women 35 and over are also using mannequins who mirror the proportions of average women.

Many in the fashion industry believe that the trend toward using real people in advertisements is due to a sense of fatigue of seeing an endless parade of skinny, expressionless models over the years. According to a recent article in *Newsweek*, much of this interest is being driven by two forces: the Internet and the increased availability of designer merchandise to the masses (e.g., Vera Wang at Kohl's or Isaac Mizrahi at Target). Internet bloggers who run sites such as *Street Peeper*, *Last Night's Party*, and *Fashionista* are creating interest in "street fashion" and what real people (not fashion models) are wearing. Although the trend of using real people is in its infancy, companies do seem to be responding to the idea. For example, the swimsuit company Lycra recruited twenty women of all shapes and sizes off the beach to model their bathing suits during the 2007 Miami Swim Fashion Week (Yabroff, 2008).

The advertisements and promotional campaigns produced on behalf of manufacturers and retailers shape the attitudes of consumers toward the brands and merchandise featured. The relationships between messages—obvious or subtle—delivered on behalf of manufacturers and the retailers selling the products can be complex. Core values related to the brands of both manufacturers and retailers can be at odds with "edgy" promotional campaigns designed to stand out and be remembered in a media-saturated world. Advertising and promotional activities are an important vehicle in creating brand recognition, customer loyalty, and consumer desire for products and retail venues. As you explore the role of advertising and promotion in the "big picture" of the fashion and retailing industries, consider to the attendant role of ethics and ethical decision making.

QUESTIONS FOR DISCUSSION

1. Despite the controversy surrounding their ad campaigns, A&F, and Calvin Klein continue to be among the most profitable apparel companies today. Therefore, it could be argued that *the ends justify the means*. What is your opinion about the ethics of apparel companies using controversial advertising?

2. Find examples of the Dove ads promoting "real beauty." What is your reaction?

3. What do you think of the criticism concerning Dove's ad campaign?

4. Visit Dove's blog on http://www.campaignforrealbeauty.com. What are some of the general opinions expressed there concerning the ad campaign? Do you find any negative reactions?

5. Visit the "Just Causes" section of the Kenneth Cole Web site (found under "About Us"). What are some of the social causes and organizations listed there, and what are their goals?

6. Do you think Kenneth Cole could reach more customers if he did not include social commentary in his ads? Why or why not?

7. Do you think it is a good idea for retailers and manufacturers to advocate social causes as part of their advertising and promotional campaigns? Explain your answer.

8. Visit *Street Peeper*, *Last Night's Party*, and *Fashionista*, the blogs mentioned in this chapter. What is your opinion of such sites as they relate to driving fashion trends?

REFERENCES AND SUGGESTED READING

Barletta, M. (2006). *Marketing to women: How to understand, reach, and increase your share of the world's largest market segment* (2nd ed.). Chicago: Dearborn Trade Publishing.

Berman, J. (September 12, 2006). Fashion designer Marc Jacobs hosts after party fundraiser to benefit NYU's interdisciplinary melanoma cooperative group. Retrieved on March 17, 2008 from http://www.med.nyu.edu/communications/news/pr_201.html

Bratskeir, A. (January 30, 2008). Diversity may be Fashion Week's latest victim. Retrieved on March 17, 2008 from http://www.newsday.com/features/lifestyle/fashionweek/ny-etlede5556549jan31,0,4847597.story

Bucciferro, M. and Morrow, E. (March 15, 2006). Federated to pay $725,000 in ad case. *Women's Wear Daily*, p. 7.

Frith, K., Cheng, H., and Shaw, P. (2004). Race and beauty: A comparison of Asian and Western models in women's magazine advertisements. *Sex Roles*, 50(1/2).

Iredale, J. (September 9, 2006). Charitably endowed. *Women's Wear Daily*, 1, pp. 14–15.

Keane, M. (January 23, 2004). Too cool Cole: The cobbler's politics. National Review Online. Retrieved on March 17, 2008 from http://www.nationalreview.com/nr_comment/ keane200401230958.asp

Kenneth Cole pours heart and sole into gay advertising. (October 2004). Retrieved on March 17, 2008 from http://www.wildemarketing.com/gay_advertising.com

Lovett, B. (November 23, 2007). Israeli fashion photographer leads worldwide campaign for healthier models. Retrieved on March 17, 2008 from http://www.medicalnewstoday.com/articles/89781.php

Peters, R. (n.d.). "Kiddie Porn" controversy: Calvin Klein ads may not be child porn but they aren't morally innocent and harmless either. Retrieved on March 17, 2008 from http://store.soliscompany.com/kpoco.html

Podmolik, M. E. (January 14, 2006). Teen stores leading the herd. *Chicago Tribune*, Business Section 2, pp. 1, 8.

Prior, M. (July 7, 2005). Dove affirms stance on beauty marketing. *Women's Wear Daily*, p. 9.

Rueters News Service (May 9, 2007). Unilever bans super slim models from advertising. Retrieved on March 17, 2008 from http://online.wsj.com/article/SB117876493685298103.html?mod=todays_us_marketplace

Sharp, R. (February 16, 2008). Fashion is racist: Insider lifts lid on "ethnic exclusion" Retrieved on March 17, 2008 from http://www.independent.co.uk/news/uk/home-news/fashion-is-racist-insider-lifts-lid-on-ethnic-exclusion-782974.html

Taylor, C., Landreth, S., and Bang, H. (2005). Asian Americans in magazine advertising: Portrayals of the "model minority." *Journal of Macromarketing*, 25(163), 163–174.

Traister, R. (2005). "Real beauty"—or really smart marketing? Retrieved on March 17, 2008 from http://www.dir.salon.com/stpru/mwt/feature/2005/07/22/dove/index1.html

Trebay, G. (October 14, 2007). Ignoring diversity, runways face to white. Retrieved on March 17, 2008 from www.nytimes.com/2007/10/14/fashion/shows/14race.html

Yabroff, J. (January 26, 2008). Rise of the real people. Retrieved on March 17, 2008 from http://www.newsweek.com/id/105585

Chapter 8

Selling: Decisions, Practices, and Professional Ethics

THE OBJECTIVES OF THIS CHAPTER ARE TO:

- Identify a variety of ethical issues surrounding sales transactions

- Recognize key qualities for effective sales

- Explore how stereotyping and discrimination negatively affect a sales transaction

- Recognize the key components of relationship selling

- Explore ways to approach sales transactions to achieve optimal outcome for both the buyer and the seller

Throughout this book, we have discussed ethical issues and doing the "right" thing in business situations. One environment particularly relevant for examining ethics in the fashion industry is that of selling. Obviously selling involves interaction between buyers and sellers, both at wholesale and retail levels, and the way that interaction is executed can be examined from many ethical angles. At the foundation of these issues are the salesperson's traits, such as fairness, honesty, courtesy, trustworthiness, sincerity, and reliability. Consider the following questions surrounding sales transactions:

- Should salespeople be responsible for buying decisions made by uninformed or uneducated consumers?
- Is it the responsibility of salespeople to educate their consumers about products when today's technology (e.g., the Internet) makes it easy to research products?

"Have you noticed ethics creeping into
some of these deals lately?"

FIGURE 8.1

- If salespeople are offered an incentive to sell a particular item, is it okay for them to encourage the purchase of that particular product over another product?
- A salesperson's job is to sell. Why are consumers surprised when salespeople try to sell them something they do not necessarily need?
- Do consumers have the right to expect salespeople to provide them with unbiased information about products?
- Should it be the responsibility of manufacturers to reimburse store buyers for merchandise the buyers selected for stores that fails to sell?

In considering these questions, one begins to appreciate how complex the connection between selling and ethics becomes. In fact, this is definitely an area in the fashion industry where many consumers believe ethical misconduct occurs on a regular basis.

Selling occurs not only between retail sales personnel and their customers but also behind the scenes during all aspects of product development and acquisition (e.g., buyers and wholesalers or manufacturer's representative.) Salespeople at all levels have been historically portrayed in a negative light, from the snake-oil salesman of the Old West to the sleazy used car salesman of today.

ISSUES SURROUNDING THE SALES TRANSACTION

Due to the complex nature of the sales transaction, and the human interaction that occurs between the buyer and the seller, perhaps no facet of business has been studied as much by scholars as the influences on the sales environment. Research has examined virtually every aspect of the sales transaction, and much of this research brings to the forefront ethical considerations. This chapter examines some of those issues and points to the importance of ethics in the sales transaction.

Attitudes Toward Salespeople

In a study done at the University of Mississippi examining consumer attitudes toward retailers, findings suggested that most consumers expect some sort of unethical behavior on the part of their local stores. Actions that consumers expected were very much related to sales and included the expectation that certain chains would pressure consumers to buy higher margin goods in order to be more profitable. Consumers also reported that retailers gave preferential treatment to some customers (e.g., white customers over black customers) and that customers were often charged full price for items that were supposed to be on sale (Hisey, 2002). Similarly, in another study, 39 percent of consumers felt that retail salespeople could not be trusted (Vitell and Muncy, 1994). In fact many consumers are suspicious of salespeople's motives especially if the salesperson is on commission. Thomas DeCarlo (2005) found that the same salesperson's tactics are processed very differently by consumers, depending on the degree of suspicion they project to the salesperson (e.g., is the salesperson just out to make the commission or is that person truly interested in helping me?). These types of perceptions are not uncommon and have led retailers such as Best Buy to stop using commission-based salespeople and instead rely more on a self-serve retail model.

Tara Radin and Carolyn Predmore (2002) examined the role that product-specific sales incentive (PSIs) or "spiffs" play in creating conflict in the sales transaction. PSIs are incentives offered by manufacturers to retail sales personnel to encourage them to sell certain products over those of the competitors. In the fashion and retailing field, PSIs are most common in the cosmetics industry. The researchers argue that although PSIs are good for the retailer because they generate sales, motivate salespeople, and provide rewards, the underlying problem is that customers generally are unaware of the incentives. This leads to a breakdown in salesperson integrity which may negatively affect the sales transaction because the incentives may motivate the salesperson to offer advice, or push a particular product, that he or she otherwise would not. The use of PSIs also raises many other questions, such as: Do consumers have the right to know that the salesperson has been offered an incentive to sell a particular product? What effect do PSIs have on fair competition at the retail level? If retail sales personnel are being rewarded monetarily with PSIs from the manufacturer, does that make it acceptable for the retailer to pay the sales personnel less? Would customers be upset if they knew that PSIs were being offered to retail sales personnel? In answer to the last question, Redin and Predmore (2002) found that knowledge of PSIs had no significant affect on younger customers' reliance on sales personnel opinions. Apparently these customers expected the salesperson to have some type of personal agenda in connection with the sales transaction. Sadly, it may also be that a perception of decline in ethics in America has lowered consumers' expectations concerning sales personnel behavior.

Conflicts for Sales Personnel

While the aforementioned questions indicate an underlying concern for customers, PSIs may also cause conflict for retail sales personnel. In fact, in one survey, some retail sales personnel viewed the incentives as "bribery." Also of concern was misleading customers about their needs in relation to the promoted product (Chonko and Hunt, 1989). On a related note, in a recent study done by *Chain Store Age* (Clark, 2006), participating retailers reported that the most prevalent corporate ethical violations were "dishonesty to vendors/suppliers" and "dishonesty to customers." The same study found that the employees viewed "dishonesty to customers" (37.9 percent) as the "most serious corporate ethical violation." Additionally, employees have reported that the primary conflict in their jobs is to manage the goals of the organization (e.g., sales quotas) with that of the customers' needs (Chonko and Hunt, 1989).

These conflicts can be very stressful, especially considering that studies have found that unethical behavior is positively related to salesperson success (Howe, Hoffman, and Hardigree, 1994), and furthermore, that successful salespeople are reprimanded less often for unethical behavior as compared to less successful salespeople (Belizzi and Hite, 1989). At the retail level, many specialty stores base their promotions on sales quotas so salespeople are under extreme pressure to perform. While some sales personnel thrive in this type of environment, others find such an environment very stressful and taxing.

Age of Salesperson and Customer

Researchers have also examined ethical issues within the sales context while considering the age of the participants. For example, how do retail sales personnel's attitudes toward older consumers affect the interaction? Does the age of the salesperson play a role in consumer perceptions? As the population ages, this becomes an increasingly important question. Julie (Johnson-) Hillery and Jikyeong Kang (1996, 1997, 2003) examined these issues and found that, in fact, both older and younger customers perceived older retail sales personnel to be more knowledgeable than younger retail sales personnel. Furthermore, consumers indicated that older retail sales personnel showed more interest in helping them, were more likely to provide clothing information, and showed more respect for them as customers. In the same studies, older consumers, when asked about service satisfaction, placed the most importance on the factor of service hospitality, which included variables related to interaction during the sales transaction (e.g., retail sales personnel are courteous and appreciate a person's patronage). The ethical issue, in regard to the age of the retail sales personnel and the consumer, becomes that of discrimination and stereotyping from both the consumer and the sales personnel. When prejudices and stereotypes guide the sales interaction, neither the customer nor the retail sales personnel benefits. To demonstrate professional ethics, retail sales personnel should approach each customer in a nondiscriminatory way, providing each customer with courtesy and consideration. If younger retail sales personnel know that consumers may prefer older retail sales personnel, the sales personnel may have to work a little harder to satisfy that customer and dispel misconceptions. Salespeople should also recognize any stereotypes that they have about older consumers and work to put those aside during their sales interactions.

Appearance of Customer Related to Dress

Sales transactions have also been examined by considering the role customer appearance plays. For example, studies have indicated that customers believe service quality depends on how they are dressed (Lee and Johnson, 1997) and that customer appearance was significantly related to the friendliness of retail sales personnel

(Lennon and Kim, 1998). Ann Paulins (2004) investigated the relationship between shoppers' dress and customer service quality offered by retail sales personnel. Her findings suggested that professionally dressed customers consistently received higher levels of customer service than those who were not professionally dressed. In addition, customers who were "dressed down," or had an unkempt appearance, received poorer customer service.

Based on the findings of the previously discussed studies, it is suggested that retail sales personnel training should include adaptive selling techniques based on developing a positive interaction rather than based on stereotypes or preconceived notions about the customer because of their appearance. Arun Sharma and Michael Levy (1995) maintain that salespeople are more successful when they correctly identify the customers' needs and dispositions and then cater each sales interaction to the individual customer. Retailers today need to emphasize the importance of providing consistent customer service regardless of the age, appearance, or dress of customers. This is especially important given the trend today for "dressing down."

RELATIONSHIP SELLING

Regardless of where the selling is occurring in the apparel chain, the job of the salesperson today has shifted from an emphasis on transaction selling (e.g., *get the sale!*) to more relationship selling (e.g., *get the sale but do it while taking care of the customers' needs!*). In other words, it is not enough for a salesperson to simply to sell the customer something; but rather, it is the responsibility of the salesperson to know their customer and to meet the needs of that customer. In order for the latter to occur, salespeople need to understand their customers on a deeper level than required in the past; thus the phrase "relationship selling," which is also referred to as "customer-centered selling." Salespeople today, on average, spend much more time with customers building relationships that must be built primarily on trust, honesty, and reliability. Of course, this takes time. Although more companies are approaching sales from this angle, the struggle many face is that the bottom line remains! What happens when a salesperson spends 6 months building a relationship with a prospective company only to have the company choose to buy someone else's products? Again, this draws attention to the ethical issue and the conflict of salespersons of putting the company's agenda above the customers' needs.

As mentioned previously, perhaps two of the key factors in the salesperson–buyer dyad are trust and credibility. Although it may take months to obtain, effective salespeople know that once trust or credibility is broken, it may never be gained again. John McCarthy (2002) discussed how each of these factors relates to ethical behavior. He stated that trust is earned and comes over time from knowledge that what the salesperson says is true, and that credibility comes from performance and not just talk. Furthermore, trust precludes any form of dishonesty, even small "white lies" that one is tempted to use occasionally to avoid uncomfortable situations. It is always best to own up to your mistakes (e.g., "your shipment is late because I forgot to place the order") rather than blaming the problem on someone else ("your shipment is late because the freight company left your order sitting in the warehouse for a week"). In this case, if the customer finds out the truth, (e.g., you forgot to place the order), they may never trust you as a salesperson again.

Database and Information Collection at Point of Purchase

Relationship selling also extends to the retail store and salesperson in their interactions with consumers. Many efforts are made at the retail level to best understand consumers therefore being able to provide better products and services. Although such information collecting is supposedly a positive for customers, in the form of better service and product offerings, several issues arise that are outlined in Box 8.1.

According to Jenn Abelson (2007), about 75 percent of merchants collect personal information about their consumers every time they make a purchase. In addition, over half share that transaction data with suppliers, manufacturers, and other business partners. Retailers track the data to better understand consumer behavior, and to provide offer incentives and tailored promotions to get the customer to spend more. Through the use of a loyalty card, retailers collect customer data at the point of purchase such as zip codes, phone numbers, names, and sometimes even credit card numbers and checking account information. Although loyalty cards often provide customers with a better price, or a reduced price on selected items, many customers may not realize that every time they use the card, retailers are tracking their consumer activity and are generally storing it in a database to help the company better understand their customers' shopping behaviors. Collecting the data is a priority for many retailers, but protecting the information is sometimes problematic and the information is often the target of thieves.

In 2007, TJX Companies, the parent company of more than 2,500 T.J. Maxx, Marshall's, and other stores, reported that hackers had broken into their computer system which contained millions of customer credit and debit card numbers along with drivers' license numbers. The breach was believed to be started when hackers intercepted wireless transfers at two Marshall's stores in Miami which eventually

Box 8.1

ISSUES TO CONSIDER CONCERNING THE COLLECTION OF CONSUMER INFORMATION AT THE POINT OF PURCHASE

1. Is the information safe and are computer systems secure where the information is kept?

2. Do the retailers need to keep the information, and for how long?

3. How do retailers dispose of the information?

4. Who has access to the data?

5. Should retailers ask for consumers' permission before sharing the information with their suppliers?

6. Do customers have a right to know how the data is being used?

7. Do the benefits to consumers outweigh the risks of data collection?

8. Does collecting the information actually help retailers serve customers better?

led the hackers to break into TJX's central databases. The information stolen, which dated as far back as 2003, was used to make fraudulent purchases all over the world (Abelson, 2007). In August 2007, TJX Companies reported that costs from the breach have reached $256 million dollars which is approximately ten times the $25 million that the company estimated just three months prior. Industry experts believe the costs could wind up being much higher depending on the outcome of class action lawsuits and government fines and sanctions (Kerber, 2007).

Similarly, a hacker gained access to 1.4 million DSW (Designer Shoe Warehouse) customers' credit card and debit card numbers along with 100,000 checking accounts and drivers' license numbers resulting in fraudulent charges occurring on some of the customer accounts. Consequently, after being notified of the breach, DSW customers had to close their accounts incurring out-of-pocket expenses for items such as having to have new checks printed. DSW, which is a major national shoe retailer, collected the consumer personal information at the point of purchase including their name, credit card number, expiration date, and other "magnetic stripe" data. In investigating the case, the Federal Trade Commission (FTC) held DSW liable for having insufficient security measures in place to protect the information but found no evidence that DSW misrepresented itself about its security practices. They also required DSW to establish and maintain a comprehensive security program to ensure the safety of consumer data. (Sotto, Finn and Swindle, 2005). As a result of the computer breaches at DSW and TJX Companies, consumer advocates are calling for better protection of such data (Abelson, 2007).

Disposing of Stored Customer Data

The two aforementioned cases involved issues of the security of storing customer data, however another issue is that of how to properly dispose of the data. In April 2007, Texas Attorney General Greg Abbott filed a suit against CVS Pharmacy for failing to protect sensitive customer data. According to the suit, CVS in Liberty, Texas, exposed hundreds of its customers to identity theft because they had disposed of bulk customer records by tossing them in a dumpster behind the store. Contained in the records were customer's names, addresses, dates of birth, and prescription information. Additionally, credit and debit card numbers, along with expiration dates were also found. The lawsuit filed charges CVS with violating Chapter 35 of the Business and Commerce Code, which is a law passed in 2005 requiring businesses to protect sensitive customer data and provides for a fine up to $500 for each compromised record (Staff, 2007).

Although the 2005 law required retailers to protect "sensitive" customer data, other databases being designed by retailers do not fall under such regulations leaving critics to call for action. For example, Limited Brands, Inc., which at the time owned Express stores began using a database to monitor, and sometimes deny, customer returns. In essence the database tracks customer returns and creates a so-called "blacklist" of customers with excessive returns (Cha, 2004; Whitaker, 2004). The National Retail Federation (NRF), estimates that retailers lose an estimated $16 billion annually to fraud on returns, and that the databases are simply a way to keep returns in check. With increasingly sophisticated technology, and the Internet, scammers are able to launder money whereby people steal store merchandise, return it for credit at stores, and then sell the slips on online auction sites at a discount (Cha, 2004). However, the NRF also agreed that the vast majority of consumers making returns do so legitimately (Whitaker, 2004).

Regardless of what information retailers are collecting, consumers should take every precaution to protect themselves against identity theft. This involves knowing about consumer rights and asking specific questions about how the information is being used and secured. Companies should make this information readily available to consumers but unfortunately that is not always the case. For example, retailers such as TJX, Macy's, and Circuit City use a company called Coremetrics to investigate consumer Web site activity—specifically when customers abandon a shopping cart. At the retailer's request, Coremetrics can retrieve personal data such as the customers' e-mail address. Unless customers click through several pages of privacy policies, and read the fine print, they would not know that the information is being collected (Abelson, 2007). On the other hand, companies like Von Maur make their privacy policy readily available on their Web site (see *http://www.vonmaur.com*) to consumers giving them the option as to whether they want Von Maur to collect, or share, their personal data.

CODE OF ETHICS FOR SELLING

Just as many retailers and apparel product companies have developed codes of ethics outlining proper employee behavior, so too has the Direct Selling Association (DSA). The DSA is the national trade association for leading firms that manufacture and distribute foods and services sold directly to consumers. Member companies include Avon Products, Inc., Jafra Cosmetics International, Inc., Mary Kay, Inc., and Jockey Person to Person. The DSA Code of Ethics, which is available in its entirety on the organization's Web site (*see http://www.dsa.org*), addresses both the consumer and the seller and ensures that member companies make no statements that might mislead consumers or other salespeople. It is enforced by an independent administrator who is not affiliated with any member companies and has the power to resolve complaints and decide on solutions. Specifically, it states:

> No member company of the Association shall engage in any deceptive, unlawful or unethical consumer or recruiting practice. Member companies shall ensure that no statements, promises or testimonials are made which are likely to mislead consumers or prospective salespeople (http://www.dsa.org/ethics/code/ #deceptive).

Codes such as the one adopted by the DSA works to increase members' credibility, and to protect customers. The code also addresses items such as timely delivery, warranties and guarantees, terms of sales, and identification and privacy.

Two universal warranties that apply to the selling arena are the *warranty of fitness* and the *warranty of merchantability*. A warranty of fitness is an implied warranty that results through interactions with a salesperson who represents the fitness of a given product for a particular purpose. For example, if you tell a salesperson that you wish to purchase a garment that can be laundered at home and the salesperson responds to your request by offering a particular outfit, there is an implied warranty that you will be able to launder that garment, successfully, at your home. Salespeople are obligated, under the warranty of fitness, to represent the goods they sell as fit for use in the manner that they state. It is recognized that consumers rely on salesperson expertise, and salespeople have a responsibility to provide accurate information. A warranty of merchantability is also an implied warranty that guarantees a product will perform in the manner in which it is supposed to. Although fashion products are less scrutinized by consumers in the area of warranties than say automobiles or electronic equipment, it is nevertheless relevant for salespeople in the fashion business to be aware that the products they sell must work for consumers as they are intended by manufacturers, and that their comments and promises to customers about how the merchandise will perform are binding.

This chapter is just a sampling of the many ethical issues that surround the sales interaction, whether it is between retail sales personnel and their consumers, or between manufacturers and retail buyers. Regardless of the parties involved, it is important to make smart decisions in the face of the conflicts or dilemmas that may arise. As mentioned previously, effective and successful salespeople need to be honest, credible, and trustworthy. Again, there is no one ideal sales position because each person will bring his or her own ethical foundation and personality to the sales interaction. The challenge is to find your match so that you can always display belief in the product you are selling and the company you are representing.

QUESTIONS FOR DISCUSSION

1. Review the questions posed at the beginning of this chapter and discuss your thoughts concerning them.

2. What is your opinion of PSI's? Should the consumer be told if PSI's are being offered to a store's sales personnel?

3. If you were the owner of a clothing store, would you incorporate a commissioned-based sales policy? Why or why not?

4. Think about a time when you had a positive encounter with a retail salesperson. What factors contributed to the favorable outcome?

5. Think about a time when you had a negative encounter with a retail salesperson. What factors contributed to the negative outcome?

6. Think about a time when you had a positive encounter with a retail customer. What factors contributed to the favorable outcome?

7. Think about a time when you had a negative encounter with a retail customer. What factors contributed to the negative outcome?

8. Discuss a time when you think appearance played a role in a sales encounter you had.

9. Do you think the advantages of data collection at the point of purchase outweigh the potential risks to customers? Discuss your answer.

10. What is your personal code of selling ethics?

REFERENCES AND SUGGESTED READING

Abelson, J. (February 3, 2007). Data thieves target retailers. *The Boston Globe*. Retrieved on August 7, 2007 from http://www.boston.com/business/articles/2007/02/03/data_thieves_target_retailers

Alonzo, V. (1999). Death of a salesman. *Incentive*, 173(10), 42–48.

Belizzi, J. and Hite, R. (1989). Supervising unethical salesforce behavior. *Journal of Marketing*, 53(April), 36–47.

Cha, A. (November 7, 2004). Retailers turning to databases to rein in customer returns. *San Francisco Chronicle*, p. A8.

Chonko, L. and Hunt, S. (1989). Ethics and marketing management: An empirical examination. *Journal of Business Research*, 13(August), 339–359.

Clark, K. (June 2006). Who are you listening to? Exclusive survey of corporate ethics. *Chain Store Age Executive*, 33–35.

DeCarlo, T. (2005). The effects of sales message and suspicion of ulterior motives on salesperson evaluation. *Journal of Consumer Psychology*, 15(3), 238-249.

Dubinsky, A, Nataraajan, R., and Huang, W. (2004). The influence of moral philosophy on retail salespeople's ethical perceptions. *Journal of Consumer Affairs*, 38(2), 297–319.

Hillery, J. and Kang, J. (2003). Understanding elderly consumers: Retail sales encounters through the utilization of focus group interviews and qualitative software. In Stewart, B. Purcell, R and Lovingood, R. (Eds.), *Research applications in family and consumer sciences*. Washington, D.C.: American Association of Family and Consumer Sciences.

Hisey, P. (May 2002). Retail: The state of ethics. *Retail Merchandiser*, 42(5), 17–18.

Howe,V. ,Hoffman, K. and Hardigree, D. (1994). The relationship between ethical and customer-oriented service provider behaviors. *Journal of Business Ethics*, 13, 497–506.

Johnson-Hillery, J. and Kang, J. (Fall/Winter, 1996). Elderly consumers and retail sales personnel: An examination of attitudes and service satisfaction. *Journal of Shopping Center Research*, 3(2), 7–22.

Johnson-Hillery, J. and Kang, J. (1997). The difference between elderly consumers' satisfaction levels and retail sales personnel's perceptions. *International Journal of Retail and Distribution Management*, 25(4/5), 126–138.

Kerber, R. (August 15, 2007). Cost of data breach at TJX soars to $256m: Suits, computer fix add to expenses. *The Boston Globe*. Retrieved on August 7, 2007 from http://www.boston.com/business/globe/articles/2007/08/15/cost_of_data_breach_at_tjx_soars_to_256m/

Lee, M. and Johnson, K. (1997). Customer expectations for service at apparel retail outlets. *Journal of Family and Consumer Sciences*, 89(4), 26–30.

Lennon, S. and Kim, M. (1998). The effect of customer's dress on salesperson's service at apparel retail outlets. *Proceedings of the International Textiles and Apparel Association*, 59.

Paulins, V. A. (2004). An analysis of customer service quality to college students as influenced by customer appearance through dress during the in-store shopping process. *Journal of Retailing and Consumer Services*, 12(5), 345–355.

Radin, T. and Predmore, C. (2002). The myth of the salesperson: Intended and unintended consequences of product-specific sales incentives, *Journal of Business Ethics*, 36, 79–92.

Sharma, A. and Levy, M. (1995). Categorization of customers by retail salespeople. *Journal of Retailing*, 71(1), 71–81.

Sotto, L., Finn, E. and Swindle, O. (December 2005). Retailer liable for failing to protect customer data. *Hunton & Williams Client Alert*. Retrieved on August 7, 2007 from http://www.hunton.com/files/tbl_s10News/FileUpload44/12641/FTC_DSW_ClientAlert_12.05.pdf

Staff (April 17, 2007). Attorney General Abbott continues aggressively enforcing identity theft prevention law: CVS Pharmacy cited for exposing hundreds of customer records. Retrieved on August 7, 2007 from http://www.oag.state.tx.us/oagnews/release.php?id=1976

Vitell, S. and Muncy, J. (1992). Consumer ethics: An empirical investigation of factors influencing ethical judgments of the final consumer. *Journal of Business Ethics*, 11, 585–597.

Whitaker, B. (December 28, 2004). Return that ill-fitting gift? Maybe not. *The New York Times*. Retrieved on August 7, 2007 from http://www.nytimes.com/2004/12/28/business/28returns.htm

Chapter 9

Ethical Consumer Decisions

THE OBJECTIVES OF THIS CHAPTER ARE TO:

- Develop an understanding of the role consumers play in decisions made by companies

- Explore various perspectives that customers consider in their decision-making processes

- Identify ways that consumers exhibit positive ethical behavior in their acquisition of goods and services

- Gain an awareness of the range of ways consumers may exhibit unethical behavior

- Consider actions that businesses might implement in response to both ethical and unethical consumer behaviors

Most of this book has focused on the responsibilities of professionals within the apparel product development and retailing industries and their decisions that carry ethical implications. Customers, however, exert a tremendous force shaping many of the policies and decisions generated by retailers and manufacturers. The behaviors and decisions of consumers often determine company policies because of the close relationship between retail sales and the bottom line. Obviously, shoplifting and abuses of merchandise return privileges adversely affect company fiscal performance. Recent estimates suggest that shoplifting costs American consumers $16 billion each year. Companies set policies that affect dressing room use, merchandise returns, and merchandise accessibility on the sales floor generally with the purpose of deterring consumer abuses and theft; however, these policies may

FIGURE 9.1

also affect customer comfort while shopping at a retailer. Consumer decisions to support (or boycott) certain products, brands, or retailers also affect sales volume, and therefore can influence businesses to be lenient in terms of customer service (i.e., adopting "the customer is always right" philosophy) in an effort to remain competitive.

Some customer activities are clearly unethical and other behaviors warrant exploration in terms of their degree of ethicalness. But many consumers' behaviors are driven by a desire to exercise ethics in their choices. The responses of retailers and manufactures to ethical and unethical behaviors of customers have direct implications for the reputations of their companies, the perceptions that customers have of the companies and, in particular, the "customer-friendly" environments that companies develop.

Many consumers are conflicted by ethical marketplace situations. Randy Cohen, "The Ethicist" for the *New York Times Magazine*, notes in his book *The Good, The Bad & The Difference*, that his chapter on commercial life is one of the longest, as commerce is one of the most common human interactions. Cohen observes that customers want to pay the lowest possible price, sellers want to be paid the highest, and this dynamic creates numerous opportunities for deception. Based on readers' questions appearing in Cohen's column, the book demonstrates that consumers are interested in determining the ethical choice.

Clive Barnett, Philip Cafaro, and Terry Newholm make the distinction between ethical consumption and the ethics of consumption in their book, *The Ethical Consumer.* Consumers who choose to exercise ethical consumption bring a Virtue Approach to their decision making. Buying Fair Trade products, supporting companies that are socially responsible, and seeking products that are sustainable or have been manufactured in environmentally friendly ways are examples of ethical consumption. Ethical consumption decisions are broadly associated with people's general ethical behaviors—such as not stealing and reporting receipt of too much change after a purchase. These behaviors reflect the values and morals of consumers and are rooted in Principled and Fairness Approaches to ethics. Obviously, consumers determine the level of success of any manufacturer or retailer. The court of public opinion can sway consumer behaviors drastically—causing both windfalls and disasters. The role of ethics should not be underestimated, both in terms of the cost of misbehavior and the value of consumers making conscientious decisions.

THE CONSCIENTIOUS CONSUMER

The underlying function in a free economy is the notion of consumer sovereignty—the concept that the consumer is all-powerful. A supplier's success in the economy depends on whether consumers will choose that company's goods over a competitor's. When consumers are sovereign, their decisions about buying products that are manufactured abroad, in nonunion settings or by children, determine whether those business practices can be supported. Likewise, consumers vote with their pocketbooks to determine whether products that harm the environment, such as some pesticides and chemical waste products, can sustain their manufacturers. As discussed in Chapter 5, there are enough different consumer perspectives to support a variety of beliefs, and therefore manufacturing processes and products. Furthermore, consumer sovereignty in a free economy assumes that consumers have adequate knowledge to make rational, deliberate decisions. Consumers often make decisions primarily based on cost and perceived quality rather than on the actual value that will be gained as an outcome of the purchase. Moreover, many of today's consumers are likely to feel so removed from the manufacturing and production processes that those types of considerations do not significantly influence their shopping decisions. In general, consumers give little thought to the conditions in which the products have been made, or even to the materials that compose the products. They may or may not realize that their purchases support behaviors by companies that are counter to their ethical beliefs. And many consumers are constrained by price—they simply cannot afford, nor are willing to pay for, a more expensive product (e.g., an item manufactured in a developing country in a facility certified to be fully compliant with international fair labor standards), even if they would prefer it.

James Roberts (1996) noted that the increased public interest in environmental and social issues is a likely result of media coverage of environmental disasters and social problems. He theorized that this interest influences consumer decision making. Despite consumers considering themselves recyclers and environmentalists, Roberts indicated that behaviors do not always reflect these attitudes because green products are expensive; price, quality, and convenience are most important in consumer decision making; consumers are confused about green products; and businesses hesitate to offer green products because of the repercussions associated with scrutiny from environmental organizations and the potential of making costly deceptive claims. Nevertheless, Roberts' survey revealed that a target market of socially responsible consumers of significant size exists, just as there is also a substantial segment of consumers who have little or no concern for social or environmental issues. Roberts cautions apparel producers and retailers, though, that while consumers may express interest in social responsibility, their behaviors may not necessarily reflect their attitudes.

Obviously, the law of supply and demand is the major driver of the marketplace; this concept can also be applied to ethical situations in the apparel product development and retailing industries. Consumers who place a high value on conscientiously produced apparel and home furnishings create a certain level of demand for those goods. If a sufficient number of consumers collectively demand such products, that demand creates a market that gives manufacturers and retailers the incentive to produce an appropriate level of supply. The key is that the price level is set relative to the level of demand corresponding to the supply. If the price cannot support continued business for suppliers (through markup that covers expenses of doing business), the producers cannot continue. When hundreds of customers in New York and Los Angeles turned out to purchase designer Anya Hindmarch's canvas bags in 2007, intended as a reusable substitute for plastic shopping bags while simultaneously making a fashion and environmental statement by declaring "I'm not a plastic bag" (Brown, 2007), the economic impact of conscientious consumerism was clearly demonstrated. In fact, the $15 bag was quickly sold in secondary markets for hundreds of dollars. See Figure 9.2 for an example of this bag.

Individual consumers and consumer activist groups go to significant effort to enhance consumer knowledge, and often to sway attitudes and influence consumer decisions with pleas for ethical behavior. Some efforts are small-scale, such as campaigns that encourage support of local economies, and others are huge, complexly structured campaigns on national or global levels. In Athens, Ohio, the chamber of commerce promotes a "Shop Athens First" campaign during the holidays to encourage consumers to keep money in the local economy. The goal of the campaign is to boost the local economy so that sales and tax dollars will remain available to support local businesses and public needs. Buy American and Buy Union campaigns build on consumer patriotism in an attempt to keep the United States economy and manufacturing industries vibrant and competitive. As Wal-Mart has

FIGURE 9.2   Designer Anya Hindmarch's very popular "I'm not a plastic bag" design

grown from a fledgling discount retailer to the largest company in the world, orga-nizations that both support the business (Working Families for Wal-Mart) and oppose it (Wal-MartWatch) have emerged and become highly visible in the media. A desire to influence consumer decisions, with the underlying message to consumers to do the right thing, is the common thread of both these campaigns.

In addition to lobbying for or against retailers and retail venues, consumers have also targeted specific products and manufacturing techniques for their ethical positions. As mentioned in Chapter 2, People for the Ethical Treatment of Animals (PETA) is a high-profile animal rights organization; its mission state-ment declares that "animals are not ours to eat, wear, experiment on, or use for entertainment." Thus, PETA's work potentially affects myriad retailers and manu-facturers. In 2005, PETA effectively persuaded J.Crew to stop selling apparel with fur components by waging a public campaign aimed at the retailer's customers; the activists highlighted the aspect of torture in fur production. Similarly, Wet Seal agreed to eliminate fur products from its merchandise assortment after a PETA campaign in 2006.

How Are Consumers Influenced?

Age, culture, and gender are demographic factors that tend to influence consumers' purchasing behaviors, and may affect ethical behavior (Hoffman, 1998). David Strutton, Lou Pelton, and O. C. Ferrell (1997) found that younger consumers (those born between 1961 and 1981) in the United States are more likely to rationalize unethical consumer behavior than their older "baby boomer" counterparts. Dong Shen and Marsha Dickson (1991) explored the relationship between consumers' culture and ethics and found that consumers identifying with American culture are more accepting of unethical clothing consumption behaviors than consumers who identified with Chinese culture. James Hoffman (1998) compared responses of men and women to ethical vignettes and found that the specific ethical issue determines whether responses from men and women will differ. In his research, Hoffman found that women respond more ethically than men in some, but not all, ethical situa-tions. Karen Callen and Shiretta Owenbey (2003) conducted research that yielded similar outcomes. They found that, in a sample of university students, women are less accepting of unethical consumer behavior than men. In addition, their research supported the notion that people who consistently follow their primary faith are less accepting of unethical consumer behavior than those who do not.

According to BMRB/Mintel International Group Ltd., a consumer media and marketing research company, only 7 percent of consumers claim that they "always

Box 9.1

WORDS CAN NEVER HURT? TEENS TICKED OFF OVER TEES

Fourteen-year-old Liz Clark of Fox Chapel, Pennsylvania, says that T-shirts sold by Abercrombie & Fitch are demeaning and offensive to girls. That's why she and other members of the Allegheny County Girls as Grantmakers group, which helps raise money for girls' causes, urged their friends and fellow students not to buy the shirts.

The T-shirts from the popular retailer have been the subject of boycotts by female students (who call them "girlcotts") in Illinois, Connecticut, and Pennsylvania. The students don't like the messages emblazoned across the front of the shirts. Some of the more tame examples of the printed text are "Blondes Are Adored, Brunettes Are Ignored" and "I Make You Look Fat."

Abercrombie & Fitch has responded to the students by pulling two of the shirts deemed most derogatory from some store shelves. The store's press release stated, "We recognize that the shirts in question, while meant to be humorous, might be troubling to some."

The controversial shirts are called "attitude tees," and Abercrombie & Fitch says it sells them because people buy them. In a statement, the company wrote, "These T-shirts have been very popular among young women to whom they are marketed." There are similar shirts for boys that have not been protested.

Abercrombie's customers are teenagers and college students, and are buying the shirts and their messages because they think they're humorous. "It's not like we wear these shirts to be serious," Alle Torbick told *The Advocate*. "We wear the shirts for fun and to laugh at them."

In the end, some say the controversy might just be free advertising that will help the stores sell more clothing. Abercrombie & Fitch has reported profit increases compared with the same time last year. Bronwyn Lance Chester of *The Virginian-Pilot* writes, "Listen up, girls: While well-intentioned, your boycott only made Abercrombie happy."

or nearly always buy or use ethical products and services" in a report about attitudes toward ethical foods (Page and Fearn, 2005). Research has not produced definitive information regarding consumers' responses to ethical and unethical companies nor the extent to which customers seek to make ethical consumer decisions. Some research indicates that consumers are likely to support ethical companies but tend not to boycott unethical ones (Simon, 1995); other studies reveal a propensity for consumers to punish unethical behavior but not necessarily reward ethical behavior (Folkes and Kamins, 1999; Spranca et al., 1991; Reeder and Brewer, 1979). It may be that attitudes toward ethical behavior are incongruent with behaviors when making purchasing selections. Emma Boulstridge and Marylyn Carrigan (2000) found that the most important criteria considered when buying products were price, value, quality, and brand familiarity. They observed that consumers select products primarily for personal, rather than societal, reasons. Even when consumers were aware of unethical corporate activity, some of them still purchased the offending company's products, particularly when they liked and regularly used those products. Graham Page and Helen Fearn (2005) identified two elements of corporate reputation that seem most important to consumers as they make purchasing decisions: (1) perception of fairness toward consumers and (2) perception of corporate success and leadership. Although consumers indicate that they care about and want to patronize companies with good business practices, Page and Fearn found that more personally relevant factors such as cost and brand appeal are more important.

Carrigan and Ahmad Attalla (2001) speculated that with respect to ethics, consumers' statements and behavior might be inconsistent, or that consumers lack the knowledge and awareness they need to make ethical judgments. The researchers used focus group discussions to explore whether "good" companies attract consumers and whether unethical companies inspire product boycotts. The focus group participants did not indicate that the company's ethical records affected their purchase intentions. The consumers they interviewed indicated an unwillingness to boycott companies they know pay low wages to laborers; similarly, those consumers were not willing to pay higher prices for goods so that they could be produced in more socially responsible ways. Carrigan and Attalla concluded that ethical companies may be admired by consumers, but—consistent with other research—consumer decisions tend not to be influenced by the level of social responsibility of companies, particularly for fashion merchandise with highly visible brand images.

Only a minority of consumers seem to combine ethical awareness with ethical intentions. A majority of consumers are relatively uninformed about companies'

Box 9.2

CUSTOMER PURCHASE DECISIONS

When asked outright whether a company's record on the environment or social responsibility influence their purchase decision, almost all respondents said that it had no influence on their decision, and that they did not care how well companies behave. One did say that it might affect about "5 percent" of their purchase decisions. Respondents did seem to consider the media a powerful information source on ethical issues, and believed that if a great deal of publicity were given to a company behaving badly then this would affect their purchase intentions. However, when it was pointed out that Nike, The Gap Inc., and McDonald's had all been very publicly exposed for poor ethics, the respondents acknowledged that in terms of these products it had made no difference to their purchase behavior:

"I like Gap clothing, McDonald's tastes good, and Nike looks and feels right."

Finally, most participants were keen to point out that if they could financially afford to discriminate against those unethical companies, then they would pay the premium for any good quality products that were produced through a more responsible approach.

SOURCE: Carrigan, M. and Attalla, A. (2001). The myth of the ethical consumer—do ethics matter in purchase behaviour? *Journal of Consumer Marketing, 18*(7), pp. 560–577, 569–580. All rights reserved. Reproduced with permission of Emerald Group Publishing Limited.

ethical behaviors and their levels of corporate social responsibility and seem to have little interest in increasing their awareness of these issues. However, a plethora of information (most in the form of personal postings and pleas) is available on the World Wide Web using the search term "ethical consumption." As media attention on the topics of Fair Trade and ethical consumerism increases, the responses of the apparel product development and retailing industries will be of keen interest.

Is the Customer Always Right?

How widespread is customer misconduct? To what extent does unethical customer behavior influence retailing and manufacturing policy? How does customer dishonesty affect the bottom line of retailers and manufacturers? Why do customers engage in unethical behavior? These topics are explored as we address the question, "Is the customer always right?"

Particularly in the retail sector, much customer misbehavior is tolerated; it is considered a cost of doing business. The convenience of shopping without barriers, such as access to dressing rooms and companies' liberal return policies, often outweighs the consequences of greater customer scrutiny. But in an increasingly competitive environment where bottom lines are of growing concern, many retailers have started to become less tolerant of some specific consumer misbehaviors. Kelly Tian and Bill Keep reported on consumer misbehaviors in their book *Customer Fraud and Business Responses: Let the Marketer Beware*, using results of their extensive study of more than 250 middle- and upper-class Americans. The authors define customer fraud as "an act or course of deception that is practiced by individuals against retailers or manufacturers with a view toward gaining an advantage in the exchange that would not be available without covertly breaking the rules or norms of customers' exchange behavior established by marketers" (p. 24). They identified seven specific types of fraudulent acts that consumers reported committing: product acquisition, product return, services acquisition, use of sales promotions, dealing with marketers' negotiators, fraud with employee accomplices, and capitalizing on marketers' pricing, collection, and distribution errors. These are described in greater detail in Box 9.3.

Some types of customer misconduct—such as shoplifting—are clearly unethical and in fact illegal. Other customer behaviors have ethical implications that are more a matter of personal values and perspective. Some examples include customer reactions to and behaviors related to return policies; consumption of counterfeit goods and black market purchases; misuse of personal discounts; and electronic file sharing. To what extent should retailers and manufacturers discourage and prevent customer misbehavior? What are your views on the ethical issues of customer behavior? How will you represent your company in response to these issues? Although you may not have clear-cut answers to these questions presently, as a professional, you will be expected to have a certain level of awareness about these matters.

EMPLOYEE RESPONSIBILITIES

Retail store employees need to be aware of the ethical aspects of customer behavior in an effort to represent the best interests of their employers. Consider this situation experienced by a sales associate:

> I ran into one problem with a specific customer that I will never forget. A family friend named June, who happens to be a very prominent woman in

Box 9.3

SEVEN TYPES OF CUSTOMER FRAUD

Product Acquisition Fraud

- Shoplifting
- Covertly Rebundling Packaged Merchandise
- Covertly Manipulating "Set" Price Information of Merchandise

Product Return Fraud

- Returning Store Merchandise to Retail Stores under False Pretenses
- Returning Merchandise to Manufacturers under False Pretenses

Services Acquisition Fraud

- Covertly Violating Norms or Rules of Service Contracts or Memberships
- Covertly Violating Norms or Rules Established for Noncontractual Service Transactions

Fraud in the Use of Sales Promotions

- Misusing Coupon and Rebate Offers
- Misusing Discount Offers
- Taking "Unintended" Advantages of Promotional Gift Offers

Fraud in Dealing with Marketers' Negotiators

- Deceiving Sales Negotiators
- Deceiving Insurance Claims Negotiators

Fraud with Employee Accomplices

- Returning Merchandise Purchased by an Employee with Discount for the Full Retail Price
- Obtaining "Free" or Discounted Goods from Employees

Box 9.3 continued from page 221
SEVEN TYPES OF CUSTOMER FRAUD

Capitalizing on Marketers' Pricing, Collection, and Distribution Errors

- Paying the Labeled Price on Merchandise that Obviously Possesses an Erroneous Price Tag
- Failing to Correct Employees' Billing or Change-Making Mistakes
- Accepting and Using Incorrectly Delivered Products without Payment to the Marketer

SOURCE: Tian, K. and Bill Keep, B. *Customer fraud and business responses: Let the marketer beware*, Quorum Books, 2002, 8–9. All rights reserved. Reproduction with permission of Greenwood Publishing Group, Inc., Westport, CT.

my hometown, stopped in the store. June sought me out to handle a return, presumably because she knew me. She insisted that I help her, even when other employees offered, and I was flattered that she sought my assistance while I was new to my job. June wanted to return two 100 percent cashmere sweaters that, as the receipt indicated, had been sent to her house from another store. Because the sweaters were sent directly from a store, there were no labels that would have been put on merchandise at the point of checkout so I overrode the computer request for information from these labels. I didn't know that I was supposed to obtain a manager's approval to do this.

June got over $100 in store credit as a result of this return. June wanted the credit put on her charge card, so at that point she went upstairs to customer service to see if the store credit could be applied to her store charge card and I went to a neighboring department to see what I should do with the sweaters because our store no longer carried that merchandise. While I was asking my fellow employee what I should do with the sweaters it became obvious to me that the sweaters were not 100 percent cashmere like the tags on the sweaters said. Upon noticing the fact that I was not dealing with cashmere, two of my fellow employees and I began to analyze the sweaters and we then realized the original labels and tags in both sweaters had been removed and new, false labels were hand sewn into those sweaters. I quickly realized that I had just taken back two sweaters that were never sold by our store. I then called the store manager and when she came downstairs I explained to her what just happened. Further detective work revealed that June had two sweaters sent to her in the mail from our store nine years ago. She apparently took the tags out of those two sweaters and hand sewed the labels into two different sweaters and had me return them. Now that it is all over and I look back on it I realize something was very wrong and I knew it at the moment, but I never thought a friend of my family would do something like that to me.

As a retail employee, what would you have done in a situation like the one described? Take a moment to carefully think about how this could have happened: What store policies were in place that enabled—or could have prevented—this type of behavior?

CONSUMER MISBEHAVIORS

Shoplifting accounts for the loss of more than $33 billion per year, according to the 2002 National Retail Security Survey. The average retail store loses 1.70 percent of its gross sales to shoplifting. Internal theft, when employees steal, accounts for some of this loss. Other activities, such as merchandise returns and damages, also have a negative impact on the bottom lines of companies.

Shoplifting and Other Theft Activities

Shoplifting is simply the act of a customer removing merchandise from a store without paying for it. The "grab and run" method of shoplifting, while prevalent, is losing favor to more sophisticated and difficult-to-catch methods of theft. Shoplifting now takes on many forms, some of which are extremely complex and connected to organized crime. In August 2007, *Women's Wear Daily* devoted a cover story to the problem of shoplifting gangs and organized in-store theft. The article (Clark, 2007) quoted Joseph LaRocca of the National Retail Federation, who indicated that there is great incentive for thieves to steal, with stolen merchandise selling for "30 cents on the dollar on the street, 70 cents on the dollar if they're sold online or, for the more enterprising, 100 percent plus tax if they're returned to the store" (p. 11). Not only do the unethical shoppers cause financial woes for retailers, they also introduce price increases for all consumers.

Interestingly, many non-shoplifting customers do not actively engage themselves in deterring theft when it occurs in their presence. Kitty Dickerson (1979) reported a study by Leonard Prestwich (1978) where 70 percent of respondents said they would report shoplifting if they observed it. Dickerson compared this statistic with a reported study by Gelfand et al. (1973) that yielded only 28 percent of shoppers actually reporting shoplifting behavior when directly exposed to it. Without the vigilance of ethical shoppers to improve shoplifting deterrence, retailers are challenged to empower their employees to observe and reduce shoplifting. When also considering the estimate that employee theft accounts for almost 45 percent of inventory shrinkage (2000 National Retail Security Survey), shoplifting can be a major impediment to retailer success.

Dressing rooms have long been an "area of opportunity" for thieves in retail stores. When dressing rooms are not carefully monitored, customers may engage in shoplifting because of the privacy afforded by dressing rooms. Thieves may stuff merchandise into bags or pockets, or may simply wear the merchandise out of the dressing room under the clothes they wore in. Shoplifters have developed ingenious ways to hide merchandise on their bodies, then walk right out of the store. Thieves often wear specially designed clothing that accommodates the merchandise being lifted and use bags lined with metal to circumvent security sensors.

A newer development is the practice of trolling parking lots for discarded receipts. Thieves take these receipts into the stores, shop for the merchandise listed on the receipt, and then return the merchandise for a cash refund.

As previously mentioned, shoplifting has also become an activity of organized crime. Online and street vending opportunities make for lucrative markets where stolen merchandise is sold to willing customers who purchase the items at bargain prices. The Federal Bureau of Investigation (FBI) has targeted organized shoplifting as part of its focus on organized crime, and has partnered with retail trade groups and retailers to break up these activities (Clark, 2007). For an insightful, yet disturbing, look into the world of a shoplifting ring, the novel *The Booster* by Jennifer Solow is a recommended read.

Merchandise Returns

Bill Angrick, CEO of online wholesale marketplace Liquidity Services, reported in an interview by Len Lewis in *Stores* (June 2007) that 5 percent of all brick-and-mortar retail purchases are returned and that returns for online retailers are double that amount. According to Angrick, fraudulent returns cost retailers $100 billion per year. David Speights and Mark Hilinski of The Return Exchange (now The Retail Equation, see http://www.returnexchange.com) reported in 2005 that approximately 9 percent of all returns in the United States are fraudulent. Return fraud is emerging as a significant problem for retailers, to the extent that many

Box 9.4

"SWEATERS BORROWED, USED, RETURNED"

My sister was going to buy some colorful sweaters to use in a family picture and then return them for a refund. When I chided her on this, she said it was the same as when I went to Barnes & Noble and looked up European restaurant numbers in the *Michelin Guide* without buying the book. What do you think?

—*M.L., Vermont*

Here's one way to sort it out: Ask a clerk's permission, or at least imagine asking a clerk (who could be incredibly charming and attractive; after all, it's your imagination). I suspect that the B&N clerk would let you look up a couple of numbers, but I'd be astonished if the clerk at the clothing store would let you borrow a wardrobe. There is not an absolute distinction between these two acts, but there is an absolute door to the store, and when merchandise passes through it, things change. At least your sister didn't plan to photograph a family dinner; it's so hard to return even a slightly used pot roast.

SOURCE: From *The Good, The Bad, and the Difference* by Randy Cohen, copyright © 2002 by Randy Cohen. Reprinted with permission of Doubleday, a division of Random House, Inc.

retailers have developed return policies that no longer reflect a perspective of "The customer is always right." Unethical consumers have developed a multitude of ways to defraud the return process.

"FREE-RENT" MERCHANDISE.   Think about the following questions: Have you ever been tempted to "rent" items to save yourself a big-ticket purchase? For example, have you ever bought and worn an expensive outfit to a once-in-a-lifetime event, then returned the garment to the store for a full refund? What about "temporarily" purchasing a big screen TV for a Super Bowl party? Many consumers who would not consider actually shoplifting decide to return merchandise that cannot be resold. Is this activity unethical? Does it harm the retailer or other consumers? Is it unethical to return virtually new or even gently worn merchandise to a store?

GIFTS WITH PURCHASE.   Retailers offer gifts with purchase as incentives and rewards for customers to buy promotional merchandise. An added advantage for

BOX 9.5
"NINE SIMPLE THINGS TO CONTROL THEFT"

1. Greet customers as they enter and as they leave the store. Be sure to look customers directly in the eye.

2. Install cameras. Even if you don't record anything, a camera can be a good deterrent.

3. Stay in touch with local police and let them know that you will prosecute all shoplifters.

4. Review film and tape after someone suspicious leaves the store to identify shoplifters.

5. Ban a known shoplifter from your store.

6. Talk with your staff frequently about shoplifting and how to handle it.

7. Check bags and backpacks at the door.

8. If your state allows civil demand or civil recovery, set up a system to fine shoplifters.

9. If you notice a change in shoplifting patterns, contact retailers in your area.

SOURCE: Rosen, J. (May 24, 2004). Fighting back against theft. *Publishers Weekly*, 28–29. Reproduced with permission from *Publishers Weekly*.

retailers is the increased likelihood that shoppers will buy additional items once they have reached the dollar amount needed for the gift with purchase. Retailers are increasing their efforts to prevent abuses by customers related to gifts with purchase, some of which occur in the following manner. When a customer spends a certain amount on regular merchandise, she or he receives a gift set. The gift is scanned into the register with the purchase to document that the customer has received it. The fraud occurs when customers purchase the amount of merchandise required to secure the free gift, then return the purchase for a refund but still keep the free gift. Is this ethical? Is this stealing? What would you do if you were the retailer?

Price Tag Switching

Price tag switching has become a prevalent method of stealing that seems to be justified by the fact that some money (albeit not the full ticket price) is paid for the merchandise.

The following actions taken by apparel product developers and retailers may counterbalance unethical consumer behavior and its effects on the industry:

- Educate customers to make them aware that shoplifting by others is costly to everyone in the form of increased prices.
- Encourage customers to keep their receipts secure (particularly do not dispose of them on store or mall property) so that their purchases do not generate unethical behavior by others.
- Offer helpful customer service in areas where shoplifting is likely to occur (dressing rooms and store corners).
- Reward customers who report shoplifting and other unethical behavior.
- Offer customer education seminars to familiarize customers with brand and logo distinguishing features so that they are more aware of copyright and trademark infringement issues (discussed in Chapter 4).

What additional strategies can you identify to address the issue of customer ethics? Which of the five activities listed above have you seen implemented? What level of success (or lack of success) have you observed with respect to these efforts?

This chapter has provided insight into the behaviors of customers when they are faced with ethical decisions. Manufacturers and retailers should consider the viewpoints of consumers as they develop policies affecting production materials and methods and retail practices in dressing rooms and for returns. Professionals need to be able to work with customers in difficult situations; keep the customers calm, communicate store policy, and keep a positive atmosphere. Furthermore, it is important to be aware of potential fraudulent activities so that you can take a proactive stance for your company.

QUESTIONS FOR DISCUSSION

1. Should companies require identification (such as driver's license) for returns? What are the benefits and consequences of such policies? How do you feel about being required to share your personal information?

2. How many types of theft have you witnessed in your work experience? Describe the situations you have observed.

3. Look into whether your state allows civil demand or civil recovery, as noted in Box 9.5. Explore what steps are required to set up a system to fine shoplifters.

4. How could you effectively implement some of the suggestions presented in the chapter to deter unethical consumer behavior?

5. Describe some customer service strategies that can deter unethical consumer behavior. What are advantages and disadvantages of implementing these strategies in a workplace?

REFERENCES AND SUGGESTED READING

Barnett, C., Cafaro, P., and Newholm, T. (2005). Philosophy and ethical consumption. In R. Harrison, T. Newholm, and D. Shaw (eds). *The ethical consumer.* London: Sage Publications.

Bloch, P., Bush, R. F., and Campbell, L. (1993). Consumer "accomplices" in product counterfeiting: A demand-side investigation. *Journal of Consumer Marketing,* 10(4) 27–36.

Boulstridge, E. and Carrigan, M. (2000). Do consumers really care about corporate responsibility? Highlighting the attitude-behaviour gap. *Journal of Communication Management,* 4(4), 355–368.

Brown, R. (June 21, 2007). Hindmarch 'green' bag a hot item. *Women's Wear Daily,* p. 8.

Callen, K. S. and Ownbey, S. F. (2003). Associations between demographics and perceptions of unethical consumer behavior. *International Journal of Consumer Studies,* 27(2), 99–110.

Carrigan, M. and Attalla, A. (2001). The myth of the ethical consumer—do ethics matter in purchase behaviour? *Journal of Consumer Marketing,* 18(7), 560–577.

Clark, E. (August 3, 2007). Retail's latest plague: Fighting back against shoplifting gangs. *Women's Wear Daily*, pp. 1, 11.

Cohen, J. (2001). Appreciating, understanding and applying universal moral principles. *Journal of Consumer Marketing*, 18(7), 578–594.

Cohen, R. (2002). *The good, The bad, & The difference.* New York: Random House.

Cordell, V. V., Wongtade, N., and Kieschnick, R. L. Jr., (1996). Counterfeit purchase intentions: role of lawfulness attitudes and product traits as determinants. *Journal of Business Research*, 35, 41–53.

Dickerson, K. (Winter 1979). The shoplifting epidemic: Some implications for consumer educators. *Journal of Consumer Affairs*, 13(2), 393–397.

Dragon International (1991). *Corporate Reputation: Does the consumer care?* London: Dragon International.

Folkes, V. S. and Kamins, M. A. (1999). Effects of information about firms' ethical and unethical actions on consumer attitudes. *Journal of Consumer Psychology*, 8(3), 243–259.

Forney, W. S., Forney, J. C., and Crutsinger, C. (2005). Developmental stages of age and moral reasoning as predictors of juvenile delinquents' behavioral intention to steal clothing. *Family and Consumer Sciences Research Journal*, 34(2), 110–136.

Gail, T., Garibaldi, B., Zeng, Y., and Pilcher, J. (1998). Consumer demand for counterfeit goods. *Psychology and Marketing*, 15(5), 405–421.

Garofoli, J. (December 18, 2005). O Christmas tree, are ye real or fake? *The Athens [Ohio] Messenger*, p. A12 [Scripps Howard News Service].

Gelfand, D., Hartman, D. P., Walden, P., and Page, B. (February 1973). Who reports shoplifting? A field-experimental study. *Journal of Personality and Social Psychology*, 276–285.

Ha, S. and Lennon, S. J. (2006). Purchase intent for fashion counterfeit products: Ethical ideologies, ethical judgments, and perceived risks. *Clothing and Textiles Research Journal*, 24(4), 297–315.

Harrison, R., Newholm, T., and Shaw, D. (2005). *The Ethical Consumer.* London: Sage Publications Ltd.

Hoffman, J. J. (1998). Are women really more ethical than men? Maybe it depends on the situation. *Journal of Managerial Issues*, 10(1), 60–73.

Joergens, C. (2006). Ethical fashion: Myth or future trend? *Journal of Fashion Marketing and Management*, 10(3), 360–371.

June, A. W. (March 17, 2006). Eight colleges sign on to anti-sweatshop plan but worry over antitrust issues. *The Chronicle of Higher Education*, A38.

Lewis, L. (June 2007). Getting a return on returns. *Stores*, 89(6), 42–43.

Littrell, M. A., Ma, Y. J., and Halepete, J. (2005). Generation X, baby boomers, and swing: Marketing fair trade apparel. *Journal of Fashion Marketing and Management*, 9(4), 407–419.

Page, G. and Fearn, H. (2005). Corporate reputation: What do consumers really care about? *Journal of Advertising Research*, 45(3), 305–313.

Prestwich, L. W. (Winter 1978). Consumer attitudes toward shoplifting. *The Journal of Consumer Affairs*, 12, 292–299.

Reeder, G. and Brewer, M. (1979). A schematic model of dispositional attribution in interpersonal perception, *Psychological Review*, 86, 61–79.

Roberts, J. A. (January/February 1996) Will the socially responsible consumer please step forward? *Business Horizons*, 39(1), 79–83.

Rosen, J. (May 24, 2004). Fighting back against theft. *Publishers Weekly*, p. 28.

Rudell, F. (2006). Shopping with a social conscience: Consumer attitudes toward sweatshop labor. *Clothing and Textiles Research Journal*, 24(4), 282–296.

Shen, D. and Dickson, M. A. (2001). Consumers' acceptance of unethical clothing consumption activities: Influence of cultural identification, ethnicity, and Machiavellianism. *Clothing and Textiles Research Journal*, 19(2), 76–87.

Simon, F. L. (1995). Global corporate philanthropy: A strategic framework. *International Marketing Review*, 12(4), 20–37.

Solow, J. (2006). *The booster*. New York: Simon & Schuster Adult Publishing Group.

Speights, D. and Hilinski, M. (2005). Return fraud and abuse: How to protect profits. *Retailing Issues Letter*, 17(1), 1–5.

Spranca, M., Minsk. E., and Baron, J. (1991). Omission and commission in judgment and choice, *Journal of Experimental Social Psychology*, 27, 76–105.

Strutton, D., Pelton, L.E., and Ferrell, O.C. (1997). Ethical behavior in retail settings: Is there a generation gap? *Journal of Business Ethics*, 16, 87–105.

Thomas, J. L., Vitell, S. J., Gilbert, F. W., and Rose, G. M. (2002). The impact of ethical cues on customer satisfaction with service. *Journal of Retailing*, 78, 167–173.

Tian, K. and Keep, B. (2002). *Customer fraud and business responses: Let the marketer beware*. Westport, CT: Quorum Books.

Tonglet, M. (2002). Consumer misbehaviour: An exploratory study of shoplifting. *Journal of Consumer Behaviour, 1*(4), 336–354.

Wee, C., Tan, S., and Cheok, K. (1995). Non-price determinants of intention to purchase counterfeit goods: An exploratory study. *International Marketing Review, 12*(6), 19–46.

Words can never hurt? Teens ticked off over tees. (December 16, 2005). *Weekly Reader, 105*(14), p. 3.

Chapter 10

Self-Promotion and Career Search

THE OBJECTIVES OF THIS CHAPTER ARE TO:

- Identify Federal laws that apply to the career search

- Identify the components inherent in an ethical job search, including résumé writing, interviewing, and job offers

- Identify the qualities that employers seek in prospective employees, particularly related to ethics

- Recognize the importance of the ethical job search

- Understand the impact that unethical actions can have on a person's career

Commonly, if people are asked about ethical issues concerning the job search, they will mention items that have to do with discrimination in hiring and illegal interviewing questions. Although these issues are definitely pertinent, many others can arise while conducting a career search. Because the fashion industry is highly competitive, finding a career requires not only a strong résumé, but also strong communication skills with regard to letter writing and interviewing. Sometimes people, especially those seeking entry-level positions, have doubts about the skills they possess and consequently think they need to embellish their skills and qualifications in some way. This chapter discusses ethical issues encountered during a career search and offers some strategies to navigate through the questions that often have no definitive answers.

"Thank you, sir. I am proud of my resume.
And I think you'll find that most of it is true."

FIGURE 10.1

EMPLOYMENT LAWS

Some practices are not just unethical, they are also deemed illegal under current Federal law. The Federal laws prohibiting job and hiring discrimination are as follows:

- Title VII of the **Civil Rights Act of 1964** (Title VII), which prohibits employment discrimination based on race, color, religion, sex, or national origin
- The **Equal Pay Act of 1963** (EPA), which protects men and women who perform substantially equal work in the same establishment from sex-based wage discrimination
- The **Age Discrimination in Employment Act of 1967** (ADEA), which protects individuals who are 40 years of age or older
- Titles I and V of the **Americans with Disabilities Act** of 1990 (ADA), which prohibit employment discrimination against qualified individuals with disabilities in the private sector, and in state and local governments

- Sections 501 and 505 of the **Rehabilitation Act** of 1973, which prohibit discrimination against qualified individuals with disabilities who work in the Federal government
- The **Civil Rights Act** of 1991 which, among other things, provides monetary damages in cases of intentional employment discrimination

These laws protect people seeking employment and also people once they become employed. All of the above laws are enforced by the U.S. Equal Employment Opportunity Commission (EEOC).

Furthermore, in terms of hiring, these laws protect job seekers from discriminatory practices such as denying employment because of marriage to, or association with, individuals of a particular religion, race, country of origin, or disability. Neither can individuals be discriminated against because of their place of worship or due to participation with a particular school associated with race, ethnicity, or religious beliefs (see http://www.eeoc.gov for more detailed information concerning these laws and their enforcement).

It is an employer's responsibility to know these laws in order not to violate them. It is also important for job seekers to know about these laws for their own protection. Employees and employers should know that because of these laws, many interview questions are considered illegal. On a very basic level, employers cannot ask prospective employees personal questions that have nothing to do with job-related requirements. Specifically, employers cannot ask questions about marital status, children or plans to have children, age, race, disabilities, religion, national origin, birthplace, or gender. (Ways to deal with such questions will be discussed later in this chapter in regard to all of the ethical issues surrounding interviewing.)

THE JOB SEARCH

Although the career search issues listed above are deemed illegal, and thus clearly prohibited, answers to other issues surrounding the career search are not so definitive. In a broad sense, these include résumé preparation, interviewing, and the consideration of job offers. As you read the following suggestions and guidelines, remember that unethical behavior of any kind will likely be detected and can have serious consequences. Remember too, that while you do have options, honesty is, as a rule, the best policy and will lead you to the most ethical choice and more satisfying long-term career.

Résumés

Steven D. Levitt, coauthor of *Freakonomics* and a renowned economics professor, cites research suggesting that more than 50 percent of people lie on their résumés. There is much discussion concerning the appropriateness of "creative" résumé writing. It may be particularly tempting for new college graduates, or other entry-level job seekers, to embellish information on their résumés because they feel that their skills and qualifications are not appropriately matched to any job for which they want to apply. This is sometimes coupled with the fact that many college students find themselves with a résumé full of babysitting, summer camp, and restaurant positions. Consequently, it can be tempting to make up titles for these positions to make them sound more impressive or to embellish the responsibilities they had at these positions. A résumé should be designed to highlight skills and experience, but the bottom line is that it is never okay to lie about anything on this document. Lies will eventually catch up to you. It may be during the interview when the prospective employer asks you about skills you have listed but do not really have. Or it may be after you've been hired, when you will be expected to have experience of some sort that you do not actually have (for example, you may be asked to deal with a Spanish-speaking customer but you are unable to do so because you are not exactly as "fluent" in Spanish as you stated on your résumé). When a lie does catch up to you, it can cost both your credibility and your job!

Rather than lying on your résumé, it is advisable to seek help from someone, whether it is a college career office or another professional, who has experience writing résumés. They will most likely help you identify related experience from those jobs that you might see as unrelated, and from volunteer activities, extracurricular activities, and even college courses. They can also discuss ways to highlight these skills in interviews. This approach is far more desirable than lying on your résumé. In fact, most employers will be considerate of students, for example, who waited tables through college to fund their education even though they may not have the specific skills associated with the job listing.

In preparing your résumé, just as it is important to not inflate your qualifications, neither should you discount your accomplishments. For example, give yourself credit for your leadership roles in class projects or in student organizations. Note that you have been recognized as the top salesperson of the week or list the size of the budget you managed as treasurer of your organization. Such responsibilities are credible ones to list on your résumé and also indicate desirable traits that employers seek. This is especially important for individuals who do not have specific work-related experiences.

Many students are concerned about their GPA because it is not as high as they would like. Consequently, they may think that employers will not check the accuracy of this number, so they inflate it. A better choice in this case is to list your *major* GPA if it is higher than your *overall* GPA. Again, never lie about this. If your GPA is not something you are proud of, then simply do not include it. However, if you are granted an interview, you should be prepared to explain why your GPA is not as high as you would like (e.g., perhaps you had to work full-time, you or a close family member had health problems one semester, you switched majors several times before finding your true calling, or you simply did not devote adequate time to your studies during some part of college). Another way to handle an undesirable GPA is to add a brief explanation. For example, you may want to state your GPA in this way: GPA: 2.2 *(because of disastrous freshman year; otherwise 3.5)*. Legally, employers have the right to ask for a copy of your transcripts to verify courses and the GPA listed on your résumé; this is becoming common practice for employers.

Yet another area of ethical reporting of work experience on your résumé concerns employment gaps. Never attempt to fill in gaps by falsifying dates of employment, or worse yet, by making up positions for a time of unemployment. It is actually quite common for people to have gaps in their employment history for a variety of reasons. If this is your situation, and are uncomfortable with it because you think it will hurt your chances for an interview, you can offer a brief explanation in your cover letter about the gaps. This is one area that companies will definitely check and you do not want to be rejected outright because you thought it was acceptable to "fudge" some employment dates. On a related note, make absolutely sure that the dates are correct. Sometimes these dates are incorrect simply because of a typo. However, when employers find false information, you will probably not be given a chance to explain this, regardless of the reason.

References

When providing references, be sure to identify the title and job position of each person listed. Additionally, the reference person's professional position may also give an indication of the relationship between you and that person. It is also helpful to include a brief statement accompanying the person's contact information that describes his or her relationship to you. If one of your references has changed jobs since working with you, you should indicate this with the phrase "formerly with XYZ Company." This will allow the reader of your résumé to more easily identify that person's relationship to you. In selecting references, avoid family members and purely personal references, particularly if you have other work experience. Remember, too, that it is essential to ask people you plan to list as references for permission to use their names. Most people would also appreciate a copy of your résumé to have on hand and to review before speaking with prospective employers (Paulins and Hillery, 2005).

Everything on your résumé must be the truth. The consequences of employers uncovering dishonesty are too great in that you will not be considered for a position—or perhaps worse, you will be hired and then fired once your dishonesty is exposed. Consider the case of Marilee Jones, MIT's dean of admissions, who spoke out nationally against teenager's embellishing their résumés. Jones was forced to resign after nearly three decades at MIT for misrepresenting her academic degrees. She listed on her résumé that she had degrees from three universities but she had no degrees from any of the schools. Imagine the humiliation she must have felt as she was forced to admit her lie, especially given the fact that she had advised people for years against falsifying their résumé. Not only did this resignation embarrass Jones but it also brought into question her integrity and credibility, as well as that of MIT, a very prestigious and well-regarded institution. Another factor to consider is the stress she must have been under worrying that she could be exposed at any time. Her downfall was the result of a phone call made by an anonymous person to the dean of undergraduate education questioning Jones' credentials (Bombardieri and Ryan, 2007).

Interviewing

Interviewing can be one of the more stressful parts of the job search for many people. It is also the part of the job search where many ethical issues can arise.

SCHEDULING THE INTERVIEW.   In our role as professors, probably one of the most common questions we are asked by students during a career search is whether they should interview with companies they are not really interested in, in order to get some "practice." Quite simply, the answer is no. There are several reasons why this is not ethical. First, you are wasting the recruiters' time (and the company's money). Campus recruiters have one goal in mind and that is to identify candidates who are truly interested in a career at their company. Interviewing when you are genuinely not interested is deceitful to yourself and the recruiter. On the other hand, you should also keep an open mind. Sometimes you will not know for sure about your interest until you interview. If you find yourself in this situation, do all the research you can, go to a career fair to find out more, and talk to other students or people who can give you information. This way you can make an educated decision about your options.

The second reason you should not interview with companies you are not interested in is because you are probably taking an interview slot from someone who actually is interested. This is especially true for on-campus interviews, where recruiters have only so much time, allowing for a limited number of interviews. Do not waste your time, the recruiter's time, and take another candidate's time if you are genuinely not interested in learning more about the opportunities available.

Lastly, if you need practice interviewing, there are plenty of options to pursue. Most college campuses hold practice interviews through the career office or perhaps a student organization. If yours does not, you can ask a professor to do a mock interview with you, enroll in a professional development class, or bring together a group of friends for practice.

SHOWING UP.   Once you have arranged an interview, you should arrive on time and be well prepared. If there is an emergency and you cannot make it to the interview, it is imperative that you call your college career office or the interviewer (you did get his or her phone number, right?) to let them know you cannot make it. You should do this as soon as you know you have to cancel; with enough advance notice, the recruiter may be able to fill the slot. Simply not showing up without a phone call is a poor reflection on you, your major, your college, and anyone who has helped you get the interview. College recruiters visit campuses where they have promising recruits, not schools where students are "no-shows."

ANSWERING QUESTIONS—ILLEGAL AND OTHERWISE.   As mentioned previously, you should be prepared for your interview. This means you should have done some research on the company, have answers ready for commonly asked questions, and also have a list of questions to ask the recruiter. You should not ask questions that have answers that are easily accessible on the company's Web site or literature. Ask for help from your professors or career office if you are not sure how to prepare. You should also review the list of illegal questions (presented at the start of the chapter) in case the recruiter asks you one of these. This occurs fairly often, so you should decide ahead of time how you will respond. Generally, most experts agree that you have three choices. First, you can simply answer the question although remember that you are not obligated to do so. Second, you can refuse to answer the question although you will want to be careful to not offend the interviewer, especially if you are interested in receiving a job offer. It is not a good idea to say, "That's an illegal question and I am not going to answer it!" Consider instead putting a question back on the recruiter—something like "Can you tell me how you think that will affect my job performance?" Your third choice is to answer the question but refocus the answer. For example, if the recruiter asks you if you plan to have children, you could answer by saying, "There's nothing in my personal life that I foresee as a barrier to my carrying out the responsibilities I will have with your company." Refocusing your answer probably highlights more of what the recruiter wants to know anyway.

The most important thing to remember during the interview is to answer the questions honestly. You do not have to divulge every bit of information about yourself but again, you should never lie about anything. For example, if you were fired from a job, and you are asked about it, you should state the facts of what happened and follow up with what you learned from the experience. Put a positive spin on negative events, and as mentioned, always explain what you learned and how you will now do things differently. Remember too, that you are not under any obligation to talk about such experiences if you are not asked about them.

Another item worth mentioning is that you should *never* discuss other candidates during your interview. You may occasionally encounter a recruiter or interviewer who tests you on this by asking your opinion about another student or candidate. There are two ways to handle this situation. First, you can say that there are many great students at your university and in your major (remain ambiguous) and you are sure the recruiter will find the most qualified candidates. The second, and perhaps best, response is to simply state that you would rather spend your time in the interview talking about yourself and your qualifications. This sends a clear message to the recruiter that you are a person of integrity; it also demonstrates your character. On a related note, you should never talk negatively about any former employers for these very same reasons.

ASKING QUESTIONS.   Chapter 2 discusses corporate culture and the importance of finding a company with which you feel a good "fit." Therefore, it is important to gain as much information as possible about your prospective employer regarding the company's views on ethics in the workplace, management styles, business philosophies, and employee policies. Employees who fit into their workplace will not only be happier at their job but they will also find themselves performing better, and consequently, growing within the company (Daniel and Brandon, 2006). Once you have established which ethical factors are most important to you, you should prepare a list of questions to make sure the company's mission and objectives match your own. See Box 10.1 for a list of interview questions that can help you uncover the corporate culture. Asking these questions, along with questions that

Box 10.1

INTERVIEW QUESTIONS TO ASK CONCERNING CORPORATE CULTURE

Questions to ask the interviewer:

- How are decisions made—and how are those decisions communicated to the staff?
- What role does the person who gets this position play in decision making?
- Does the organization emphasize working in teams?
- What are the organization's priorities for the next few years?
- Are there established career paths for employees in this position?

Questions to ask other employees (if you get the chance to meet with them, or if you know someone who works at the company):

- What ten words would you use to describe your company?
- What's it really like to work here? Do you like it here?
- Around here, what is really important?
- How are employees valued around here?
- What skills and characteristics does the company value?
- Do you feel as though you know what is expected of you?
- How do people from different departments interact?
- Are there opportunities for further training and education?
- How do people get promoted around here?
- Around here, what behaviors get rewarded?
- Do you feel as though you know what's going on?
- How effectively does the company communicate to its employees?

SOURCE: Dr. Randall Hansen. Uncovering a company's corporate culture is a critical task for job-seekers. Retrieved March 17, 2008 from http://www.quintcareers.com/employer_corporate_culture.html. Reprinted with permission of author.

are specific to your job responsibilities, will provide you with the information you need to make a more informed decision once a job offer is made.

TRAVELING FOR A SECOND ON-SITE INTERVIEW.   Many companies hold second interviews on-site at the corporate headquarters or at a training store; this usually involves travel for the interviewees. Through the research you have done and the first round of interviews you have completed, you should have a sense of whether the company is a good match for you. If you are still interested in the job, your on-site visit will provide you with a great learning opportunity and help to finalize your decision about joining the company (should an offer be made). However, let's assume you have interviewed with The Gap Inc. and the company offers to fly you to San Francisco to interview at the corporate headquarters. You have always wanted to visit California and, after all, this is a free trip. However, if you are not genuinely interested in working for The Gap Inc., you should not accept the offer—period. First, and as mentioned previously, you are probably taking an interview slot away from someone who truly wants to work for The Gap Inc. Second, the company will spend considerable money on candidates they choose for on-site visits and it is not ethical for you to use their resources just to travel. Remember too, this visit would be like all business trips in that you are not traveling to sightsee and have fun, but rather to learn more about the company. Usually, although there may be a short tour of the city you are visiting, you will for the most part, be inside at a corporate headquarters or store for the majority of your trip. Imagine how unpleasant it would be to spend a stressful day of interviewing at a company for which you have no interest. When you receive the offer for an on-site visit and you are truly not interested, you should withdraw yourself from consideration so that the company may invest its time and resources in a more interested candidate. Be polite in doing so and never burn bridges. You never know when you will run into these same businesspeople again in the future.

But if you truly are undecided, and still have some interest, then the on-site visit is a good idea. It will give you a chance to gather more information, meet many of the people you will be working with, and get a better idea about how you may or may not fit into the company culture. If you remain objective through the second round of interviews, an on-site interview should definitely help you make the best decision when the job is offered.

PRESENTATIONS TO THE COMPANY.   A recent column in the *Wall Street Journal* highlighted the precautions a prospective employee should take when asked to make a presentation as part of a job interview. The column, "What to do when they don't hire you, but steal your ideas," examines the experience of a job seeker who was asked to create a marketing strategy for the company's sales force. After spending over 50 hours preparing the report, and two days presenting it to the prospective company executives, the job seeker did not get the position. However, he soon discovered that the company had incorporated his proposed strategy— even calling it by the same name! Although we hope this is not frequent practice, as business proposals and presentations become more common as part of interviewing, prospective employees should take measures to protect themselves in this area. *Wall Street Journal* columnist Joann Lublin (2006) suggests that, if acceptable, the interviewee provide the company with examples of projects he or she has done in the past rather than designing something new. If the company insists that you design your presentation to their needs, another protection strategy is to leave out important details necessary to execute your plan. If you provide handouts, or do anything to express yourself in writing, it is important to add a copyright symbol to the material in addition to a statement that makes it clear that the material is for the sole purpose of the job interview. Lastly, you should draw attention to the materials in the thank-you note, stating that you were pleased to discuss your materials and ideas with them.

EXPENSES FOR TRAVEL.   If your site visit involves travel, other than a short trip by car, most companies will make the travel arrangements for you. Additionally, the majority of the time your expenses will be prepaid by the company. However, some companies may ask you to keep receipts for all travel-related expenses and will reimburse you afterward. In these situations, you should be prudent in the expenses you incur (e.g., do not order a $50 breakfast from room service) and you should not claim any personal expenses (e.g., dry cleaning, phone bills). Keep all your travel and lodging receipts to submit and follow all directions for doing so meticulously. Companies will notice how you handle this responsibility and it will consider it as a reflection of the type of employee you will be. Never take advantage of this situation.

THE JOB OFFER

The second most common question we hear from students conducting a job search is: "Is it okay to accept a job while I wait to hear about another one that I want more?" There is a simple answer to this question—NO! The most serious ethical breach a person can make in the job search is reneging after accepting a position. This is a case in which your ethical behavior will have to outweigh what may actually be best for you, and it also illustrates how sometimes it is difficult to do the right thing. While it definitely is in your best interests to have a job, it is not ethical to accept one as a precaution in case nothing better comes along. Your word of acceptance will be viewed as a contractual agreement; only in the case of extreme circumstances (e.g., sickness, death in family) would it be acceptable to withdraw an acceptance. Once you do accept a position, you should stop interviewing immediately and withdraw your name from consideration at all other companies that have job-offer decisions pending. If you have been interviewing through your college placement or career office, most also require that you notify them when you accept a position.

You may find yourself in the situation where you have not heard from all the other interviewers before you receive a job offer from another. Suppose you have interviewed with Company XYZ and it is your top choice among all prospects. However, Company XYZ has not yet made any decisions. In the meantime, Company ABC calls and makes you an offer and needs to know within a week if you plan to accept. Company ABC is your second choice. This is actually a great situation to be in, although it can be somewhat stressful if you do not know how to handle it. In this case, you should call Company XYZ immediately and tell your contact there that you have another offer. Explain that XYZ is your first choice and ask when you might expect to hear from the company. This call actually works to your advantage. First, you may have immediately become more attractive to Company XYZ simply because someone else has made you an offer. Second, knowing that you need to make a decision may actually help accelerate Company XYZ's decision.

A word of caution concerning multiple job offers: You should NEVER fabricate an offer to give yourself a better bargaining position at another company. Remember that most college recruiters will talk to each other and the chances of your being found out are high. When that happens, you will find yourself in the position of having no job offers. Besides being dishonest with the recruiters, you are not giving yourself enough credit for your credentials. A job offer that is based on anything other than your own credibility and honesty will never be satisfying.

Timeliness

Once you have received an offer, you should adhere to any timelines the company gives you concerning your decision. In the exceptional case where you cannot meet the timeline (perhaps you are waiting on other decisions), you should politely ask the company for a brief extension and explain that you need just a little more time to make sure the decision you make is the right one. But do not be surprised if the company pressures you for a decision and denies your request for an extension. After all, the goal of the interviewer or recruiter is to get you to join the company. Be prepared for how you will handle this.

Rejecting an Offer

If you receive an offer that is not right for you, you should turn it down in a way that will leave a good impression with the company. A polite phone call is sufficient; you may also want to follow up with a brief letter. Regardless of how you notify the company, it should be done in a timely manner—and, as mentioned before, you should never burn bridges. There's always a possibility that in the future you may want to work for that company or that company might even become a client of yours.

SEARCHING FOR A POSITION WHILE YOU ARE EMPLOYED

Because this is a college textbook, the discussion in this chapter has so far reflected the perspective of a college student. However, there are some additional and related ethical issues regarding the job search when a person leaves his or her first permanent position and moves on to another. First, to protect yourself, you should be as discrete as possible and not let your co-workers know that you are looking for other opportunities. This information puts them in an awkward position and it could also result in your being fired prematurely if it is discovered by your supervisor.

Second, do not use the office equipment or supplies at your present job when searching for another job. For example, do not type or copy your résumé or communicate in any way with prospective employers on your office computer. Invariably you will leave your résumé, or a cover letter, laying around (usually in the copy machine) for the wrong person to find.

Because you are employed full-time, you will also need to be creative in terms of taking phone calls and scheduling interview appointments with potential employers. It is probably best to give prospective employers your cell phone number and the times you will be available to speak with them. These periods should be during lunch hours, breaks, or before or after work hours so that you are not spending company time looking for another position. The other option is to provide a voice mail with an outgoing message that lets callers know either what time you will be available to answer the phone or what time you will return their call. You will also need to schedule interviews before or after your current working hours, or during your lunch hour. Most prospective employers will respect the fact that you are currently working and will be flexible in scheduling around your commitments. You may need to take personal or vacation time to conduct interviews. You should plan ahead so that your current employment environment functions as well as possible in your absence. It is not acceptable to call in sick to go to a scheduled interview. In fact, this could easily be discovered, placing you in a precarious position with your current employer.

As you move on from your first permanent position, remember to follow all the guidelines for ethical behavior, as you did when you accepted the current company's offer. Also, as you move on from each position, it is very important to leave on good terms, including not gossiping about or criticizing your current employer.

Lying or acting unethical at any stage in the job search can result in your being eliminated from further consideration. Employers will verify transcripts, credentials, and references. Therefore, make sure all of yours are truthful and accurate, making it as easy for the interviewer as possible. You should also keep in mind the top qualities that employers seek in new employees and make sure your résumé and actions reflect these qualities (see Box 10.2).

You will be faced with ethical dilemmas throughout your job search, situations in which your decisions affect others. For example, when you promptly notify a potential employer that you will not be accepting that company's job offer, this

---

BOX 10.2

WHAT ARE THE TOP PERSONAL QUALITIES EMPLOYERS LOOK FOR IN COLLEGE GRADUATES?

The top personal qualities/skills employers seek, according to NACE's *Job Outlook 2007* survey, are:

1. Communication skills (verbal and written)

2. Honesty/integrity

3. Interpersonal skills (relates well to others)

4. Motivation/initiative

5. Strong work ethic

SOURCE: Reprinted from *2007 Job Outlook*, with permission of the National Association of Colleges and Employers (NACE), copyright holder.

opens a slot for another person who may be eagerly awaiting a position. One of the biggest distinctions between etiquette and ethics is just that. While etiquette reflects positively or negatively on you, your ethical decisions have the most direct effect on, or reflection of, others. For example, if you are interviewing and conducting a job search through your university's career office, all of your actions are a direct reflection on your university. Not showing up for an interview or lying on your résumé may lead employers to believe that your university does not instill in students the values they are seeking, which may mean that they stop recruiting at your university. At all stages in the job search, and even as you enter the professional arena, you are representing the university, your professors, others in your major, and even your professional references. In that regard, it is unethical to shed a negative light on them—even if you can "justify" it for yourself.

Throughout this book we have described a variety of ethical issues that are faced daily in the fashion industry. In most cases, we have intentionally avoided the presentation of definitive decisions or judgments regarding the "right" decisions. It is our intention that you will consider the information provided, establish your own ethical base, and make the "right" decisions for you that reflect those beliefs.

QUESTIONS FOR DISCUSSION

1. What is the best thing to do if you are asked an illegal question during a job interview? Practice how you will respond to an illegal question.

2. Are there some "illegal" questions that are more inappropriate than others? If so, what type of questions?

3. Review the questions in Box 10.1 designed to explore a company culture. What other questions would you like to ask? Which of the questions in the list are most important to you?

4. Review the list of qualities that employers seek (in Box 10.2). Give specific examples of how you exhibit those qualities.

5. What are some of your school accomplishments that could be listed on your résumé?

6. Why do you think people lie on résumés?

7. After considering the issues outlined in this chapter, what specific actions have you witnessed that you would now consider unethical with regard to the job-search process?

REFERENCES AND SUGGESTED READING

Bombardieri, M. and Ryan, A. (March 26, 2007). MIT dean of admissions resigns for falsifying resume. *The Boston Globe*. Retrieved on March 17, 2008 from http://www.boston.com/news/globe/city_region/breaking_news/2007/04/mit_dean_of_adm

Daniel, L. and Brandon, C. (March 2006). Finding the right job fit. *HRMagazine*, 51, 62–67.

Doyle, A. (2007). Illegal interview questions. Retrieved on March 17, 2008 from http://jobsearch.about.com/od/interviewquestionsanswers/a/interviewquest.htm

Hall, B. (2007). Conduct ethical job searches. Retrieved on March 17, 2008 from http://content.monstertrak.monster.com/resources/archive/jobhunt/hall

Lublin, J. (November 28, 2006). What to do when they don't hire you but steal your ideas. *Wall Street Journal*. Retrieved on March 17, 2008 from http://online.wsj.com/article/SB116466744405433753.html?mod=todays_us_marketplace

Miami University Career Services. Some ethical considerations to guide your job search. Retrieved on March 17, 2008 from http://www.units.muohio.edu/careers/students/infobriefs/ethical.pdf

Paulins, V. A. and Hillery, J. L. (2005). *Careers! Professional development for retailing and apparel merchandising*. New York: Fairchild Publications, Inc.

Steen, M. (2005). The ultra-honest resume: How to write a resume that passes the verification test. Retrieved on March 17, 2008 from http://hotjobs.yahoo.com/resume/The_Ultra-Honest_Resume__20060921-121229.html?subtopic=Resume+Basics

U.S. Equal Employment Opportunity Commission. (2004). Federal Laws Prohibiting Job Discrimination Questions and Answers. Retrieved on March 17, 2008 from http://www.eeoc.gov/abouteeo/overview_laws.html

Credits

CHAPTER 1

1.1 © *The New Yorker* Collection 2003 Roz Chast from cartoonbank.com. All Rights Reserved.

CHAPTER 2

2.1 © 2007 Arnie Levin from cartoonbank.com. All Rights Reserved.

CHAPTER 3

3.1 Veer

CHAPTER 4

4.1 David C. Chen/Getty Images/Stock Illustration

4.2 Copyright © 2005. *Good Housekeeping* (October 2005).

4.3 Doeringer, P. and Crean, S. (2006). Can fast fashion save the US apparel industry? *Socio-Economic Review*, 4, 353–377. Reprinted with permission of Oxford University Press.

4.4 Reprinted with permission of Chanel, Inc.

CHAPTER 5

5.1 Alex Mares-Manton/Getty Images/Asia Images

5.2 AP Images

5.3 Domina, T. and Koch, K. (1997). Reprinted with permission of the International Textiles and Apparel Association and the *Clothing and Textiles Research Journal*, 15 (2), 96–102.

Index